The Internet
for Busy People

Connect to the Net and Set Up Mail

See "Key Setup Information, No Matter What Mail Program You Use" in Chapter 4, and see also Appendix A.

Write down your key information here so you can find it again easily next time you have to set up your Internet access (or when traveling).

CONNECTION:

Dial-up number: _____

Travel numbers:

City:_____ #:_____

City:_____ #:_____

Your IP address (if you have to supply it):

_____ . _____ . _____ . _____

Your DNS addresses (if you have to supply them):

_____ . _____ . _____ . _____

_____ . _____ . _____ . _____

Tech support phone number and/or e-mail address:

_____

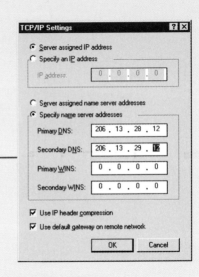

MAIL & NEWS

Your e-mail address:

_____@_____

Your outgoing (SMTP) mail server:

_____

Your incoming (POP3) mail server:

_____

Your news (NNTP) server:

_____

Other useful addresses or info:

_____

_____

Locate a Long Lost Friend or Relative

See "Finding People and Businesses" in Chapter 3.

Is Mary in Missoula, or somewhere in Mississippi—and does she have e-mail? Find out by turning to WhoWhere? (http://whowhere.lycos.com/**) or Yahoo! People (**http://people.yahoo.com/**).**

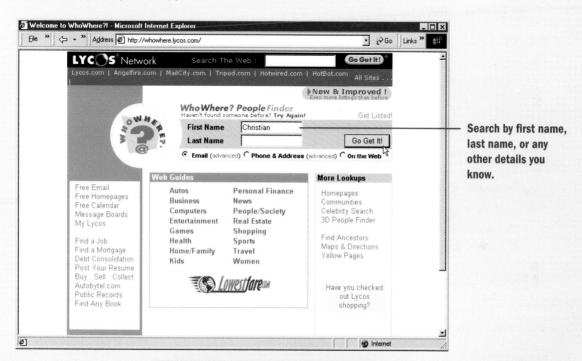

Search by first name, last name, or any other details you know.

When adding your name so others may find you, consider making entries using your maiden names (when applicable) or your home town as a child, so old friends can look you up without knowing your recent life history.

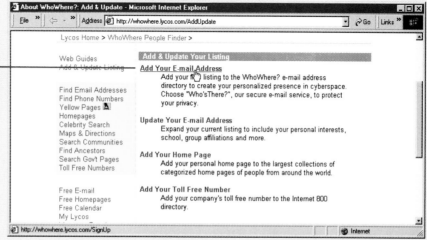

Shop Around the Clock

See "Buying Things" in Chapter 1.

Books? Software? T-Shirts? No crowds, no waiting.

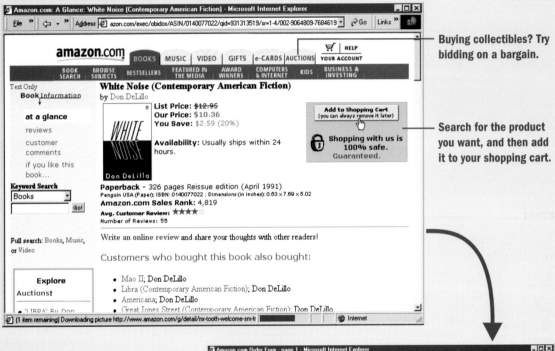

Buying collectibles? Try bidding on a bargain.

Search for the product you want, and then add it to your shopping cart.

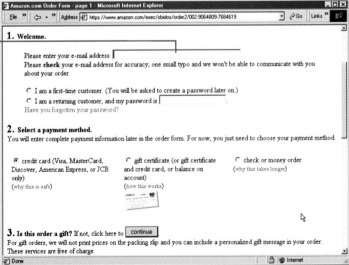

When you're ready to check out, submit your order, sit back, and relax. You'll have to fill in some personal information, as you would for a mail order.

Book Your Own Travel

See "Making Travel Plans" in Chapter 1.

Some services will send you the lowest fares, published weekly, to the destinations of your choice.

Most travel sites require registration.

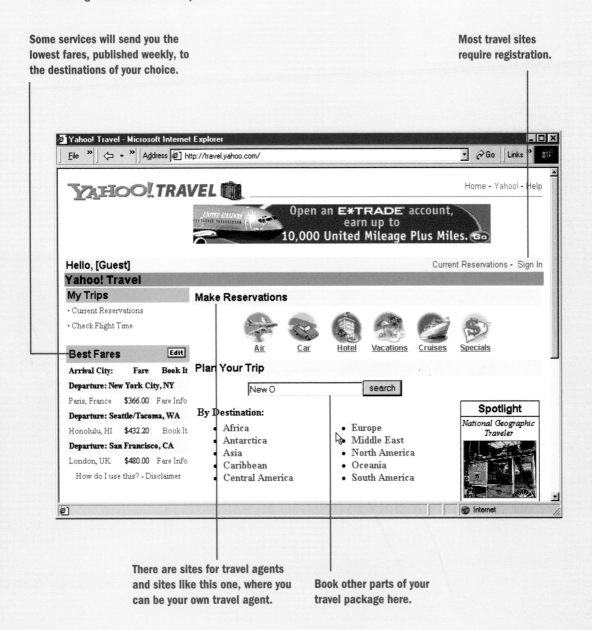

There are sites for travel agents and sites like this one, where you can be your own travel agent.

Book other parts of your travel package here.

Track a Package

See "Tracking Packages" in Chapter 1.

Where, oh, where can your package be? If you sent it by Federal Express, it's easy to find out online at http://www.fedex.com/.

It's still easier to find a package if you have the airbill number handy.

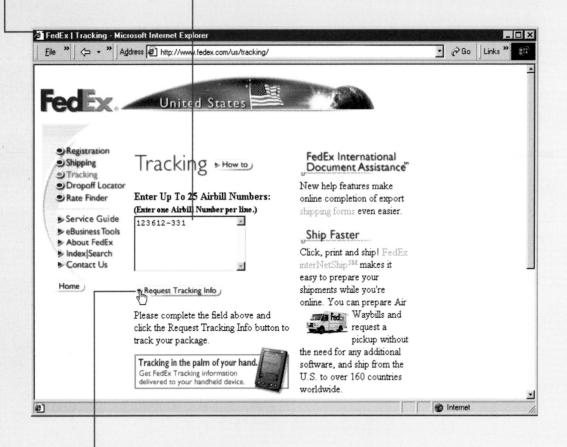

After you click here, a status report tells you what's happening to the package, and, if it has already been delivered, who signed for it.

Try Out New Software

See "Finding Software" in Chapter 3.

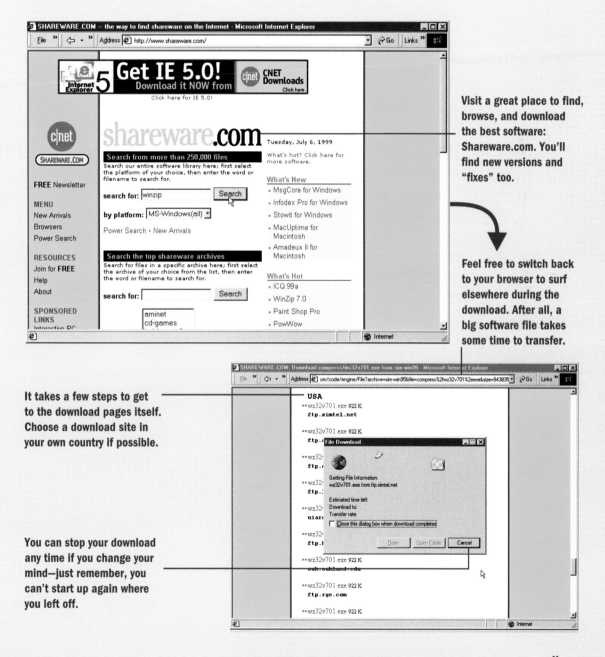

Visit a great place to find, browse, and download the best software: Shareware.com. You'll find new versions and "fixes" too.

Feel free to switch back to your browser to surf elsewhere during the download. After all, a big software file takes some time to transfer.

It takes a few steps to get to the download pages itself. Choose a download site in your own country if possible.

You can stop your download any time if you change your mind—just remember, you can't start up again where you left off.

Get a Free Webmail Account

See "Using a Free Webmail Account for Roaming Access" in Chapter 5.

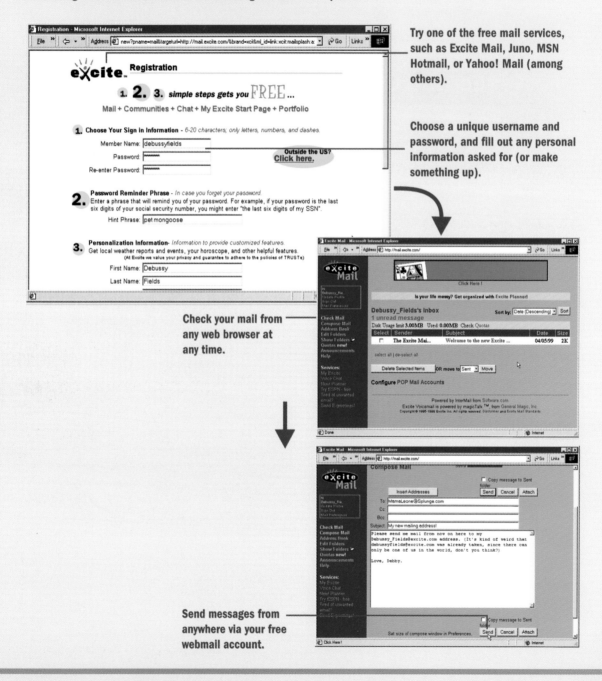

Try one of the free mail services, such as Excite Mail, Juno, MSN Hotmail, or Yahoo! Mail (among others).

Choose a unique username and password, and fill out any personal information asked for (or make something up).

Check your mail from any web browser at any time.

Send messages from anywhere via your free webmail account.

Manage Multiple E-Mail Accounts

See "Managing Multiple E-mail Accounts" in Chapter 5.

Set up each account separately
in your mail program.

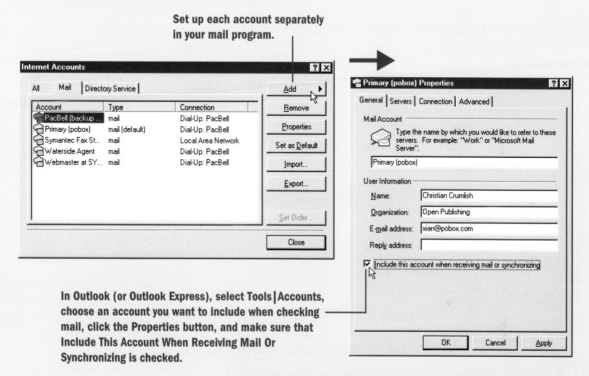

In Outlook (or Outlook Express), select Tools|Accounts,
choose an account you want to include when checking
mail, click the Properties button, and make sure that
Include This Account When Receiving Mail Or
Synchronizing is checked.

In Outlook (or Outlook Express) and
other programs, you can specify the
return address from which you are
sending by clicking the little button
to the right of the send button and
then selecting the account from
which you mean to send.

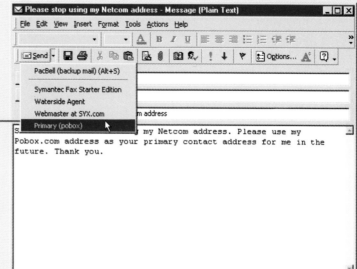

Screen an Investment Choice

See "Researching and Tracking Investments Online" in Chapter 6.

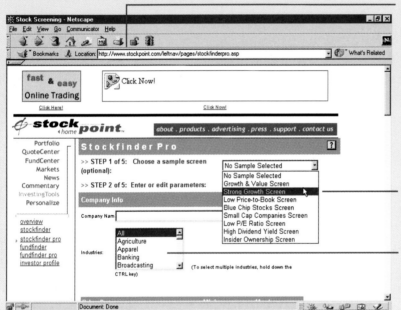

To screen a stock (for example), compare it with similar choices:

1. **Drop by Stockpoint.com's screening tool at** http://www. stockpoint./leftnav/pages/ stockfinderpro.asp**.**

2. **Choose a "screen" (a standard by which to judge the stock compared to others).**

3. **Specify or limit the statistics by which you wish to judge the stock and related stocks, and then click Search (not "Go," as the instructions read).**

Now look for research tools at a personal-finance portal such as Quicken.com (among others), to look up company news, secretary filings, historical financials, and more about the stock or stocks you're screening.

Here's some of the information that comes up for Salon.com at http://www.quicken.com/ investments/quotes/**.**

Make and Publish a Web Site

See "Creating Web Pages with Microsoft FrontPage Express,"
"Creating Web Pages with Microsoft Netscape Composer," and
"Creating Web Pages with Microsoft Word" in Chapter 7;
"Publishing Your Web Pages" in Chapter 8.

Create web documents using the menu commands and toolbar shortcuts in FrontPage Express, Netscape Composer, or Word 2000.

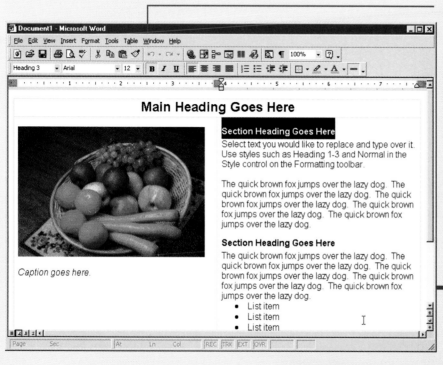

Publish web sites with the Web Publishing Wizard (Programs | Accessories | Internet Tools | Web Publishing Wizard), with File | Save As in Word, or with Web-content management programs such as FrontPage 2000, Dreamweaver, Drumbeat 2000, or GoLive.

The Internet

for Busy People

Millennium Edition

The Book to Use When There's No Time to Lose!

Christian Crumlish

OSBORNE

Osborne/**McGraw-Hill**

Berkeley / New York / St. Louis / San Francisco / Auckland / Bogotá
Hamburg / London / Madrid / Mexico City / Milan / Montreal / New Delhi
Panama City / Paris / São Paulo / Singapore / Sydney / Tokyo / Toronto

A Division of The **McGraw·Hill** *Companies*

Osborne/**McGraw-Hill**
2600 Tenth Street
Berkeley, California 94710
U.S.A.

For information on translations or book distributors outside the U.S.A., or to arrange
bulk purchase discounts for sales promotions, premiums, or fund-raisers, please contact
Osborne/**McGraw-Hill** at the above address.

The Internet for Busy People
Millennium Edition

  234567890 DOC DOC 90198765432109

ISBN 0-07-212116-5

Publisher   Brandon A. Nordin
Associate Publisher and
Editor-in-Chief   Scott Rogers
Acquisitions Editor   Joanne Cuthbertson
Project Editor   Cynthia Douglas
Editorial Assistant   Stephane Thomas
Contributing Author,
Chapter Six   William L. Valentine, IV, CFA
Technical Editor   Thomas Powell
Copy Editor   Sally Hancock
Proofreader   Mike McGee
Indexer   Claire Splan
Computer Designers   Roberta Steele, Gary Corrigan
Illustrators   Beth Young, Brian Wells, Bob Hansen
Series Design   Jil Weil
Cover Design   Damore Johann Design, Inc.

This book was published with Corel VENTURA.

To bnisbet, ngm, syrup, brooklyn, bad6,
zeigen, mal, k9luna, aweilec, annette, and mijoyce

About the Author

Christian Crumlish is a writer, editor, literary agent, book packager, and publisher. He co-founded the online magazine *Enterzone* and writes computer books for people who are as busy as he is. He is the author of the best-selling *The Internet for Busy People, Third Edition* and *FrontPage 2000 for Busy People*, as well as being the co-author of *Web Publishing with Netscape for Busy People*.

CONTENTS AT A GLANCE

CONTENTS

Acknowledgments

First I'd like to thank Stephen Mack, Nicholas Meriwether, and Richard Frankel, all of whom contributed to earlier editions of this book. William L. Valentine, IV, CFA, tutored me on the fine points of online personal finance and contributed a number of his columns to Chapter 6 of this book. I very much appreciate his sharing the benefits of his expertise with the readers of this book.

Stephane Thomas kept an eye on the schedule and worked with me to get everything in (more or less) on time, always with a pleasant and reassuring attitude. Thomas Powell proved once again to be a fine technical editor with a perspicacious eye, and Sally Hancock's careful copyedit clarified the occasional thickets of verbiage my writing can fall prey to (to which my writing can fall prey?). Thanks, too, to Mike McGee for his sharp-eyed proofread. A special thanks to Cynthia Douglas, my hardworking project editor, for managing the editorial and production processes according to her usual high standards. Cynthia made this job much more manageable for me.

Thanks to for Joanne Cuthbertson for recruiting me to work on this kooky, wacky, zany, madcap Busy People series. I'd also especially like to thank the sales, marketing, and publicity teams at Osborne. You guys deserve a lot of credit for the success of this book so far.

As anyone who's ever been around a publishing house can tell you, it's one thing to plan a beautiful design but quite another thing to implement such a design and make it look as good—or better— than the sample pages. The art and production team has raised my personal standards for design, layout, and typesetting. Thanks to Gary Corrigan and Roberta Steele for laying out the pages, and special, special thanks to graphic artists Bob Hansen, Brian Wells, and Beth Young, who managed to keep the many phases of screen art under control amid often frantic circumstances.

Thanks much to the international military-industrial complex for underwriting the Internet in the early days. Sincerest thanks to all of the active citizens of the Net, who are busy volunteering their time and information and building communities based on communication. Thanks to Briggs, geebers, my family, the *Enterzone* gang, the antiweb list, the merry punsters, BATG, Zerochildren, and many more.

Introduction

This book is for people with only a night or a few lunch hours to learn how to explore the Internet. (In the words of radio station 1010 WINS in New York City, "Give us 22 minutes; we'll give you the world.") The digital revolution has given with one hand, creating all kinds of efficient ways to communicate electronically and organizational wizardry, and taken away with the other, accelerating everyone's expectations, constantly moving the goalposts. The eruption of the Internet, the Web, and in-house intranets, has, if anything, picked up the pace.

How busy have you become lately? Has your job mushroomed with sprawling layers of responsibility? Do you feel like you have almost no time for anything? How often do you hear people say things like "Fax me that draft," "e-mail me those statistics," "our product release deadline's been moved up due to competitive pressures," or "it took longer than we thought—can you make up the time on your end?"

I Know You're in a Hurry, So . . .

Let's agree to dispense with the traditional computer book preliminaries. You've probably used a mouse, held down two keys at once, and have heard of this vast global network called the Internet. If you don't yet have Internet access, or if you're not sure what type of connection might already be available to you, start off by flipping to Appendix A, where I explain the different types of connections and how to find and select an Internet service provider (ISP).

So, now let's cut to the chase. After reading the first few chapters, you'll be able to:

- Browse (and search) the World Wide Web
- Send, receive, and reply to e-mail
- Find and join electronic mailing lists
- Chat with others instantaneously and keep connected while traveling.

Later chapters will show you how to manage your personal finances online, you how to design, create, and format web pages, and what to do when the time comes to publish web sites on the Internet (or on a local intranet).

As I mentioned, Appendix A is a primer for getting connected to the Internet. Throughout this book, I suggest web addresses (also called URLs) that you can visit for more information or to obtain free Internet programs and other software. All of the web addresses in this book are collected for your easy reference (and kept up-to-date) on the Web at the Busy People's Bookmarks page (**http://opublish.com/ busy2k/bookmarks/**). Material on FTP, Telnet, Usenet, and Gopher that was cut from earlier editions of this book can also be found online at the book's web site (**http://opublish.com/busy2k/**), along with addenda, errata, answers to frequently asked questions, a reader's forum, and more.

Things You Might Want to Know About This Book

This book uses examples and illustrations showing the Windows 98 versions of most Internet programs and features, but just about all of the information in the book applies equally well to other types of computers and operating systems, including Macintosh and Unix systems and even earlier versions of Windows. Macintosh users will find references for all the most important Mac Internet software in this book.

You can read this book more or less in any order. I suggest cruising Chapter 1 and reading Chapter 2 first, but you can start just as easily with Chapters 4 and 5 (which deal with e-mail) or by jumping directly to Chapter 3 to learn how to search the Web. Use the book as a reference. When you're stuck, not sure how to do something, know there's an answer but not what it is, pick up the book, zero in on the answer to your question, and put the book down again. Besides clear, coherent explanations of this all-over-the-map network of networks, you'll also find some special elements to help you get the most out of the Internet. Here's a quick run down of the other elements in this book.

Blueprints

Blueprints in the front of the book depict and demonstrate key tasks and goals you can accomplish on the Net.

Fast Forward

Each chapter begins with a section called *Fast Forward*. They should always be your first stop if you are a confident user, or if you are impatient or habitually late. You might find everything you need to get back in stride. Think of Fast Forward as the *Reader's Digest* version of each chapter. This shorthand may leave you hungry, especially if you are new to the Internet. So, for more complete and leisurely explanations of techniques and shortcuts, read the rest of the chapter.

EXPERT ADVICE

Timesaving tips, techniques, and worthwhile addictions are all reported under the rubric of *Expert Advice*. Force yourself to develop some good habits now, while it's still possible! These notes also give you the big picture and help you plan ahead. For example, I suggest that you use an "offline" newsreader program to save on connect-time charges while reading Usenet newsgroups.

Is This for Me?

Some resources can save you time and others will waste as much as you've got. Any new topic that may or may not be useful for a busy person starts with an *Is This for Me?* box, in which I spell out the pros and cons of tangling with the topic.

Cautions

Sometimes it's too easy to plunge ahead and fall down a rabbit hole, resulting in hours of extra work just to get you back to where you were before you went astray. *Cautions* will warn you before you commit time-consuming mistakes.

Definitions

Usually, I explain computer or networking jargon in the text, wherever the technobabble first occurs. But if you encounter words you don't recognize, look for this bookworm in the margin. *Definitions* point out important terms you might not know the meaning of. When necessary, they're strict and a little technical, but most of the time they're informal and conversational.

Netiquette

There are some well-established guidelines for behavior on the Internet, most often referred to as "netiquette," that keep the Net cooperative and help everyone get along. Civility and familiarity with the traditional ways of doing things go a long way in helping you communicate with the total strangers you'll meet online. *Netiquette* boxes will tip you off to standard practices and faux pas to avoid.

Bookmarks

Throughout the book, key web addresses are pulled out into *Bookmark* boxes, so you can find them again easily when you check the book again later. By the way, these addresses, also called URLs, are notoriously long and strangely punctuated. Often, a web address does not fit on a single line of text. To avoid introducing spurious characters that will actually make the addresses incorrect, web addresses are wrapped without hyphens or any other special characters added, usually after a slash (/) or dot (.) character. So, for example, to point your Web browser at **http://ezone.org/ez/**, just type the entire address on one line without any spaces or breaks (and don't type the comma at the end—that's just part of this sentence).

Let's Do It!

Ready? Let's dive into the Internet before the next big thing comes along!

Incidentally, I'm always happy to hear your reactions to this or any of my other books. You can reach me through the publisher, on the Net (**busy2k@syx.com**), or at the book's web site (**http://opublish.com/busy2k/**).

CHAPTER 1

Browse, Buy, and Bid on the Web

INCLUDES

- Understanding the World Wide Web and the Internet
- Browsing your own computer the way you do the Web
- Understanding Internet jargon
- Saving time on the Web
- Hyperlinks, web addresses, and channels
- Making bookmarks and getting updates
- Using any web browser

Use the Web Without Wasting Time ➡ pp. 15–16

- Keep a goal or destination in mind.
- Save references to interesting destinations for those occasions when you have the leisure to browse freely.

Browse the Web ➡ pp. 18–19

Most of the time, you'll browse by pointing to and clicking hyperlinks, which are specially highlighted text or images that lead your web browser to new destinations.

Enter Web Addresses ➡ pp. 20–22

Web addresses (also called URLs) that you type directly into the address box of any browser can be long and difficult to remember. Here are some ways to get around that problem:

- Whenever possible, avoid typing them by hand. Instead, copy URLs from e-mail messages and other online sources and then paste them into your browser's address box.
- When copying by hand, be very careful to copy them exactly.

Make a Bookmark ➡ pp. 25, 29–31

- In Internet Explorer, select Favorites | Add To Favorites. (Internet Explorer calls bookmarks *favorites.*)
- In Netscape, click the Bookmarks button and select Add Bookmark.

Go to a Bookmark ➡ pp. 25, 29–30

- In Internet Explorer, select Favorites | *Favorite-item.*
- In Netscape, select Bookmarks | *Bookmarked-item.*

Stay Calm When Your Browser Fails to Connect to a Site ➡ pp. 35–36

Don't panic. The Internet is sometimes busy. Click the Stop button and try again by clicking the Reload or Refresh button. If you repeatedly fail to connect, try again later.

In the past few years, most of us have been getting busier and busier, feeling more stress from work and family and relationship obligations, and maybe even feeling that we're falling further behind in some areas. I'm sorry to report that the Internet will probably not alleviate your pressure. It won't put more hours in the day or help you prioritize. It can easily become a time sink; an always-ready source of low-level self-distraction. If you thought solitaire or Tetris were addictive, then approach the Internet with care!

Now, I don't want to paint myself as some sort of whistle-blowing naysayer. I'm a card-carrying Internet addict, and I have trouble imagining how I could conduct my life without it. Then again, I work in this business, and I've learned long ago that my enthusiasm is not universal. The fact is, I'm part of the Internet-hype economy. Much as I'd like to deny it, I'm out in front in a barker's uniform ushering you in. Fine, that's my role and it pays the rent, but as you enter the tent let me just warn you to keep your wallet tightly gripped and be careful with your time.

The Internet: Not Useless!

All doom and gloom aside, the Internet is a fascinating and, in some sense, a *living* resource, and I have little doubt that you can quickly find information and people through it. (It beats a Ouija board, let me put it that way.) My job here is to try to cut through all the tedious software details and ever-changing computer business market buzzword campaign slogans and try to give you a clear-eyed concept of what exactly the Internet is, what it can do for you, and what it's no good for.

At the moment, one of my favorite sites is AltaVista's new translation program, Babelfish at **http://babelfish.altavista.digital.com/** (if u cn rd ths url u cn bcm a wbmstr n gt a gd jb). I let it chew on a paragraph of my writing and—well, let me allow the translation engine to restate this chapter's second paragraph in its own unique words:

> Now I would not like to paint me more naysayer as any assortment of whistleblowing. I am a card, the Internet addicted one carry and I have trouble exposure, as I mean life span without her lead could. On the other hand I am work in this business, and I experienced before long time that my enthusiasms are not. The fact is, I is hypewirtschaft a section the Internet. Much, since I would like to deny it, am I out in the front side in one barkeruniform you inside in-leading. My role and it are fine pay the rent, but, since you entered the tent, let me even you warn, your briefcase to hold fixed accessed and with your time take care.

So, I rest my case. The Internet: not useless.

The Web Makes It Easy to Get Around the Internet

The most important advance in making the Internet easy and convenient to explore has been the development of the World Wide Web (a method for viewing much of the Internet) and elegant programs called *web browsers* that enable you to view and thumb through the myriad sources of information, communication, and software out there.

Now, browsing the Internet is a simple matter of running one of these programs and jumping to a destination. Because of the flexibility of the web medium, you can even use a web browser to gain access to items that are out there somewhere on the Internet, but not directly on the Web. The web browser acts as a sort of umbrella interface for the entire Internet.

The Marriage of Your Computer and the Web

In fact, if Microsoft or the various business consortia arrayed against it manage to realize their lusty dreams of greed, one day everything you do with your computer will resemble a web-browsing experience. This has been the conventional wisdom derived from the popularity of the Web: people like the web interface better than the Mac-style interface.

So single-clicking is in. The web-page metaphor is hot, in theory. In reality, the web interface is an "eh, not bad" way to browse the global computer networks and the resources made available on them, but it's no universal computer, Darjeeling tea-type solution. Really, Microsoft and its foes are just treating the web consumer market as a new mindshare battlefield. It seems that Microsoft intends to leverage its dominance of the computer desktop into a gatekeeper role for the Internet itself (as the U.S. Department of Justice charged last year, eventually forcing MS to offer a version of Windows without built-in access to the Internet, while pursuing an antitrust action that is still underway at the time of this writing). The Java Majority plans to gang up on MS long enough to hold it at bay until they can themselves compete to control this entire new market.

Meanwhile, you benefit (sort of), as Internet access (theoretically) gets easier and cheaper. We'll see.

Jargon to Watch For

Before we get any deeper into unavoidably geeky terminology, check out Table 1.1 for a briefing on the jargon you'll encounter on the Web (and the Net). But don't let the terminology get in your way. The point is to sit back and browse, following your own instincts. Let the geeks and gurus yak in the lingo. For one thing, new buzzwords crop up all the time. A year or so ago, no one ever heard the "P" word before, "portal" site. Now every web page with high traffic, from Netscape's home page to Yahoo!, is referred to by the magical golden (in the stock market sense) word. We had jumping-off points, directories, search engines, and home pages before. Only the names have changed. My point is, learn enough of the jargon to keep up with conversations, but don't get too distracted by the buzzword of the month.

A Network of Networks

Most of us are too busy to spend all day discussing the history and technology of the Internet and all the fascinating trivia associated with it. You can get those anecdotes anywhere. (For that matter, you can get

Jargon Term	What It Means
Bookmark	A saved link to a web address; also called a *hotlist entry* or *favorite place.*
Browser	A program used to connect to sites on the World Wide Web.
Channel	A web page that is set up for continuous updating.
Client	A program, such as a web browser, that connects to a centralized server program and obtains information from it.
Client-server model	A method of sharing computer and network resources by centralizing some functions with a server and allowing individual clients to connect to the server to perform those functions.
Dialer	Software that connects your computer to an Internet service provider.
FTP	File transfer protocol. Also used to describe Internet public file archive sites (FTP sites).
Home page	The central document or default start-up page of a World Wide Web, or an individual's page.
HTML	*Hypertext markup language;* the language (consisting mainly of formatting tags) used to describe a document for the World Wide Web, including both structural formatting and hyperlinks.
HTTP	*Hypertext transport protocol;* the technique used by web servers to dispense information to web browsers.
Hyper	Nonlinear, capable of branching off in many directions; the term can be used alone or as a prefix.
Image map	A clickable image that connects to different URLs depending on which part of the image is clicked.
Information Superhighway, Information Highway, Infoway, Infobahn, and so on	Terms coined to describe a possible information infrastructure, using coaxial or fiber-optic cables, that would upgrade the existing system. (These terms correspond to nothing in the real world; the Internet is not a superhighway.)
Integration	The convergence of two technologies into one (such as the mythical convergence of TVs and computers).
Internet	A collection of networks and computers all over the world, all of which share information, or at least e-mail, using agreed-upon Internet protocols.
Link	A specially designed word or image that, when clicked, takes a web browser to a new page or other destination (an embedded web address).
Modem	The box that connects your computer to a normal phone line.
Multimedia	Refers to the incorporation of many different media, often including text, pictures, sounds, video, animation, and so on.

Table 1.1:　World Wide Web Jargon

Jargon Term	What It Means
Net	A loosely defined term meant to suggest the loose association of all or most computers on the planet. This term generally refers to a more inclusive set of linked networks than just the Internet, but it also corresponds roughly to the Internet.
Netcasting	Publishing web content on a continuous basis to subscribed viewers (also called *webcasting* and *push*).
Page	On the World Wide Web, an HTML document.
Portal	A major web site that large numbers of visitors use as a starting point on the Web.
Push	See *Netcasting*.
Server	A piece of software or machine that acts as a centralized source of information or computing resources (such as web sites, Gopher menus, FTP archives, and so on) available to clients.
Site	A location on the Internet, often the host of one or more servers, or a set of related web pages.
Web	The World Wide Web.
Webcasting	See *Netcasting*.
World Wide Web	A subset or cross-section of the Internet technically composed of a set of mutually hyperlinked documents and objects stored on web servers, but commonly taken to include any resource on the Net that can be reached with a web browser.

Table 1.1: World Wide Web Jargon *(continued)*

them for free once you're on the Net.) Suffice it to say, the Internet is not really a coherent network in the same sense as a local area network, such as you might find in an office, or a wide area network, like you might find on a university campus.

Actually, the Internet is a loosely and redundantly linked collection of smaller networks and individual computers, all of which agree to share (some) information using the various Internet protocols as a *lingua franca*.

If you ask what the Internet is like or how it works, you'll get the sort of range of answers obtainable from blind men touching different parts of an elephant. The Internet is like a cloud. The Internet is like a web. The Internet is like a tree. I suggest you think of the Internet as a black box.

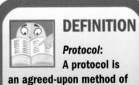

DEFINITION

Protocol:
A protocol is an agreed-upon method of communication used by two computers or two programs to interchange information—but busy people don't have to worry about it.

Stuff goes in one end and comes out the other. Forget trying to figure out what happens in the middle. Why did the chicken choose a particular path through the Internet? To get to the other side.

On the Beaten Track

To compare advertisements on the Web with those on television, some people use a pull vs. push metaphor: TV ads are pushed toward you, but web ads pull you toward them, ceding you more control.

The Web is a weird conglomeration of major media outlets, underground or alternative publishing ventures, self-promotion, home movies, and billboards. Amidst all this chaos are some big players, usually tied to major publishing empires and supported by advertising. One nice thing about advertising on the Web is that you can generally avoid it simply by not clicking the links to sponsors' sites. On the other hand, you'll be forced to see (and wait for) the art associated with a link when a web page that includes an ad is loaded.

The web browser you use determines where you start (what home page you start on), and therefore what primary links are available to you and whose list of cool or new sites you see.

Companies or other organizations can customize the browsers they distribute to their employees or clients, in the same way ISPs, computer hardware, operating systems, and software manufacturers can.

Some of the big names or owners of major pages you'll hear about include:

- **Netscape**   Makers of the most widely distributed web browser
- **Yahoo!**   One of the most comprehensive web directories
- **Wired.com**   The first major commercial web publication
- **CNN**   Yes, the Cable News Network
- **clnet**   The online publishing network
- **W3C.org**   The World Wide Web consortium
- **Amazon**   The most notable of the large scale e-commerce ventures

EXPERT ADVICE

You can always customize the home page of a browser to point to your own personal favorite page or list of sites, as explained in Chapter 2.

- **Microsoft**   Thrown for a loop (briefly) by the Internet, this software behemoth has developed a broad, coherent web presence

You'll have no trouble finding these sites because all roads lead to them. Many of them function as jumping-off points to other similar high-gloss sites.

Is the Web a New Kind of TV?

So if CNN and ESPN have some of the most popular, most expensive, most close-to-supporting-themselves-via-advertising web sites, does this mean that the Web is really a new kind of TV? No, it doesn't, but those who have thrived in the one-to-many media model would like to emphasize those capacities of the Internet. Others would argue that the Net is inherently many-to-many, and must naturally evolve differently from TV.

Still, there is WebTV, which puts the Internet on your TV screen (without cable speed, alas), and does not require that you own a computer. This means the Internet is neither a subset of the computer world nor of the TV world, but is rather a specific tool in its own right. It will naturally share some of the advantages and disadvantages of other existing media, and it promises to be omnivorous, possibly incorporating TV-quality broadcasting on standard computer screens, as well as more convenient Web-based information access with hand-held computer devices.

And on the integration front, Microsoft owns part of the cable television channel MSNBC and together they produce the MSNBC web site and web channel, so that's a form of integration already (integration, by the way, is the buzzword that implies two technologies becoming one, as in TVs and computers merging into one appliance). ZDNet and clnet also produce technology-oriented television shows tied in with websites.

What Can You Use the Web For?

So the Web is the easiest way to get around the Internet, but what can you use it for? What are the practical applications? More and more new services are coming online all the time, but the following are some of the things you can do on the Web right now:

- Shop for products and buy them online
- Find and download software
- Make travel plans
- Do financial planning
- Research medical conditions
- Look for a new job
- Join in on ongoing discussions
- Read some of the wealth of information published on the Web
- Search for people or information

Buying Things

Figure 1.1 shows the Amazon.com online bookstore web site (**http://www.amazon.com**).

IS THIS FOR ME?

This is a question you must ask yourself repeatedly. There are degrees of involvement with the Internet, and as a busy person you shouldn't get anymore involved in or distracted by the Net than you would allow yourself to be by any other diversion. If it helps your business communication to use e-mail, by all means use it. If you can find resources you need quickly and easily on the Web, it would be foolish not to explore it. If your enterprise has a legitimate purpose that could be served more efficiently through a Net presence, then look into it.

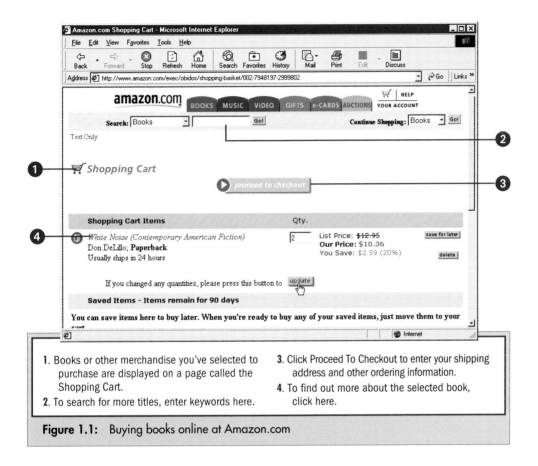

1. Books or other merchandise you've selected to purchase are displayed on a page called the Shopping Cart.
2. To search for more titles, enter keywords here.

3. Click Proceed To Checkout to enter your shipping address and other ordering information.
4. To find out more about the selected book, click here.

Figure 1.1:   Buying books online at Amazon.com

Outside of ordinary retail, the hottest trend in web shopping is auction sites such as eBay.com, where ordinary individuals bid on each others' collectibles (see Figure 1.2). Auction sites make especially good use of the Web because they bring together buyers and sellers and broker the transactions. Because of the success of the eBay model, many other auction sites have cropped up, and most of the portal sites have added an auction feature in the relentless effort to offer everything in a single place. There's even a site called iTrack (**http://www.itrack.com**) where users can monitor auctions at multiple sites.

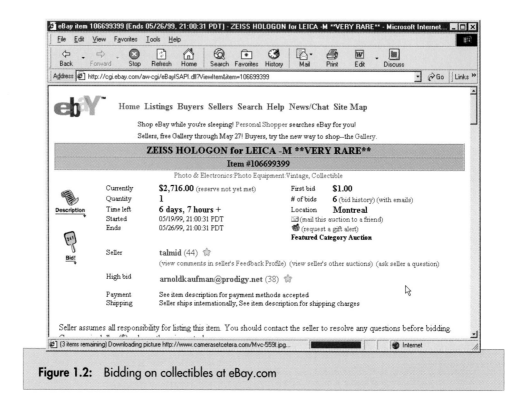

Figure 1.2: Bidding on collectibles at eBay.com

There's more on finding and downloading software in Chapter 3.

Getting Software

Figure 1.3 shows me downloading WinZip—it's easy!—from clnet's Shareware.com web site.

Making Travel Plans

Figure 1.4 shows Microsoft Expedia, a site where you can research and book your own airline flights.

For much more concrete advice on investments and money management online, see Chapter 6.

Investments and Money Management

Financial advice and information on the Net ranges in quality from highly regarded tip sheets to bum steers of questionable provenance. The Motley Fool site got its start on AOL and puts its money where its mouth is in its own portfolio (see Figure 1.5).

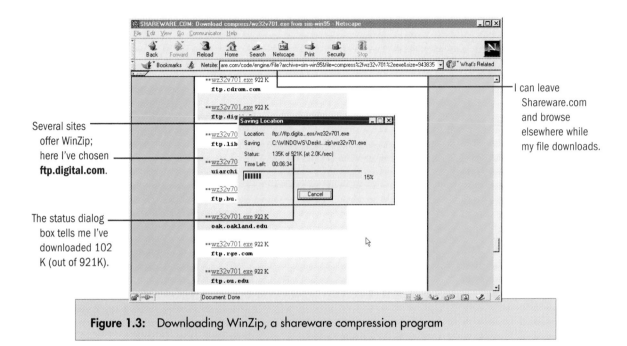

Several sites offer WinZip; here I've chosen **ftp.digital.com**.

The status dialog box tells me I've downloaded 102 K (out of 921K).

I can leave Shareware.com and browse elsewhere while my file downloads.

Figure 1.3: Downloading WinZip, a shareware compression program

Both of these round trips are the same price.

I'm hoping to get away to New Orleans in March.

You can fine-tune your travel dates and times.

Figure 1.4: Sites such as Expedia offer travel-agent style flight information packaged with other services, such as weekly updates on best prices for flights to a destination you select in advance.

Get quotes for specific stocks.

Follow real-world portfolio demonstrations.

Get up-to-the-minute market reports and analysis.

Figure 1.5: Get investment advice from self-proclaimed fools and others.

Health/Medical Research

There are support groups and updates on research for just about any medical condition (see Figure 1.6).

Job Hunting

These days, unemployment is coming down and jobs are hunting for people. One of the fundamental benefits of a large-scale network such as the Internet is the brokerage of large groups of buyers and sellers or, in this case, hirers and job-seekers. This isn't going to change the it's not what you know, it's who you know rule, but at least you're no longer limited to answering blind want ads in your local paper. Figure 1.7 shows a searchable job resource for openings in the non-profit sector. (See Chapter 3 for more on searching.)

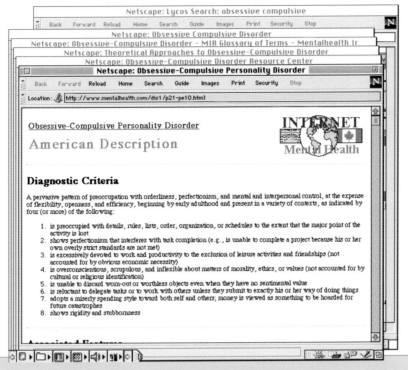

Figure 1.6:   A basic search I conducted for the parents of a child suffering from obsessive/compulsive disorder pinpointed many helpful resources.

Tracking Packages

The Internet can even help you solve problems in the real world, such as looking for a missing package from a delivery service (see Figure 1.8).

Using the Web Without Wasting Time

The biggest impediment to making efficient use of the World Wide Web is that it's essentially a digressive medium, perfectly suited for long asides and fascinating tangents, and is less well suited for hard-core, finite research.

This is Opera, a perfectly good (in fact, fast) browser that isn't made by Netscape *or* Microsoft.

I found this site when doing a quick search on the phrase "job hunting."

Opera v3.0 - [Job Search]

File Edit View Navigation Lists Mail News Preferences Window Help

Search Jobs

Home

To search job listings, you may target the jobs that you wish to scan by selecting any one or more of the following:

Select jobs by salary range:

Select job type:

Any

Select jobs by employer name:

Select jobs by job title

Any
$20-30,000 $30-40,000
$40-50,000 $50-60,000
$60-70,000 $70-80,000
$80-100,000   Over $100,000

Limit search to jobs posted within last 2 weeks

http://www.nonprofitjobs.org/sjob.cfml   100%

This search page at **www.nonprofitjobs.org** helps you look for work in the nonprofit sector.

Figure 1.7: You can be as specific or as flexible as you like when searching for jobs with this form.

CAUTION

With most browsers, once you back up and then head in a new direction, the branch you explored earlier will disappear from your history path. This is one important reason why you should make bookmarks.

There are two things you can do to make more efficient use of your time on the Web. The first is something I cannot emphasize strongly enough: make bookmarks. Make Bookmarks. MAKE BOOKMARKS! The Web rambles this way and that, and you're bound to visit some interesting sites and then never see them again because you won't remember exactly which tangents you followed to get there. You can always remove bookmarks that you end up not needing, so make a bookmark every time you arrive at an interesting-looking site. Later, you'll be glad you did.

The other good advice I can offer is to separate out your business or educational use of the Web from your recreational use. To save time working on the Web, set yourself a goal and head for it as directly as you can. If, along the way, you are tempted by the siren call of interesting links, note them or make bookmarks for them, but put off visiting them for another time.

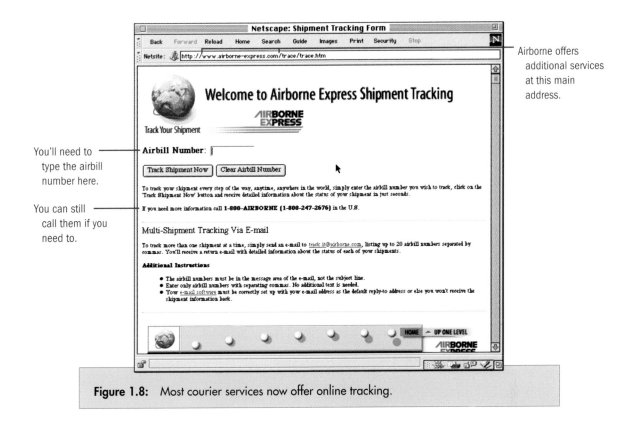

You'll need to type the airbill number here.

You can still call them if you need to.

Airborne offers additional services at this main address.

Figure 1.8:   Most courier services now offer online tracking.

If You've Seen One Web Browser, You've Seen 'em All

If you need to get, install, or set up Microsoft Internet Explorer or Netscape Navigator, see Chapter 2.

If I've whetted your appetite to check out the World Wide Web for yourself, then it's time for you to fire up a web browser and start exploring. There are quite a few browsers out there, but the two you're most likely to encounter are Microsoft's Internet Explorer and

---

EXPERT ADVICE

If any web page takes more than 90 seconds before even beginning to load, stop the browser and try again or come back later. You're too busy to sit there twiddling your thumbs while computers fail to connect to each other.

Netscape's Navigator. Since 1994, each company has released four new versions (not including bug-fixed versions) in an ever-escalating features war.

I'll show you how to set up and use both of these browsers because the odds are that you'll have access to at least one, if not both of them. Even if you end up using some other browser, most of the features will be the same. First, I'll give you a basic rundown of how to work with any browser. Then I'll give you the specifics for Internet Explorer and any details that differ for Netscape.

Web Browser Basics

No matter what kind of web browser or Internet connection you have, the overall process of running a browser and connecting to the Web is more or less the same. Sometimes the terminology or the actual mechanism varies from program to program, and not all browsers share the exact same set of capabilities, but the differences are getting smaller with every revision. The features war that I alluded to earlier means that browsers are squirmy things, changing all the time (so long as you keep upgrading, that is).

With any web browser, you'll need to know how to

- Start the program
- Navigate the Web by following links
- Move backward and forward along your recent path
- Type a web address to go to that location directly
- Turn off graphics for speedy browsing (for graphical browsers only, naturally)
- Make and return to bookmarks
- Assign a favorite web page as your starting page (discussed, along with other customizations options, in Chapter 2)
- Search the Internet (see Chapter 3 for the full lowdown)

Once you have these basic techniques down, browsing the Web is simply a matter of starting your program and then following links, visiting bookmarks, entering addresses directly, and searching.

If you don't have an Internet connection or don't know whether you are connected, see Appendix A for information on how to shop for and select an Internet service provider (ISP). If you are connected to the Net but you don't have a web browser available, see Chapter 2 for information on how to obtain and install Microsoft Internet Explorer or Netscape Navigator.

When people talk about addresses on the Internet, they usually mean web addresses (URLs) or e-mail addresses (see Chapter 4).

EXPERT ADVICE

Another thing you'll have to get used to is updating your software from time to time. If you ever notice that the program in front of you lacks a feature I'm describing in the book, you may need to upgrade your web browser. If so, see Chapter 2.

Sure, you'll encounter some variations: pages that are split into frames like a TV dinner, sites that ask you to register and/or enter a password to proceed, secure connections between your browser and a host so you can purchase products online without exposing your credit card to snoops. But the basic routine—the motions of pointing, clicking, bopping from site to site—doesn't change.

Your Internet connection must be up and running for your web browser to work. See Appendix A for more on determining your type of Internet connection.

Clicking Links and Going Back and Forward

Most of the time, you'll go from page to page on the Web by clicking hypertext links. These are images or highlighted words that, when clicked, jump you to another page or section of a page. Most web browsers also have special links built in. Usually a browser has an icon (placed near the top right-hand corner) that leads directly to the browser's own home page, and other buttons or menu items that take you to directories, search pages, new site announcements, and so on. Even if you start by visiting one of these built-in destinations, you'll soon be proceeding by clicking links.

Many high-end pages these days sport image maps, which are clickable images that connect to different URLs, depending on where they are clicked.

Your mouse pointer changes (usually from an arrow to a pointing hand, as shown here) when you point to a link. Your browser's status bar will usually show the URL destination of the link to which you're pointing, although some web designers substitute explanatory text down there. On some websites, link image or text becomes animated when pointed to. Web designers call this "rollover."

EXPERT ADVICE

If you ever get tired of waiting for a page to appear, press the Stop button and then either try again (click Reload) or go somewhere else.

CAUTION

Some addresses will take you to one page and then immediately whisk you off to another. If you're ever taken to a page where you don't want to be, just use your Back button to head back to familiar territory.

Once you've followed a few links, you'll either find something interesting or you'll feel that you're running into a dead end. If you find something interesting, make a bookmark (more on that later in this chapter). If you don't, you can always retrace your steps, back and forth, using your browser's Back and Forward buttons (or jump several pages at a time by choosing from a list of recent sites).

Use these buttons to retrace your steps.

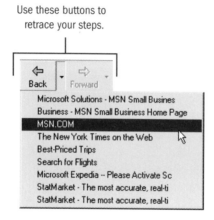

DEFINITION

URL: Uniform resource locator. The URL is a standard form of address for any file, object, or resource (any information unit) on the Internet. Pragmatically, a URL is an Internet address expressed in a form that any web browser can understand. Web addresses usually start with http:// (or something else followed by ://) and usually end with .html or just a trailing / to indicate the default file in a folder.

Typing Addresses Directly

In a perfect Internet, every interesting destination on the World Wide Web would be accessible via a single click of the mouse. But because the Net evolves so quickly, there is no single comprehensive listing anywhere that covers everything you might ever want to see. Sometimes you'll learn about an interesting spot on the Web from a book or newspaper article, or even from a friend. In that case, the location on the Web will be expressed in the form of a *URL*.

In most web browsers, you can type the address directly into the location box. Windows 98 includes not only a box you can add to your taskbar that can launch your default web browser (pointed at the address you enter), *but also* a box built into every folder window that can start only Internet Explorer. MacOS 8 offers a similar Apple menu feature (Connect To), which opens a location box that launches your default web browser when you enter a web address.

Table 1.2 shows you six sample URLs.

URL	What It Points To
http://altavista.digital.com/	The main page (also called the *index* or *default file*) of the AltaVista server at the Digital Equipment Corporation Site. (AltaVista is a search engine.)
http://ezone.org/ez/	The home page of a magazine called *Enterzone* on a server called ezone in the domain of not-for-profit organizations (.org).
http://www.emf.net/~estephen/zeigen.html	An HTML document called *Zeigen's Dilemma*, located in the personal directory of the owner of the site (Stephen Mack) on the web server of his service provider, EMF.
ftp://ftp.cdrom.com	The public file archive of an online CD-ROM retailer.
gopher://gopher.netcom.com/	A menu on a Gopher server (which is technically not a web document, but which can be reached via the Web) on a machine in the network of Netcom, an Internet service provider.
news:news.announce.newusers	A Usenet newsgroup. Note that most URLs correspond to a specific document somewhere out there on the Internet, but the Usenet URLs usually point to an entire newsgroup.

Table 1.2: Five Sample URLs and Where They'll Take You

Don't worry about learning the system for naming URLs. Before long, they'll be completely hidden. For now, just be sure to spell the URL correctly, carefully copying it character for character (and making sure to duplicate the capitalization as well, as parts of URLs are case-sensitive), if you plan to use it to reach a destination.

If you *are* forced to copy a web address from paper, beware of some common typographical errors. Web addresses rarely end in periods, for example, so if you see an address printed with a period at the end, it's probably just punctuation in the sentence and not part of the address. Addresses often end with the letters html or with a forward slash (/). Web addresses sometimes have a ~ character (called a *tilde* or *squiggle*) in them, and sometimes newspapers will mess up and leave it out entirely or put it on top of a letter of the alphabet instead of within the address.

Depending on your mail program, people may be able to send you e-mail with an attached web address so that all you have to do is

You can leave a trailing "/" off of most addresses.

CAUTION

If you copy a URL from a newspaper or book, be prepared to deal with typos. Often URLs gain or lose hyphens in key places when typeset in "old-fashioned" publications.

double-click the attachment and your mail program will start your web browser and go directly to the attached address.

If you are sent a web address (a URL) via e-mail or some other onscreen medium, then you can select and copy the address and then paste it directly into your browser's address box. This saves you the trouble of retyping and eliminates the risk of making a typo. In some e-mail programs, you can click or double-click any web address to jump to your browser and visit the page directly.

Fixing an Incorrect Address

If you type an address and receive an error message rather than the web page or resource you were looking for, try trimming the address. Just follow these steps:

1. Select the final file or directory name in the URL and delete it.
2. Press ENTER.
3. If you still don't get where you want to go, repeat the process until you get down to just the root web address with no path folders or file name (**http://***something.thing*/).

Printing a Web Page

Even though most people read web pages online, jumping from page to page like a TV-watcher skirting advertisements, you can easily print an interesting page to read at your leisure or to send to someone who lacks Internet access. Just click the Print button (or select File | Print) and then click OK.

DEFINITION

Search engine: A large database of Internet addresses that users can visit on the Web and query to search for resources.

Domain name: Every computer on the Internet can be identified (and addressed) by a domain name consisting of, from right to left, a primary domain (such as com, edu, net, mil, or gov), a subdomain (such as gateway2000, princeton, pacbell, or whitehouse), and an optional host or site name (such as www, garnet, or grateful), all separated by dots.

EXPERT ADVICE

On a page with multiple frames, your browser will print the current frame (either the one you've clicked or the one that appeared most recently). Frames don't always have visible borders and only in the Mac version of Netscape is it easy to tell which frame is selected (it gets a thick black border). Background images—even watermark-type images—may or may not print by default, depending on your browser and version. Recent versions of both browsers, however, give you more control over what aspects of a page will print.

Internet Explorer, the New Champion

Slow and steady wins the race, they say, and true to form, Microsoft has gradually whittled away at Netscape's headstart in the browser competition and has finally become the most popular web browser around. Microsoft's Internet Explorer can be downloaded for free from its web site (**http://www.microsoft.com/ie/**). Internet Explorer's close ties to the Windows platform might slow its acceptance among Macintosh and Unix users, but these ties will inevitably help it prosper if Microsoft succeeds in integrating the web interface into the company's dominant operating system product.

If you need help obtaining a copy of Internet Explorer, see Chapter 2.

Microsoft Terminology

Partly as a consequence of Internet Explorer's compliance with Windows 95 standards, some of the terminology it uses differs from that used elsewhere on the Internet. To save you from committing embarrassing *faux pas* in front of Internet purists, the following table provides you with some translations.

What Others Call It	What Microsoft Calls It
A link	A shortcut
Bookmarks (or hotlist)	Favorites
Images	Pictures
Reloading a page	Refreshing a page

Starting Internet Explorer

In Windows 98 and later, Internet Explorer is integrated with the old Explorer folder-window system, and you can jump to the Web at any time by typing a web address in the location box at the top of a window or by clicking the Internet Explorer icon that appears at the upper-right of all folder-windows. (On the Mac, you start Internet Explorer the same way you do any other program.)

To start Internet Explorer, you can also double-click the Internet Explorer icon. Internet Explorer starts you at a page called Microsoft Internet Start (see Figure 1.9). This page may change, and as with any browser, you can assign a different page as your startup page (see Chapter 2 for how to do that).

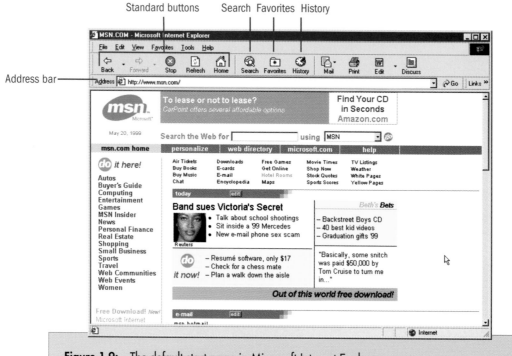

Figure 1.9: The default start page in Microsoft Internet Explorer

If you have an older installation (or if your PC came installed with AOL), you may be started off at a different page called Welcome to MSN! If so, go to *http://www.msn.com/* to get with the new program.

If you've used Internet Explorer before, you may have noticed that Microsoft has changed the start page that automatically comes up when you start the program. Microsoft has been sorting out their web strategy for the last few years, and in the meantime, a number of different home pages have come and gone.

Microsoft has now settled into a fairly coherent system:

- Its home pages relate to the giant software company and its products.

- The MSN home pages are of more general interest. MSN refers to Microsoft's online service the Microsoft Network. MSN started as an America Online-type online service but has retooled itself as a web presence with special content and services for MSN members as well as Internet Explorer users.

- There have been four different versions of Internet Explorer in the past few years, and each has had a different default home page. If your computer once had an earlier version installed, you may find that even your up-to-date Internet Explorer starts at the old page.

Ever since version 3.0, Internet Explorer's buttons have appeared in a new style that may be unfamiliar to you. Buttons don't look raised in this scheme. Instead, they appear to light up when the mouse pointer passes over them. The standard Windows 98 folder windows have also been retooled to look this way, as will the upcoming versions of other Microsoft applications.

Favorite Places

Internet Explorer saves shortcuts to your favorite web pages in a folder called Favorites. Instead of adding a bookmark to your hotlist, as various other web browsers refer to it, you add a page to your Favorites, but the idea is the same.

There are a couple of ways to add a page (such as the *Wall Street Journal* page) to your Favorites folder:

- Select Favorites | Add To Favorites.
- Right-click (or, if you're a Mac user, click and hold). When a shortcut menu pops up, choose Add To Favorites.

A dialog box called Add to Favorites, looking like a standard Save As dialog box, appears.

Internet Explorer will invite you to subscribe to the page (see "Channels" later in this chapter for an explanation). Change the name for the shortcut if you like and then click the Add button. The page will then appear on the Favorites menu as well as in the Favorites folder. Any time you want to return to a favorite page, you can select Favorites and choose the page from the menu.

To get rid of a less-favored shortcut or to rearrange your favorites, select Favorites | Organize Favorites, select the shortcut, and press DELETE or move or rename it. Then click Close. Internet Explorer stores your favorites in a normal folder on your computer's hard disk, but if you click the Favorites button, the contents of the folder appear in a bar down the left side of the window.

E-Mail with Internet Explorer

Clicking a mailto link (shortcut) in Internet Explorer automatically launches whichever e-mail program you have integrated into your operating system and your local network (if any). See Chapter 4 for more on the differences among various mail programs.

Smart Updating

Microsoft's Active Setup system enables you to upgrade your Internet Explorer (and other MS software) automatically. To update the most recent version of Internet Explorer (MSIE for short), choose Tools | Windows Update. Active Setup will ask you for your OK to check for components on your system. Click Yes. (If the program didn't check with you, Microsoft would be accused of snooping on your computer.) This connects you to an Update page at one of Microsoft's web sites (see Figure 1.10). Follow the simple instructions to add any piecemeal component to your setup.

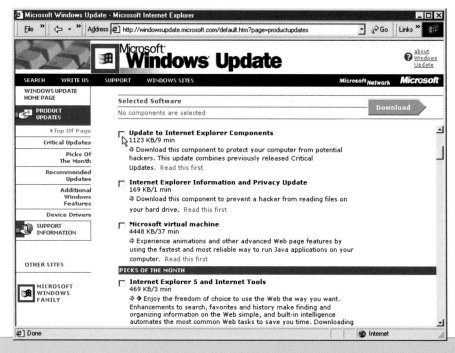

Figure 1.10: Microsoft's Active Setup is designed to keep you coming back for more.

Netscape, Now the Challenger

According to some research, about half of web browsers in use are still versions of Netscape. Odds are you'll end up in front of Netscape sometime if you haven't already.

Starting Netscape

There are two ways to start Netscape:

- Double-click the Netscape icon (don't worry if yours looks different—they change it all the time).
- Open your computer's Start (or Apple) menu and select Netscape (or, if necessary, thumb through the appropriate submenus and *then* select Netscape).

   (If this is the first time a version of Netscape will be run on your computer, you'll be asked to register the product and be offered a digital ID: you can opt yes or no at each step, and then a Netscape License Agreement dialog box will appear. Read the agreement and then click the Accept button.)

   Netscape will start and connect you to the Netscape home page, called Welcome to Netscape (see Figure 1.11).

Netscape is locked in a tight struggle with Microsoft for dominance of the Web as a new platform, interface, and market. Netscape has made its basic product free and its software code available to developers in an attempt to head off Mister G.

The figures in this book will generally show Windows screens, but I'll always point out differences in the Macintosh version of Navigator (such as shortcuts for commands) as they come up. (So don't feel left out, Mac users.)

Location toolbar

Navigation toolbar

Personal toolbar

This ad is a clickable image

Clickable hypertext link

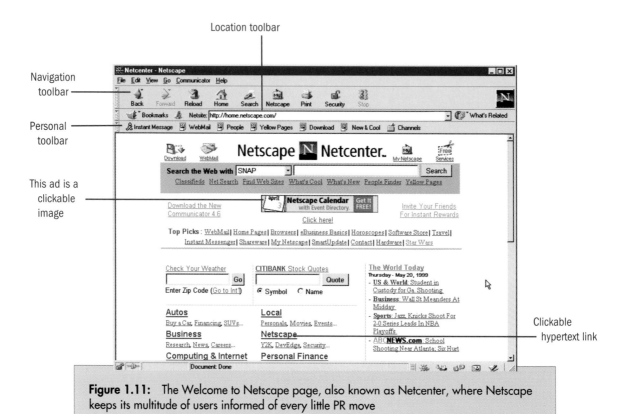

Figure 1.11: The Welcome to Netscape page, also known as Netcenter, where Netscape keeps its multitude of users informed of every little PR move

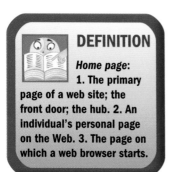

DEFINITION

Home page:
1. The primary page of a web site; the front door; the hub. 2. An individual's personal page on the Web. 3. The page on which a web browser starts.

You can return to your browser's startup page at any point by clicking the Home icon on the toolbar.

Using Your Startup Page as a Starting Point

When you start your browser, it has to open at some location. The lingo is that it starts off "pointing at" some address on the Web. Most browsers come configured to start you on a page maintained by the maker of the browser. Some may come configured to start you at your company's or department's home page on the Web.

Usually, the startup page will have all kinds of useful jumping-off points for random web surfing, for specific information resources, and for search utilities that can lead almost anywhere on the Internet.

Netscape's Built-In Directory Links

Your browser may also have some useful links built in to its menus or toolbars. Netscape's personal toolbar menu points to a number of different starting places, some maintained by Netscape, some by independent companies competing for Netscape's audience. Netscape's directory of the Net is produced by Yahoo!, the oldest popular directory site (on the Internet, dating back to 1994 qualifies something as old). To see it, click the Internet button on the personal toolbar.

To take a look at the leading Internet directories and search sites, click the Search button on the Navigation toolbar. This takes you to Netscape's Net Search page (more on this in Chapter 3), which features the dominant front doors to the Net, with different ones featured prominently at different times.

Making Bookmarks

If you get to a page you find interesting, but you don't have the time to explore it and all of its links completely in one sitting, make a bookmark for that page. I recommend making bookmarks often. They're easy enough to get rid of, but without them, it can be very difficult to find your way back to a page you only vaguely remember from an earlier web session.

To do so, click the Bookmarks button on the Location toolbar and select Add Bookmark.

You can also right-click on a page (or click and hold with a Macintosh) and choose Add Bookmark to make a bookmark there, or you can right-click on a link (Mac users click and hold) to bookmark a page without even visiting it first.

After you add a bookmark, the page will appear at the bottom of the Bookmarks menu the next time you pull it down.

You can continue following other links or backtrack and go off in another direction. When you find another interesting page, bookmark it, too. (Notice that the previous bookmark you added is now on the

DEFINITION

Directory: An edited, categorized, usually searchable catalog of resources on the Internet.

Search Site: Also called a search engine; a searchable, usually unedited (inclusive), sometimes categorized listing of resources on the Internet.

You can also jump directly to a search page by typing two or more words (separated by spaces) in the Location box (next to the Netsite label).

EXPERT ADVICE

You can have Netscape check to see if any of the pages you've bookmarked have changed since you last visited them. To do so, in the Bookmarks window, select the bookmarks you want to update unless you want to update them all, choose View | Update Bookmarks, choose All or Selected, and then click Start Checking.

DEFINITION

Bookmark: A saved reference to a web address which enables you to return to that address instantly at any time. Also called a hotlist entry or a favorite place.

bookmark list.) Now you can return instantly to any of your previously bookmarked pages by selecting it from the Bookmarks menu.

At first this approach works best. Soon, though, you will fill up your Bookmarks menu and you'll have to create submenus and file your bookmarks into different categories. To organize your bookmarks, select Bookmarks | Edit Bookmarks to open your Bookmarks in a window for editing. Often you'll find that you've bookmarked the same page two or more times. Other times you'll find that a bookmarked page no longer exists or, more to the point, no longer interests you. In either case, you can easily remove bookmarks from the Bookmarks window by selecting them and then pressing DELETE.

Once you've run out of space on the menu, even after deleting unwanted bookmarks, you can make submenus (just like subdirectories) in the Bookmarks window by selecting File | New Folder. Type a name for the submenu in the Bookmark Properties dialog box that appears, press ENTER, and then click OK (see Figure 1.12).

You can then drag your existing bookmarks into folders based on their categories. To revisit a bookmarked page that's filed in a submenu folder, click the Bookmarks button, select the submenu, and then click the bookmark.

As of Netscape version 4.5 and later, you can file bookmarks directly into existing submenus when you first make them. To do so, click the Bookmarks button, select File Bookmark, and then choose the submenu name you want, as demonstrated in the following illustration:

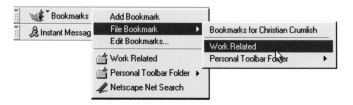

Bookmark Properties   ✕

General

Name: New Folder

Location (URL):

Description:

There are no aliases to this bookmark   Select Aliases

Last Visited:

Added on: 1/28/1998 6:47 PM

OK   Cancel   Help

Figure 1.12:   Making submenus is the only way to keep your bookmarks under control in the long run.

Saving an Image to Your Computer

If you see an image on a web page that you'd like to save on your own computer, you can snatch it easily with Netscape. Just right-click the image you want to save (click and hold with the Macintosh) and choose Save Image As. A Save As dialog box will appear. Change the filename if you want and specify the location where the image will be saved. Then click the Save button.

Previewing a Page Before Printing

If you want to preview a page before printing, don't click the Print button or select File | Print. Instead follow these steps:

1. Select File | Print Preview. This starts a Print Preview mode similar to that of a word processing program.

2. Click the magnifying glass icon anywhere on the page to zoom in to that place, to see how well Netscape renders the page for

Back
Forward
Reload
Stop

View Source
View Info
View Image (resumes.gif)

Set As Wallpaper
Add Bookmark
Create Shortcut
Send Page

Save Image As...

Copy Image Location

NETIQUETTE There's nothing wrong with saving other people's images on your computer. Just don't republish the art on the Web or in any other medium without the expressed permission of the artist and original publisher.

EXPERT ADVICE

You can save the text contents (as well as the embedded hypertext links) of a web document in the form of an HTML (.html or .htm) file, in much the same way as you save images. Select File | Save As and then save the document.

---

printing. (Some web pages won't look good or won't be legible when printed.)

3. Repeat step 2 to zoom in closer and then, after three clicks, zoom back out again.

4. If everything looks OK, click the Print button.

Figure 1.13 shows pages in Print Preview mode.

S ee Chapter 4 for an explanation of Internet e-mail.

Sending E-Mail from Netscape

There are two ways to send e-mail while browsing the Web, but each of them uses the exact same mechanism in Netscape. Some web pages

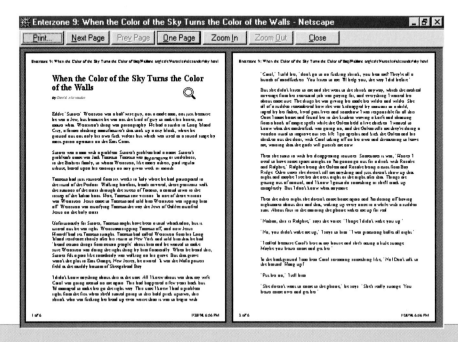

Figure 1.13: You can preview a page before printing it.

have e-mail links, also referred to as mailto links (because the URL of such a link starts with mailto:, as in **mailto:busy2k@syx.com**). Click one of these links and Netscape will open up a mail dialog box with the e-mail of the recipient automatically in place, drawn from the link URL. These links allow web publishers to invite easy interaction from the audience.

However, you don't need a mailto link to send e-mail from within Netscape. You can also select File | Send Page (to send a copy of the page you're viewing to someone) or File | New Message (CTRL+M or COMMAND+M). This brings up a mail message window (see Figure 1.14). Netscape suggests a subject (the title of the page) and, if you chose to mail the document, pastes the current URL into the first line of the message window and includes the document itself as an attachment.

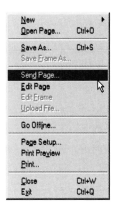

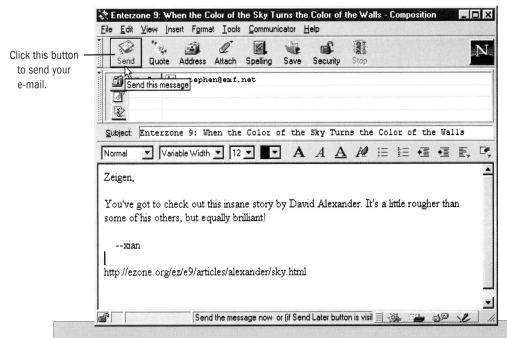

Click this button to send your e-mail.

Figure 1.14: Send e-mail to anyone on the Internet from within Netscape, and include the text content of your current web page if you like.

In earlier versions of Netscape, the Send Page command was called Mail Document. Netscape and other software developers seem to change command and menu names frequently from version to version, most likely in half-hearted efforts to standardize or improve the interface. Try to think of the meaning or use of the commands you encounter and you'll weather the changing nomenclature more easily.

Smart Updating

Netscape has automated the process of upgrading your software when improvements have come down the pike for various components. Any time you want to check to see if you're due for an upgrade, select Help | Software Updates (or click the SmartUpdate link on the Welcome to Netscape page at **http://home.netscape.com/**). Figure 1.15 shows Netscape's web-based update page.

Quitting Netscape

When you're finished browsing and have made bookmarks to all the tantalizing loose ends that you plan to pursue later, quit Netscape by selecting File | Exit. Then get back to work!

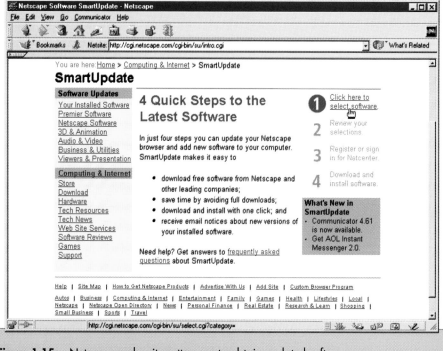

Figure 1.15:   Netscape makes it pretty easy to obtain updated software.

Using a Different Browser

There are many different browsers available. If you have one other than the two I've described, I think you'll be able to follow along, taking into account that some commands may appear on different menus or with slightly different names, and that some of the latest features may not be supported.

One up and coming browser, Opera (**http:// www. operasoftware.com/**), is favored by some for its speed and responsiveness. Many claim that it is a less bloated program than the other browsers that are caught up in the features war.

All Circuits Are Busy

The Internet is still a haphazard collection of networks and you won't always be able to make the connection you want. Sometimes, especially during peak hours (traditionally, the normal work week in the U.S., but patterns are changing), your browser will fail to connect to the page you want. In general, all traffic on the Internet is highest during these times, and popular servers can slow down or even crash when hit by too many clients. Even sites that are available 24-hours a day, seven-days a week need to shut down occasionally for maintenance or in the event of a crash.

You'll see an error message, perhaps alluding to a "failed DNS server look up" or what have you, but ignore it; it's usually just your browser's knee-jerk guess as to what went wrong (a symptom of a busy or overworked network). Most of the time, all that happened was that some attempt to connect along the route timed out; that is, gave up before connecting successfully.

Sometimes your browser won't acknowledge that it's hung up somewhere. Instead it will just keep churning away as if it's really loading a page, but nothing new will happen, and the thermometer-like readout that shows the progress will stop moving. When your browser gives up, whether it admits it or not, press the Stop button and try again.

Lately, my experience suggests that usage patterns may be changing with weekends becoming the busiest times for dial-up users on the Net. This suggests that recreation, more than business, is driving the Net's popularity.

Another problem you may run into is not knowing the exact address of or any specific route to the information or site you want to reach. In that case, you'll want to use one of the many search mechanisms available on the Web. See Chapter 3 for more information on searching.

Some Final Questions

Here are a few more naturally occurring questions about the Net that I find myself answering all the time:

How Can I Keep Up with the Web?

There's really no way you can keep up with the Web. It's changing and evolving so rapidly, I'm not sure it even makes sense to talk about keeping up with it. However, there are a few things you can do to stay in the loop.

One thing I'd recommend is subscribing to *Netsurfer Digest*. To check it out, visit its home page at **http://www.netsurf.com/nsd/**. Read the latest issue and see if you'd like to receive it. It comes more or less weekly and is sent as an e-mail message (with web formatting). All sites are linked directly from the newsletter pages.

Another good place to visit is the clnet online home page (**http://www.cnet.com**). So far, clnet is the leading online source for Internet information.

How Hard Is It to Publish on the Web?

Putting up your own pages on the Web is easier than you might think. See Chapter 7 to learn how to build your own web site and Chapter 8 to learn how to set up shop on the Internet.

How Do I Find Information on the Net?

For the web browser to become a truly useful front door to the Internet, it has to enable you to reach out and find specific information quickly and accurately. Browsing the Web from site to site, following whims and distractions, is a new mode of entertainment and has its place, but there's more to the Web than just channel surfing. If you want learn how to zero in on specific information, resources, or people, go on to Chapter 3.

There's More . . .

Now you know the basics of getting onto the Internet and finding sites, information, programs, and people to talk to out there. But there's more to this book than coverage of the World Wide Web. That's because, contrary to all the hype you may have heard recently, there's a lot more to the Internet than just the Web. In fact, the area of the Internet with the highest volume of usage (discounting huge binary files, such as graphics) is still (and probably always will be) electronic mail. Chapter 2 shows you the ropes for using specific web browsers, and Chapter 3 introduces you to the fastest shortcut on the Net that helps you search directly for keywords. But after that, you'll plunge into the world of e-mail, mailing lists, discussion groups, and so on.

You don't have to read this book straight through. Pick the chapters that interest you. The whole book is thoroughly cross-referenced, so you won't miss anything (unless you want to). Whenever possible, I will include useful or informative web addresses where you can get hands-on experience or find information on any given topic.

Don't let me hold you back! The best service I can render in this book is to offer you a grounding in what's happening on the Internet and to show you how to work the controls of your browser and other software. After that, you have an entire globe full of information and ideas to explore. I'll point you down some likely pathways, but mainly I'm going to get out of your way and let your natural interests draw you toward your own destinations. Welcome to the Internet.

CHAPTER 2

Stuff to Do Once to Make Your Life Easier

INCLUDES

- Choosing a strategy for the Net and the Web
- Setting up Internet Explorer
- Setting up Netscape
- Customizing your browser
- Choosing a different startup page
- Customizing your startup page
- Buying stuff online

Install Internet Explorer ➡ pp. 46–48

1. Click a Get Internet Explorer link (or go directly to **http://www.microsoft.com/ie/download/**).
2. Click the product you want and then click Download Now! on the page that appears.
3. Specify the version of Internet Explorer you want, again, and click Next.
4. Click one of the download links that appears. If it fails to connect (it happens), click Reload.
5. Choose to run the installation file automatically upon download.
6. Approve the suggested folder for installing Internet Explorer (or specify another folder), and then let the setup program do the rest.

Install Netscape ➡ pp. 50–51

1. Click a Download link on the Netscape home page (or go directly to **http://home.netscape.com/download/**).
2. Scroll down to the Download Netscape Browsers and Accessories section and choose the version of Netscape you want.
3. Click the Download link.
4. Specify the platform of your computer, your language, and the version of Netscape you want (yes, again!).
5. Click the Download For Free link. If it fails to connect (it happens), click Reload.
6. Choose a directory for the file from the Save As dialog box. Your browser will download the file (it will take a while).
7. Double-click the file you downloaded, which starts the installation program, approve the suggested folder for installing Netscape (or specify another folder), and then let the setup program do the rest.

Customize Your Browser ➡ pp. 55–64

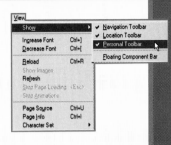

Use Internet Explorer's View menu and Internet Options dialog box (Tools | Internet Options) or Netscape's View | Show submenu and Preferences dialog box (Edit | Preferences) to change the look and feel of your browser. Changes I recommend include the following:

- Minimizing the buttons and doodads on the screen
- Turning off link underlining
- Changing your startup page

Choose a Different Startup Page for IE ➡ p. 57

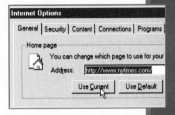

1. Go to the page you want to use as your starting page.
2. Select Tools | Internet Options.
3. On the General tab, click the Use Current button.
4. Click OK.

Choose a Different Startup Page for Netscape ➡ p. 62

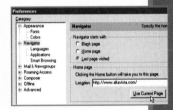

1. Go to the page you want to use as your starting page.
2. Select Edit | Preferences.
3. Select the Navigator category.
4. Click the Use Current Page button.
5. Click OK.

One common complaint people have about the Internet is the do-it-yourself, erector-set mentality of much of the software. To get a reasonable Internet setup on your computer, you may have to install several different programs and fiddle with them to get them to work together. Then you may want to upgrade some of your programs from time to time, when improvements come out or after annoying headaches are solved by later versions.

The only way to enjoy smooth Internet access is to decide on an approach to take ahead of time. Determine how much poking around you're willing to do, how easy you want things to be, and how much pizzazz you want to extract from your Internet connection.

Your Web and Net Strategy

To keep yourself sane when you start dipping into the Internet, take a minute or two now to envision how you're going to use the Net and how much of your time you want it to consume. I'll describe three different approaches to Internet use—you determine which fits you best.

The Easiest Way

By fully released, I mean completely tested and officially released, in contrast to beta versions of most programs, which are often widely available and widely in use on the Net, but not fully tested or ready for prime-time release.

The easiest approach to Web and net access is to use as few programs as possible and to use only the fully released, stable versions of each program. This strategy is similar to my hardware strategy, which is to buy not the latest thing, but the next-most-latest thing, which is usually much cheaper. With Internet tools, it's not so much the money that you save (this approach may even be a little more expensive than others), but the hassle. Stable, fully released software will break down less often and the various programs will tend to be compatible (if not capable of all the latest tricks). This is definitely the approach you want to take if you're equipping an entire office or project. Within a single company, you're better off if everyone is using the same tools (within reason).

To minimize the number of different programs you have to install and set up, you can rely primarily on your web browser and tools that plug into it. This is one type of "easy," since it reduces the amount of configuration and setup you have to do. On the other hand, you may want to opt for maintaining separate mail or news programs. Regardless of what approach you take, I will tell you how to install and configure your extra (non-web) Internet tools.

If you're completely new to the Net and the Web, consider signing up for a free month with an online service (such as AOL) to get yourself oriented with the fewest number of new programs to learn. If you like what you find, you'll probably want to switch to a flat-rate Internet service provider (or ISP; see Appendix A for more on shopping for access).

Beta Tester

If you're always looking to eke out a little extra performance from your computer and you're interested in the improvements available in upcoming software releases, then you might want to take the permanent beta tester approach and use software as soon as it's released for testing, upgrading whenever new (even interim) versions come out.

This approach has two real drawbacks:

- You have to download and upgrade software frequently.
- Beta software is not always dependable and can crash on you or freeze your machine.

The counter arguments to these objections, by the way, are as follows:

- You have to download and upgrade software frequently no matter what.
- All software sometimes freezes computers.

One additional benefit of being a beta tester (beyond that of experiencing the latest advances in technology) is that you don't have to pay for beta software since it's not in actual release yet. You are

DEFINITION

Download:
To transfer a file from a remote site to your own computer. Conversely, upload means to transfer a file from your own computer to a remote site.

doing a favor for the company that makes and publishes the software by testing it for them (provided, of course, that you report the bugs you find or make other suggestions for improvements).

Multimedia Monster

The third approach—using all the multimedia features the Internet presents—requires some investment in hardware as well. To explore the most advanced (and exciting) tools that the Internet has to offer, you need to make sure first of all that your computer is equipped to play sounds; store (enormous) video files in memory and play them back at a reasonable speed; display high-resolution graphics and redraw the screen quickly; record with a microphone, camera, video camera, and scanner; and so on.

On the software end, you need to download new web-browser plug-in software (more on plug-ins later in this chapter) and set it up to work with your browser and your Internet connection. This software may enable you to see other people (video conferencing); interact with online programs and environments; play games; and edit and post sounds, video, or other multimedia contents to the World Wide Web or to an intranet (a local, private web).

Microsoft Versus Everybody Else

Why should you care about industry gossip like this? Only because the leading products set the de facto standards, and when a single product or technology "locks in," you're stuck with it—anyone remember Betamax?

For most people on the Net (aside from the diehard, Unix-loving, text-only, Lynx-using few), the question of which web browser to use has narrowed to just two: Microsoft Internet Explorer and Netscape Navigator. In terms of sheer percentages as well as number of different computer platforms covered, Netscape took an early lead by giving away for free a browser that was better than all of its competition at the time. Since then, Microsoft has taken a similar tack and has patiently whittled away at Netscape's market share.

If Internet Explorer were the product of any other company than juggernaut Microsoft, it would not be considered an equal contender for web domination, despite the fact that (at least on the Windows and, to some extent, Macintosh platforms) it matches Netscape, more or less, feature for feature, and has put Netscape in the position of playing catch up. While Netscape has a natural constituency among those who prefer Internet diversity to Microsoft monoculture, there's no denying that Microsoft can buy its way into any market if it really wants to (and it does).

As of this writing, the U.S. government is playing a role in determining whether and to what degree Microsoft will be able to leverage its dominance of the PC desktop to create a similar lock on Internet access. The Justice Department may therefore determine whether, for instance, an Install Internet Explorer icon appears on your Windows desktop or not. But no matter how the chips fall, there will be nothing to prevent you from using the browser of your choice.

Netscape's suite of tools, Communicator, has been criticized for being bloated and including software tools not everyone wants with their browsers. In response to this, Netscape has also made a stand-alone version of Navigator available. Microsoft solves the downloading problem by making sure an up-to-date version of IE is built into all new versions of Windows and comes with each new application software release (such as Office 2000, and its component parts), but IE is also quite bloated.

Personally, I still prefer Netscape, but I wish there were a viable alternative to either of these please-all/ please-none choices and I may just switch to Opera (*http://www.operasoftware.com/*) one of these days.

Downloading, Installing, and Setting Up Internet Explorer

As for downloading Internet Explorer, the first question is, silly as it may sound, Do you have access to the Web yet? You may, if you have an online service (such as AOL) or access through work or school and some other web browser (or an earlier version of Internet Explorer itself).

If you don't, then you have two choices. You can walk into (or call) a computer software store, buy a shrink-wrapped copy of Microsoft Internet Explorer, and then install it from the disk in the box. Alternatively, you can sign up with a service provider or accept some other offer that includes a copy of Internet Explorer on a disk (and, as before, install the software from the disk).

Let me start by explaining how to download Internet Explorer (using any browser), assuming that you already have access to the

If you have Internet Explorer installed already, skip on ahead (unless, that is, you want to upgrade to a newer—or beta—version and your existing version is earlier than Internet Explorer 4.0).

EXPERT ADVICE

If you use Windows, you can see if Internet Explorer is already installed on your computer by checking Start | Programs | Internet Explorer.

Web. If you have Internet Explorer on a disk (or plan to get it that way), just skip ahead to the section Installing Internet Explorer. If you belong to an online service, you may already have Internet Explorer on a disk or installed with the main program, or you can usually download Internet Explorer directly from the service's archives (search for, or go to, Internet Explorer). You may not get the most recent version this way; if you don't, read the upcoming section, Upgrading Internet Explorer.

Internet Explorer and Windows 98 (and 2000)

Internet Explorer is now fully integrated into Windows 98, as it will be in the upcoming version of the operating system, Windows 2000, unless the U.S. Department of Justice rules otherwise. This means that you probably don't have to download the program from scratch but can simply upgrade whatever version is built into your system at the moment.

Downloading Internet Explorer

If you're upgrading a version of MSIE earlier than 4.0, jump ahead to "Upgrading Internet Explorer." If you're upgrading a more recent version of MSIE, select Help | Product Updates and then follow the instructions.

1. Point your browser to **http://www.microsoft.com/ie/download/** (or click any Get Microsoft Internet Explorer button).

2. Click the product you want and then click Download Now! on the page that appears.

3. You may have to specify the version of Internet Explorer you want (get the latest) again, and click Next.

4. If you see a security alert like the one shown here, click Yes, or check the box to prevent similar alerts in the future and then click Yes. (You may see more than one alert.)

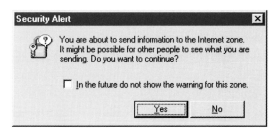

5. Choose a language (probably U.S. English) and click Next.

6. Choose a download site, in your own country if possible, and click Next. If it fails to connect (it happens), click Reload.

7. Click OK to save the installation program to disk, or click Run This Program From Its Current Location to start the installation automatically and then skip to the next section. (The latter approach is faster, but does not enable you to reinstall from disk later should you ever need to.)

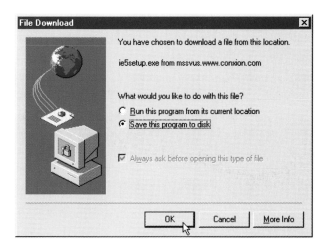

8. Choose a directory for the file from the Save As dialog box, and click Save.

Installing Internet Explorer

To install Internet Explorer (if you did not run the installation program directly from the Microsoft site), double-click the file you downloaded, which starts the installation program, approve the suggested folder for installing Internet Explorer (or—one time only—set up a special folder for such purposes, whether you call it *temp* or *downloads* or *installstuff* or whatever, and specify it for such purposes ever after), and then let the setup program do the rest.

Upgrading Internet Explorer

If you've customized Internet Explorer and you want to keep all of your preferences without having to set them again, one by one, be sure to install the new version over the old one.

Once you've got Internet Explorer 4.0 or later running on your computer, you can upgrade it or add components at any time by selecting Help | Product Updates and following the instructions from the Internet Explorer Component Download page, as discussed in Chapter 1.

See Chapter 4 for more on mail.

Setting Up Personal, Mail, and News Information

Internet Explorer comes with a mail and news program called Microsoft Outlook Express. Although designed specifically to work well with Internet Explorer, Outlook Express is a conventional news and mail reader that can stand alone and work with any other Internet tools.

For mail and news, all you can set up in Internet Explorer is which mail and news programs to use. To check your setup, select View | Internet Options, click the Programs tab, and then choose mail and news programs from the pull-down boxes provided. (Click OK when you're done.)

I'll explain how to use Outlook Express in Chapter 4, but I will mention here that its menus are inconsistent with Internet Explorer. If you want to set up or change mail or news settings, you must first select Tools | Accounts. To change an existing account, select it, click the Properties button, and then change the server or user names in the dialog box that appears. To add a new account, click Add | Mail (or Add |

News) and then permit the Internet Connection Wizard to walk you through the necessary steps. It's all part of Microsoft's master plan.

As for Internet Explorer itself, from now on, you can just run the program and forget about the setup (unless you choose to customize it, as explained later in the chapter).

Downloading, Installing, and Setting Up Netscape

The process for getting a copy of Netscape is not as streamlined as I'd like it to be, but you get used to it. The first question, which may sound silly, is Do you have access to the Web yet? You may, if you have an online service (such as AOL) or access through work or school and some other web browser (or an earlier version of Netscape itself).

If you don't, then you have two choices. You can walk into (or call) a computer software store, buy a shrink-wrapped copy of Navigator, and then install it from the disk in the box. Alternatively, you can sign up with a service provider or accept some other offer that includes a copy of Netscape on a disk (and, as before, install the software from the disk).

Let me start by explaining how to download Navigator (using any browser), assuming that you already have access to the Web. If you have Navigator on a disk (or plan to get it that way), just skip ahead to the section Installing Netscape. If you belong to an online service, you may already have Netscape on a disk or installed with the main program, or you can download Netscape directly from the service's archives (search for, or go to, Netscape). You may not get the most recent version this way; if you don't, read the section Upgrading Netscape, coming up.

> I f you have Netscape installed already, skip on ahead (unless, that is, you want to upgrade to a newer—or beta—version and your existing version is earlier than Netscape 4.0).

EXPERT ADVICE

If you're upgrading a version of Netscape earlier than 4.0, then jump ahead to "Upgrading Netscape." If you're upgrading a more recent version of Netscape, select Help | Software Updates and then the follow the instructions.

Downloading Netscape

Before starting, think about whether you want to download the entire Netscape Communicator suite (including the mail and news component called Messenger, the web editor called Composer, a paging system called AOL Instant Messenger, and the channels viewer called Netcaster), or just the web browser (Navigator). You can always upgrade or add components in the future.

Here's how you download Netscape:

1. Point your browser at **http://home.netscape.com/download/** (or click the Download link on Netscape's home page).

2. Scroll down if necessary, and click the version of the product that you want (most likely the latest).

3. Click the Download link. If it fails to connect (it happens), click Reload.

4. Choose a directory for the file from the Save As dialog box. (By the way, even if you've never heard of FTP before, you're using it now.) Your browser will download the file. (It will take a while.)

Installing Netscape

To install Netscape (or to upgrade a pre-4.0 existing version), double-click the file you downloaded to start the installation program, approve the suggested folder for installing Netscape (or specify another folder), and then let the setup program do the rest. Once everything's unpacked and set up, you can answer No to the last few questions Netscape asks you (unless you *want* to read the latest release notes or visit the Netscape web site to register the software immediately, but I recommend choosing No unless you have a lot of spare time and patience).

Upgrading Netscape

If you're installing an upgrade version of Navigator, you should do so in the same folder as the older version *unless* you're installing a beta version or a version you're not sure you want, in which case you should install it in a different folder and leave your older installation of Navigator untouched.

For Windows users, if you've customized Netscape and you want to keep all of your settings without specifying them all over again, be sure to install the new version over the old one (without first uninstalling the old one). This is not an issue on the Macintosh; your preferences are stored separately.

Once you've got Netscape 4.0 or later running on your computer, you can upgrade it or add components at any time by selecting Help | Software Updates and following the instructions from the Netscape SmartUpdate page, as discussed in Chapter 1.

Setting Up Personal, Mail, and News Information

The first time you run Netscape, you'll be asked to read and accept a license agreement. Then the program will start and attempt to connect to the Netscape home page.

Some providers fill in this information for you.

Chapter 4 explains more about e-mail and touches on Usenet news and other types of newsgroups.

The first thing you should do is tell Netscape who you are and what your e-mail address is (along with some other basic mail and news information). Select Edit | Preferences. On the left-hand side of the dialog box that appears, click the little plus-sign icon (+) next to the Mail & Groups and then select Identity.

Fill in your information:

1. Click in the Your Name box; type your name as you want it to appear on your outgoing e-mail, and then press TAB.

2. Type your e-mail address (if you know it) and press TAB twice.

3. Optionally fill in the organization box (see Figure 2.1).

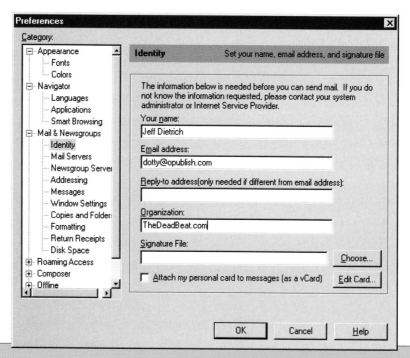

Figure 2.1: Name, e-mail address, and organization entries in Netscape's Preferences dialog box

At this point, you may want to give Netscape your mail and news information. No matter what programs you end up using for mail and news reading, you'll have to enter this information into those programs. The only reason to tell Netscape is so that you can use Netscape Messenger for mail and news.

To set up Netscape for mail and news, follow these steps:

1. Click the Mail Server category.

2. If there's no Incoming Mail Server listed, click the Add button. If a server is listed there already, click the Edit button.

3. If it's not there already, type the address of your incoming-mail server and press TAB twice.

4. Type your username (the left-hand component of your e-mail address, up to but not including the @), and click OK.

5. If it's not already entered, click in the Outgoing Mail (SMTP) Server box and type the Internet address of your outgoing-mail server (your provider or system administrator should tell you this—it's often, but not always, the same as the outgoing server) and press TAB (see Figure 2.2).

6. Click the Newsgroup Servers category, and then click the Add button and type the address of your news server, if it's not entered already.

7. Click OK.

If the content of the Outgoing Mail (SMTP) Server box at the top of the dialog box is just the word mail, or if that box or the news server box is empty, then you'll have to get the addresses of your mail and Usenet news servers from your service provider's technical help staff or from your network's system administrator (and then you'll have to type the server names in these boxes exactly).

That's all you have to deal with. Click OK to accept your preferences. From now on, you can just run the program and forget about the setup (unless you choose to customize Netscape—see "Customizing Your Web Browser" later in this chapter).

DEFINITION

Server:
A network machine that handles heavy-duty jobs such as sorting and routing mail, maintaining archive sites, and serving web pages to multiple clients.

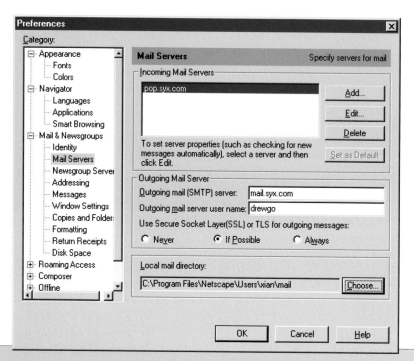

Figure 2.2: Netscape keeps making the mail and news setup process a *leetle* more complicated with each new version of the program (never a good practice).

Customizing Your Web Browser

Most web browsers allow you to change some of their basic settings, affecting mainly appearance. (There are also advanced preferences you can set, but let's not get into that level of detail.) For the two major browsers, I'll tell you how to change the look of the screen (you don't have to—you can leave it just the way it is; most people do) and how to change the startup page. I'll tell you what my personal preferences are, but this is really a matter of taste and comfort, and in fact, your preferences will most likely change if you use your browser for a long time.

Customizing Internet Explorer

Because I use Internet Explorer as an alternative or back-up browser, I often leave it set up the way it installed itself. When I find myself using it a lot, though, I eventually do customize it to more or less duplicate my Netscape preferences (covered in the next section).

Keep Toolbars Under Control

Internet Explorer usually hides its Links buttons (direct links to useful starting places) at the right end of the Address Bar. Double-click the handle (the raised double-groove) to the left of the word Links to expand the Links buttons and hide the Address bar. Double-click again to change it back.

The toolbars are pretty flexible. You can experiment a little with clicking on a toolbar's handle (at its left edge) and dragging it up or to the right. As you move it around, watch as the toolbars constantly rearrange themselves. At first the interface seems a little squirmy, like mercury, but after a while you'll find it very easy to push the toolbars up and out of your way.

You can remove any toolbar by unchecking it on the View menu (or right-clicking—that's click-and-hold on the Mac—and unchecking the toolbar's name), but I recommend leaving things as they are, since the toolbars are so easy to push around.

To minimize the size of the main Navigation buttons, right-click on any toolbar and uncheck Text Labels.

EXPERT ADVICE

When you want to get maximum use of your screen space, click the Full Screen button. The toolbars will go to the top of your screen and the window edges will melt away. When you want to return to the normal mode, click the Full Screen button again.

Turn Off Link Underlining

As I mentioned in the Netscape section, I personally think underlined links ruin the look of most pages (although I admit this is a matter of taste), so I tend to turn off link underlining as soon as I remember to.

To turn off link underlining, select Tools | Internet Options and click the Advanced tab in the Internet Options dialog box. This brings up a forbidding looking list of mostly esoteric options. Fortunately, you can ignore most of what's there (and you can always click the Restore Defaults button if you don't like the effects of your changes; the downside is you'll get all the old warning messages again, too).

Scroll down to Underline Links in the Browsing category (you can double-click any of the icons to collapse or re-expand the list of options in that category), and choose Never if you want link underlining off completely or Hover if you want links to appear underlined only when the mouse pointer is on them (see Figure 2.3). Then click OK.

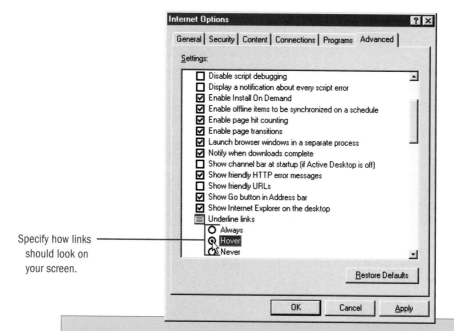

Specify how links should look on your screen.

Figure 2.3: You may prefer the Hover option for links, which makes the underlining appear dynamically whenever you point to a link.

Choose a Different Start Page for Internet Explorer

When you run Internet Explorer, it will connect you to its default home page, Microsoft Internet Start. If you decide you'd like to have Internet Explorer start you off somewhere else automatically, follow these steps:

1. Browse to the address where you'd like to start in the future.
2. Select Tools | Internet Options.
3. Click the General tab.
4. Click the Use Current button (see Figure 2.4).
5. Click OK.

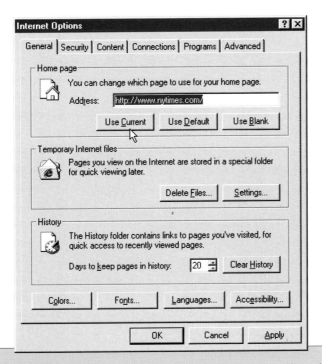

Figure 2.4: Changing IE's startup page frees you from having to pass through Microsoft's portal site every time you visit the web.

EXPERT ADVICE

If you have several web pages you want easy access to, you can add them to your Links toolbar by selecting Favorites | Organize Favorites (as discussed in Chapter 1) and then dragging any particular favorites into the Links folder.

DEFINITION

Cookie: A short text entry stored on the user's computer, identifying the user's preferences to the server of the web site that originally stored the entry.

Setting a Cookie Policy

Microsoft's web site and those customized for Internet Explorer specifically often use cookies to customize and streamline their sites for return visitors. Follow these steps to change how Internet Explorer deals with cookies:

1. Select Tools | Internet Options.
2. Click the Advanced tab (see Figure 2.3).
3. Scroll down to the Security category (the last item is a subcategory, Cookies).
4. Next, choose one of the following:
   - To accept cookies without any confirmation dialog boxes, click Always Accept Cookies.
   - To harass yourself constantly with alerts about cookies, click Prompt Before Accepting Cookies.
   - To refuse all cookies, Click Disable All Cookie use.
5. Click OK.

IS THIS FOR ME?

Cookies are fairly harmless. Microsoft's own web sites and active content customized for MSIE rely fairly consistently on cookies (and certificates to authenticated add-ons, as we'll get to in the next section). If you want to protect your privacy to a degree just short of paranoia, then turn off cookies, but be prepared to deal with a less automated Web experience.

EXPERT ADVICE

For Windows users, to display a channel as a screen saver, right-click on your desktop, choose Properties, click the Screen Saver tab, and select Channel Screen Saver from the Screen Saver list. Then click OK.

Active Channel Options

The main thing you can set up with Active Channels is how they (and Internet Explorer) start up. In the Browsing category of the Advanced tab of the Internet Options dialog box (see Figure 2.4), click to check (if it's not already checked) one of the following:

- Show Channel Bar At Startup if you always want the channel bar accessible when you start Internet Explorer.
- Launch Channels In Full Screen Window to make sure channels don't look like normal web pages.
- Launch Browser In Full Screen Window if you want all the web pages you visit to look like channels.
- Enable Scheduled Subscription Updates if you want channels to be able to update themselves automatically according to schedule.

All of these except Launch Browser In Full Screen Window should be checked by default, as long as no one has messed with your setup.

Customizing Netscape

You've no doubt seen the familiar Netscape window in newspapers, magazines, books, and on TV shows. Usually it's the Macintosh version of the screen, since most publishers use Macs, but it's always the just-out-of-the-box setup, with all toolbar buttons showing words *and* pictures; the most amount of detail possible. As with all programs, very few people change the basic settings of Navigator, but it's worth at least knowing how to. Most of the Netscape illustrations in this book show *my* preferred setup, the way I think the screen looks best, but you'll be able to follow along perfectly well no matter what preferences you choose.

Keep Toolbars Under Control

I have nothing against toolbars, but they take up a lot of your precious screen real estate. When possible, I like to scoot them out of the way. For instance, if you find that you never use the Personal toolbar (the bottom one), you can fold it up by clicking its little handle at any time...

...or take even its handle and edge off the screen by selecting View | Show | Personal Toolbar (to *un*check it):

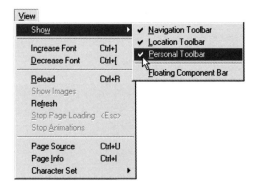

(You can restore it later by selecting View | Show | Personal Toolbar again.)

When you want to maximize the window, you can fold up all the toolbars:

You'll want to keep the Navigation toolbar visible most of time, but you can reduce the size of the buttons once you get the gist of what the main ones do. To do so, select Edit | Preferences and choose the Appearance category in the Preferences dialog box (see Figure 2.5).

Turn Off Link Underlining

I'm going out on a limb here, but I feel strongly about this: web pages look much better without underlined words all over the screen. Links are already a different color from the rest of the text (usually blue versus black), and the default underlining draws unnecessary emphasis to link words and destroys the typographical design of a web page.

recommend not messing with the default color settings.

To turn off link underlining:

1. Select Edit | Preferences.

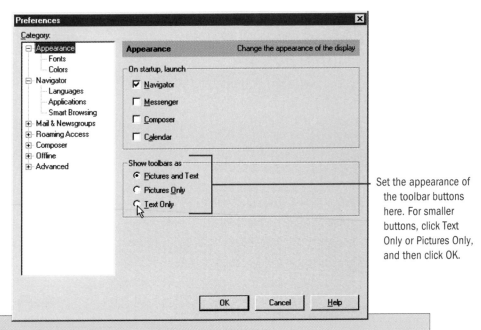

Figure 2.5: Navigation buttons with Pictures Only on them are smaller than the default that has Pictures And Text. Smallest of all are the Text Only buttons.

2. Click the Colors category (under Appearances) in the Preferences dialog box.

3. Click to uncheck Underline Links in the Links area.

4. Click OK.

Choose a Different Home Page for Netscape

You don't have to start at the Netscape home page every time you run Navigator. There are two things you can change: the browser's home page, and whether the browser starts up at the home page, at a blank page, or at the page you visited last (you can always click the home button to get to the designated home page).

If you come across a page you like enough to use as a jumping-off point (such as CNN, Yahoo!, any of the search pages discussed in Chapter 3, or any of the special start pages various web services offer to create for you), then you can make it your browser's home page (the N button will still always take you to the Netscape *company* home page).

1. Go to the chosen page (such as **http://www.altavista.com/**).

2. Select Options | Preferences.

3. Click the Navigator category in the Preferences dialog box.

4. Click the Use Current Page button in the Home page area.

5. Choose Blank Page or Last Page Visited in the Navigator Starts With area if you want to change how Netscape starts up.

6. Click OK.

If you have several web pages you want easy access to, you can add them to your Personal toolbar (you may have to restore it with the command on the View menu) by simply visiting the pages and then dragging the bookmark icon from the Location toolbar to the Personal toolbar. (The Personal toolbar can be edited as a submenu of your Bookmarks folder, as discussed in Chapter 1.)

CAUTION

There is a slight security risk to starting with the last page visited in that it reveals to the next user of your browser where you've been browsing. For that matter, anyone who knows how to look at your history file can figure that out. To be absolutely paranoid, click the Clear History button in the History area.

> ### IS THIS FOR ME?
>
> **Cookies are fairly harmless. For the most part they are used to store registration (log-in) information for sites on your computer so you can revisit those sites without hassles in the future. If you want a one-click shopping experience at popular sites such as Amazon.com, surrender your cookie information voluntarily or deal with the hassle of inventing and recording passwords for each such site you plan to revisit. Still, if you're getting confusing dialog boxes about cookies or if you're worried about web sites being able to store information about you on your computer, this section will tell you how to control how Netscape handles cookies.**

Setting a Cookie Policy

In the last few years, some web sites have started using a method to customize and streamline their sites for return visitors. As a result, various users have become concerned about the cookies used in this method to store basic information on the users' own computers. To some it seems intrusive, to others harmless. I don't get my knickers in a twist about cookies, but I understand why it might bother a person to have a web site squirreling away data about that person on his or her own machine. Many commercial sites these days rely on cookies, and if you turn them off, such sites may no longer work for you.

Follow these steps to change how Netscape deals with cookies:

1. Select Edit | Preferences.

2. Choose the Advanced category (see Figure 2.6).

3. Next, choose one of the following:

   • To accept cookies without any confirmation dialog boxes, click Accept All Cookies and make sure the Warn Me Before Accepting A Cookie checkbox is unchecked.

   • To limit Netscape to cookies that can only be read by the originating site (most cookies, actually, but this is to reassure you), click the choice that begins with Accept Only Cookies That… (and uncheck Warn Me…).

   • To refuse all cookies, click Disable Cookies.

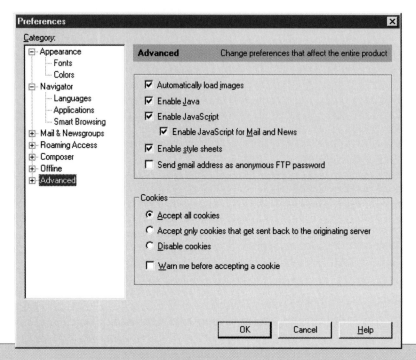

Figure 2.6: Tell Netscape how you want it to deal with cookies.

- To harass yourself constantly with alerts about cookies, check the Warn Me... box.

4. Click OK.

Downloading Plug-Ins and Add-Ons

You can download and install a number of third-party programs to extend the capabilities of your web browser. In the early days of web browsers (two or three years ago), the only way to enhance a browser's features was to inform it of stand-alone helper applications the browser could start up externally (to display an image, for example). While helper apps (as they're often called) still exist, more and more programs are emerging, designed specifically to plug directly into a web browser and increase its own ability to display or handle additional file formats. Still, the process of installing plug-ins was a

Any new components invented by the maker of your browser can be added automatically with automatic software updates, as discussed in Chapter 1.

technical hassle for most users until the recent versions of Internet Explorer and Netscape.

Now, when your browser encounters a file format it doesn't recognize, it has the capability of offering to go and get the necessary plug-in, install it, and proceed with displaying the media in the new format.

There are too many of these plug-ins for me to list them all here, and most of them will be useful to you only if you visit specific web sites that require them to function fully. Some of these plug-ins can produce astounding results and display fascinating effects, but many of them are bulky and take up a lot of disk space and memory when they're running. Your web browser by itself is a bit of a resource hog. Think back to your Internet strategy. If you want to explore the limits of multimedia available online, be ready to install many plug-ins. If you'd rather keep things simple, you may want few or none.

Choosing Plug-Ins

If you have the disk space and the interest in getting additional programs, here are three must-have plug-ins:

- Macromedia's Shockwave
- RealNetworks' RealPlayer
- Adobe Acrobat Reader

Shockwave enables your browser to handle files that can include animation, sounds, and interactive elements (things that respond differently depending on where you click, for example). Shockwave's new Flash animations features have my designer friends all fired up. You can download Shockwave from **http://www.macromedia.com/ shockwave/** or just wait until your browser stumbles into it and then follow the instructions on the dialog box that appears.

RealPlayer is the most popular format for *streaming* audio, video, or even animation files. Streaming files can start playing soon after they start downloading (as opposed to only once they're fully downloaded). The data comes to your computer in a stream and is processed

CAUTION
If you get your Internet access through a business that protects its data behind what's called a "firewall," some plug-ins may not work for you.

continuously until it plays through. You can download RealPlayer from **http://www.real.com/** (or wait until it's needed).

Acrobat is a software program which creates a compact portable document format that enables publishers to design sophisticated publications and make them available on the Web without the limitations of HTML, the coding language normally used for web documents. To view this document format from your browser, you can download the Acrobat Reader plug-in from **http://www.adobe.com/acrobat/** (or wait 'til it comes up).

Internet Radio Formats

Advertisers and experts from traditional media continue to experiment with ways to simulate broadcasting online, to "push" content, sound, or media, usually in exchange for your attention to advertisements. The emergence of adequate, economical, concise sound-file formats—such as MP3 (.mp3) and Shorten (.shn)—have brought music transmission to the forefront of new media developments on the web. Several approaches to live sound and video are still vying for dominance. Some websites require a single specific format, and others hedge their bets and support multiple formats, from MP3, to Windows Media format, to Real Player. I'll briefly touch on three examples.

IE's Radio Toolbar

Right-click on any toolbar in Internet Explorer and choose Radio to open the Radio toolbar. Choose Radio Stations | Radio Station Guide on the toolbar to see some sites that broadcast in the Windows Media format. Click a station's button in your browser to hear its broadcast. If music doesn't start playing as soon as the new pages finish loading, click the Play button in the Radio toolbar.

The Radio Stations button's drop-down menu remembers recent stations you've tuned into, and has an Add To Favorites button for those you want to add to the Radio folder of your Internet Explorer favorites.

WinAmp Plays Everything

Windows users can download the WinAmp plug-in as shareware from **http://www.winamp.com/** to get a player capable of playing multiple formats, with its own built-in mini-browser for finding music sites. Both major browsers can make use of this player. Figure 2.7 shows the WinAmp player streaming music from an "ambient" MP3 radio station listed among the ten most popular (of the moment) at the Shoutcast site (**http://www.shoutcast.com/**).

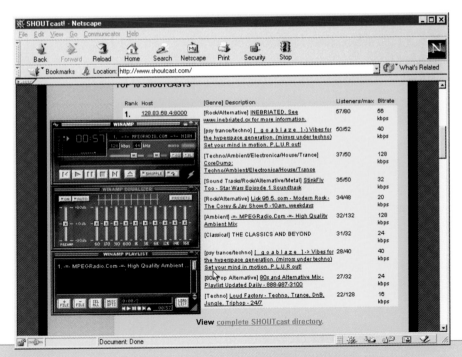

Figure 2.7: I've synchronized my chakras while catching up on my e-mail listening to ambient techno mixed over this WinAmp player.

RealPlayer and MP3 Sites

The RealPlayer is still a popular plug-in or stand-alone sound player with its own proprietary format. Most music sites try to support RealPlayer (even if they also support other proprietary formats, such as Windows Media, or open formats such as MP3). By default, the Drum n' Bassment show at Radio-V (**http://www.radio-v.com/**) launches a Java window with a RealPlayer control panel plugged into it (see Figure 2.8).

My basic point is, there's no need to lock yourself into any single playback program or file format. Don't even worry about it. These things have a way of sorting themselves out. Meanwhile, download scrappy, new, nonbloated shareware soundplayers and see if you like music coming out of your computer's speakers while you're doing other things.

Figure 2.8:   Checking out a fresh mix via RealPlayer at Radio-V

Security, Credit Cards, and Online Purchases

The Internet and the Web are open systems, not designed with security as the paramount consideration. Understandably, there's been a lot of concern in the past few years about how to make Net transactions secure and how to reassure potential consumers that they can safely send sensitive information, such as credit card numbers and expiration dates, over the Internet without compromising their security. (Never mind that most consumers take bigger risks with their credit information in restaurants every day.)

Many people are unsure what to think about cookies. As currently employed, they seem relatively safe and anonymous. Still, it doesn't take a Strangelovian paranoia to worry about sites sharing cookies, compromising your security, possibly enabling megacorps to correlate all this seemingly disconnected data about you.

Reputable commercial sites online, starting but not limited to those catering to children, must now post clear statements of their policies on privacy, specifically to what use they intend to put any information you've offered them in exchange for access.

Secure Connections

Both Internet Explorer and Netscape use similar solutions. They both have the ability to create secure connections with certain types of web servers out there on the Net (conveniently, for the most part, with servers made by the same company as the browser in question) and can notify you that the connection is secure whenever it is. Internet Explorer, for instance, displays a lock on the right side of the status bar if the current page is secure. You can get more information about a page's security by using the File | Properties command and clicking the Security tab.

Similarly, Netscape displays an open padlock in the lower-left corner of the screen when the connection is *not* secure (most of the time), and it displays a closed padlock when it is. See Netscape's View | Page Info command or click on the padlock icon for a more detailed security report.

Certificates of Authenticity

Both Internet Explorer and Netscape, when you first install them, also offer you the option of installing a certificate for security purposes. You are not obliged to use the system they offer, however, and there are other third-party systems available. Both browsers display a message when you connect to a secure server. Furthermore, when you do attempt to send any type of information to a server, both browsers will warn you if the connection is not a secure one (though they give you the option of turning off the warning screen if you find it intrusive).

These warning messages can become annoying because they pop up so frequently. A very real danger is that you will get in the habit of clicking OK to ignore these warnings, so that they become meaningless. For now, you may want to remind yourself to keep your credit cards private and uncheck the Show This Alert Next Time box.

There's More . . .

Now you know how to set up your most basic Internet tools, and you can start wandering the Web. If you get tired of poking around aimlessly, Chapter 3 will show you how to search for specific topics and zero in on exactly the resources you want online. After that, you'll see how to use the Internet's most common communication tool, e-mail, and how to participate in ongoing and live discussions. Finally, you'll learn how to connect to remote sites, and create and publish web documents.

Find Things (and People) on the Web

INCLUDES

- Guessing Web addresses
- Letting the browser help you find a site
- Working with portals
- Searching with keywords
- Refining a search
- Searching for software
- Finding e-mail addresses, phone numbers, and snail mail addresses

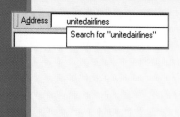

Guess Addresses and
Let Your Browser Sort It Out ➔ pp. 74–75

1. Type a single word (such as a company's name) into your web browser's address box and press ENTER.
2. Choose from the suggestions your browser comes up with.
3. Backtrack and visit other related sites to zero in on your goal.

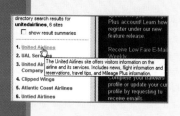

Use IE's Search Bar for Web Searching ➔ pp. 75–77

1. Type a word or two into IE's address bar.
2. Click links on the Search Bar that appears in the left side of the IE window.
3. Preview sites in the main browser window.
4. Close the Search Bar when you're finished with current search.

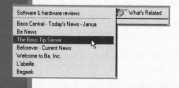

Look for Related Sites with Netscape ➔ pp. 77–78

1. Type a word or two into Netscape's address bar.
2. Click links on the Netcenter page that appears in response.
3. Click What's Related and choose from other sites related to the current site.

Let a Portal Do Your Walking ➔ p. 78

1. Start from **Yahoo.com** or **Netscape.com** or **Msn.com** or any other omnibus "portal" site (or perhaps even your browser's default startup page).
2. Click on a link for a major category or listed subcategory.
3. Keep clicking subcategories to narrow your search.
4. Visit reviewed sites or perform keyword searches to zero in on your goal.

Use a Search Engine ➡ pp. 78–82

1. Go to a search engine site, such as **Altavista.com**, **Excite.com**, or **Hotbot.com** (or just use whatever search engine is affiliated with your all-purpose favorite portal site).
2. Type one or more keywords (more is better) separated by spaces, and press ENTER.
3. Visit returned sites or continue refining your keyword list.

Refine Your Searches ➡ pp. 82–85

- Enter more keywords to match by placing a + (plus sign) in front of each word.
- Find phrases (words that have to appear together) by entering them between quotation marks.
- Rule out keywords to avoid by placing a – (minus sign) in front of each.

Find Software, Shareware, and Freeware ➡ pp. 87–88

1. Start at the home page for the software or the company that makes it, or for shareware, start at Shareware.com.
2. Search for, or follow links to, the link for downloading the software (for commercial software, this will require credit card purchase or some equivalent), shareware, demo, or freeware.
3. Download the software.

Hunt for E-Mail Addresses ➡ pp. 88–89

- Visit **http://whowhere.lycos.com/**, type the first name, press TAB, type the last name, and click the Go Get It button.
- Visit **http://people.yahoo.com/**, type the first name, press TAB, type the last name, and click the Search button.
- Visit **http://www.bigbook.com/**, to look for business (commercial addresses).

As you've probably noticed by now, the Internet (not to mention the Web) is a nebulous, amorphous, constantly changing, regularly shifting blob of a network. Fortunately, there are brave souls out there working hard to make it comprehensible as well as searchable. So when you're looking for information on a rare disease, planning to go scuba diving in South America, or looking for a new job, try searching the Net using some of the methods described in this chapter. I'll point you toward some useful search engines, give you some basic search tips, show you how to find software, and run through some of the methods you can use to look for individual e-mail addresses and other information about people.

Guessing Web Addresses

If you're looking for a specific web site (as opposed to a topic), you may be able to guess the address of the site's home page. Many companies, for example, have home pages with an address in the form **http://www.***CompanyNameHere***.com**. Often you can easily try one or more possible variations of this format to see if you can find the page you want. University sites generally end in .edu, noncommercial sites often end in .org, and government sites usually end in .gov. Another variation to try sometimes is .net, since commercial, educational, and noncommercial sites may have the net domain name in their address.

The Internet Explorer and Netscape browsers both assume that you want an address starting with http://, if you leave out that part. For some addresses, they'll even assume the www. at the beginning and the .com at the end if you type just a single word. This means, for example, that you can type just **ibm,** as shown here, and IE will take you there but may also open its Search Bar to give you alternative choices (discussed in an upcoming section). Netscape, when you type **ibm**, will connect you with **http://www.ibm.com.**().

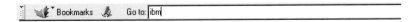

For less well known domain names, Netscape will sometimes return a web page listing the likely address along with some alternatives at its Netcenter portal.

For both of these browsers, if you type two or more words separated by spaces, the words are treated as a query by the search engines affiliated with the respective software company's portals.

Letting Your Browser Handle the Search

Both Internet Explorer and Netscape offer search facilities accessed through their address boxes, linked to search engines affiliated with their portal sites (MSN and Netcenter.com, respectively). If you haven't bookmarked your favorite search sites yet, then using your browser's built-in search page is the easiest way to perform a search.

Internet Explorer's Search Bar

If you type one or more words in Internet Explorer's address box, first IE tells you it assumes you're asking to do a search.

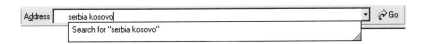

When you're done typing keywords, press ENTER. By default, IE opens the Search Bar, lists the matches there, and opens the most likely matching site in the main browser window.

EXPERT ADVICE

To change how IE interprets what you type in the address bar, select Tools | Internet Options, click the Advanced tab, and then under the Search From The Address Bar category, choose what IE should do when searching—Display Results, And Go To The Most Likely Site (this is the default), Do Not Search From The Address Bar, Just Display The Results In The Main Window, or Just Go To The Most Likely Site—and then click OK.

If none of the matching sites register as likely enough to show in the main frame, IE will instead show a message to that effect. Click a link to one of the returned sites to see it in the main window (see Figure 3.1).

You can also click the Search button in the IE Standard toolbar to open (or close) the Search bar at any time. With the search bar open,

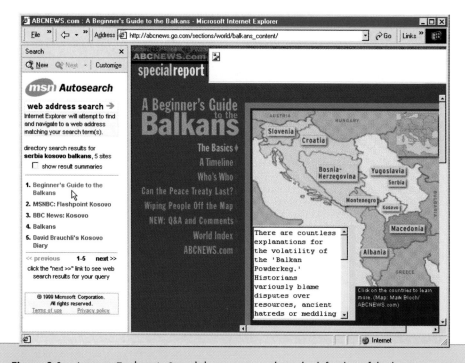

Figure 3.1:   Internet Explorer's Search bar appears along the left edge of the browser window so that your search criteria can stay on the screen even as you check out the various results.

you can enter and refine searches in the MSN/Goto.com search box. We'll get to search strategies in general later in this chapter.

Searching and Finding Related Sites with Netscape

If you type two or more words into the Netscape address bar, Netscape will treat them as a query and send them to its Open Directory server, returning with a list of sites that match some or all of your keywords on one of its Netcenter (portal) pages. Figure 3.2 shows the first few results from a search on the words "biotech venture capital."

Click a link to visit a matching site. With versions 4.5 and later of Netscape, if it's close but not exactly right, try clicking the What's Related button on the right side of the Location toolbar. A menu listing related sites (or links to further searches or related Open Directory categories) will appear after a few moments.

DEFINITION

Keyword:
(Also key word.)
A word which, when specified with other words in a search, can single out documents or database entries that contain the specified word or words. Good keywords are those that narrow down the number of matching results as much as possible.

I f Netscape's Open Directory server can't find any matches for your search, Netcenter sends your request to the Google search engine.

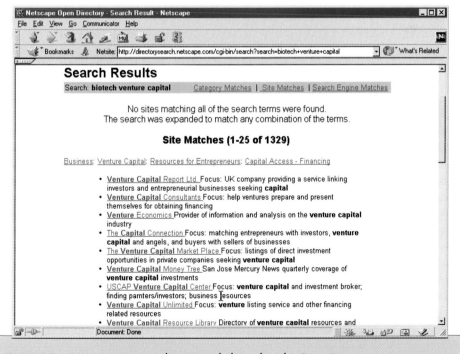

Figure 3.2: Netscape invites volunteers to help update the Open Directory resource to which it automatically refers search terms.

The premier directory-turned-portal site is Yahoo! at *http://www.yahoo.com/*.

You can also click Netscape's Search button at any point to return to an Open Directory search page and enter new search terms. You may alternate between searching and choosing sites from the What's Related menu to zero in on your goal.

Working with a Portal

You may find the search pathways built into your browser more than adequate, or perhaps you'd rather decide for yourself where you want to start your searches on the Web. Most of the popular directories and search sites have teamed up with (been bought by, or turned into) major portal sites (web sites with the highest amount of traffic). You can start at any portal and hunt for your topic by categories through an edited guide to the web, or enter keywords to search an indexed database of web sites constantly being updated by automated "webcrawler" software.

Despite the technical difference between search engines and directories, on the surface they look very much the same. Most directories are now searchable, and many search engines also include subject categories (and even reviews), much like a directory. In the long run, this distinction will probably become blurrier and eventually disappear.

At any directory—oops, I mean portal—page, you can hunt your way through categories and subcategories to zero in on your goal (see Figure 3.3).

Searching with Keywords

When I first discovered the Web, I used it mostly by browsing. I wandered randomly through the hyperlinks of the Web, sometimes stumbling over stuff I found really interesting. After a while, I found this approach took up too much of my time. Along the way I had developed the habit of making bookmarks, so from that point on I generally went directly to my favorite bookmarked sites (although I still did a lot of browsing, especially from my favorite starting points).

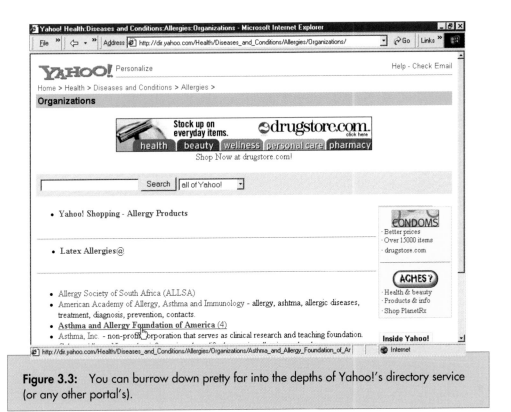

Figure 3.3: You can burrow down pretty far into the depths of Yahoo!'s directory service (or any other portal's).

Finally, I realized that I was limited to the precincts of the Web I had explored before (or could get to in a number of jumps from sites I already knew about), and I started guessing addresses and searching for sites. Now most of the time I use the Web like this: I run my browser (usually Netscape), go to the AltaVista search page (**http://www.altavista.com**—at times, I've even made the AltaVista page my startup page), enter a keyword or two, and click the Submit button. Then I'm off and surfing.

Actually, there are several different senses in which you can search on the Web. For example, with any web browser, you can search the text of the current page. This can be useful with very long pages. You will also sometimes encounter pages with the notice, "This is a searchable index." Pages with this notice have been designed so that if you type a keyword (or words) in the box provided and press ENTER, you'll receive whatever matching information is available.

I n Internet Explorer or Netscape, press CTRL+F to search for a particular word on the current page.

Finally, you'll encounter pages, such as those outlined in the next few sections, that are really front ends for search engines. A *search engine* is a program that connects you to a database of web addresses. These databases are generally compiled by computer programs (called *webcrawlers, spiders,* or *robots*) that explore the Web, catalog pages they find, and send references back to the main database. Search engines therefore can often give you huge numbers of pages in response to a query, though sometimes without much context or filtering. You get what the robots found.

These search engines often give you more control over your search than just entering a word or two. These pages usually contain full-fledged forms with most of the features you probably associate with dialog boxes (list boxes, checkboxes, and so on). You fill out just as much of the form as is necessary, click a button to submit your form, and then await the results. Some databases have just the titles of documents stored; others have entire documents or abstracts with keywords.

The best way to look for a specific topic is to perform a keyword search using one of the many search engines. Each of the competing search sites has

CAUTION

Because the information on the Net ages so quickly, often the pages you find from a search will already have been moved or changed. Try using several search engines to perform as thorough a search as possible.

DEFINITION

Search engine: A computer program, especially one accessible via the Web, that can be used to search a database or index of web sites, Internet resources in general, or other reference sources.

HotBot is powered by Inktomi (same as MSN's Goto.com Search bar).

CAUTION

If you're trying to buy something over the Web and you're about to send your credit card number and expiration date, answer this question before you submit it: Are you the type of person who tears up your credit card carbons? If you are, then you should cancel the transaction.

EXPERT ADVICE

One other thing about search engines (before I show you some): sometimes, when you click a button to submit a form, your browser will display a warning dialog box to tell you that your transmission is not secure (as discussed briefly in Chapter 2). If all you're doing is searching, then there's nothing to worry about and you can go ahead and click Continue.

different special features that allow you to express sophisticated search requests (called queries), but all of them perform basic searches in about the same way.

- **AltaVista** http://www.altavista.com/
- **Excite** http://www.excite.com/
- **HotBot** http://www.hotbot.com/
- **Lycos** http://www.lycos.com/
- **Infoseek** http://infoseek.go.com/

EXPERT ADVICE

I'd recommend that you make some bookmarks for these sites since you'll probably want to visit them more than once. In addition to using AltaVista as my startup page, I also have a few other search engines at the top of my bookmarks.

There are also sites that query multiple search engines for you all at once:

- **Search.com** http://www.search.com/
- **Metacrawler** http://www.metacrawler.com/

A Basic Search

The simplest type of search involves a single keyword. If there's an obvious single word associated with your topic, you can try typing it

EXPERT ADVICE

You can also widen your search by trying to hit multiple search engines with a single query. Besides MetaCrawler, other all-in-one search sites include SavvySearch at *http://www.savvysearch.com*, SuperSeek at *http://w3.superseek.com/*, DogPile at *http://www.dogpile.com/*, and many more listed by Yahoo! in its All-in-One Search Pages category at *http://dir.yahoo.com/Computers_and_Internet/Internet/ World_Wide_Web/Searching_the_Web/All_in_One_Search_Pages/*.

in a search query form and clicking the button (usually called *Submit*). You may discover that your search turns up relevant and irrelevant results, especially if your keyword has more than one meaning. In that case, you can try again, entering two words (separated by a space) to see which web pages the engine finds that include both words.

EXPERT ADVICE

You can often get more exact search results by searching for two or more words. In most search engines, you can put two or more words in quotation marks to require that they be found all together in a phrase. Also, try more than one search engine, as their results can differ substantially.

You can perform more advanced search techniques requiring that documents meet additional criteria. For example, you can require that some or all of the search words appear in every document returned, that two or more words be found close together (or in a phrase), or that documents contain one word and exclude some other word.

Refining Your Search

As mentioned earlier in this chapter, the first step in putting together a focused search is to come up with additional keywords. Putting a single word into the form on a search engine works great for a quick-and-dirty, scattershot search, but it won't work if you're trying to be thorough and exhaustive. To begin with, try to come up with as many unique words that will help zero in on the information or file you want.

Database searching is a branch of computer science and it can be an infinitely subtle topic. Furthermore, the different search engines often use different commands and even different search principles, so I can

---

IS THIS FOR ME?

If you're finding your way around the Web just fine or are even a bit overwhelmed by the number of different tangents you're being distracted by, then you probably don't need to deepen your web searching just yet. If you're having trouble finding what you're looking for or if you're trying to make more directed searches, read on.

---

only show you so much. I'll give you a grounding in the concepts of advanced searching and I'll show you a few practical examples with my favorite search engine, AltaVista.

Another limitation of web-based searching is that not everything on the Internet is visible or well-documented on the Web itself. Sure, you can *reach* most of the Internet via the Web, but that doesn't mean that every file stowed away in an archive, every Telnet-based card catalog, and every Gopher menu ever created is indexed in the huge databases you're searching. People were searching the Net for resources long before the Web and its directories and search engines came along, and I'll give you a briefing on some of these predecessor search methods for those times when you need to tease out well-hidden material.

Some search engines do a better job than others of telling you their capabilities. Some have a link to an advanced search page where you can fill in a more elaborate form. Others offer more-or-less complete documentation of their features. Still others have linked pages of search tips or hints.

Generally, the way to focus a search is to specify additional keywords and look for certain relationships among them. The most common relationships are those used in Boolean logic: And, Or, and Not. These relationships are symbolized in different ways by different search engines, but the concepts are universal.

CAUTION
A typical rule that can differ from engine to engine is how capitalized keywords are matched. Additionally, some search engines look for pages that contain all of your search terms, while some search engines look for pages that contain any or most of your search terms.

Example #1

In most search engines, just putting words one after another, separated by spaces, indicates that you're looking for matches of any of the words. This is an Or type of search (in the Boolean sense): you'll find documents containing *apple* OR *pie* (or both, but that's not required). If you think about this, you'll realize that just stringing words together in this way does not narrow your search; it expands it to include any documents containing the second word as well as all those containing the first word.

To limit the hits that match your list of words, you can specify that each word (or some core set of them) *must* be found or you're not interested. This is the And type of search (the second common Boolean connector). In most search engines, you indicate that a word must be found by preceding it with a plus sign. Thus, if you're looking for documents containing both the words *apple* AND *pie*, you usually type

```
+apple +pie
```

The third basic step to take to refine your searches (besides adding additional words and specifying that some *must* be present) is to require that some words be found next to each other (or close to each other, depending on the capabilities of the search engine). This requirement can be handy if you're looking for a specific phrase, or if you just want to make sure of the context of certain ambiguous words. In many search engines, you indicate phrases by surrounding the words in question with quotation marks, like so:

```
"apple pie"
```

When performing a search, you'll sometimes be surprised by the unexpected matches you get to your keywords, often unintended connotations and coincidences. Fortunately, you can also filter out some responses if you can identify a keyword to be found in all or most of the bogus matches. This brings into play the third common Boolean connector: Not. In many search engines, you indicate that you are searching for phrases containing some words *and not* others by preceding the latter with a minus sign, like so:

```
apple -computer
```

Example #2

Suppose you want a copy of the football schedule for the University of California at Berkeley (the California Bears). Just type

```
Cal Bears football schedule
```

in the search box of any search engine (more on these later in this chapter). The first set of pages returned in this simple search is largely irrelevant. Since you don't want the Bears' basketball schedule, you can exclude basketball pages by putting a minus sign in front of the word "basketball." Add the year to concentrate on the current schedule. A more refined search might put a plus sign in front of "schedule," to indicate that the word schedule must appear somewhere on the page. Also, you can consider adding Berkeley and California as well as Cal, so pages that mention the California Bears are returned. A successful search string might be

```
California Cal Berkeley +Bears +football +schedule
-basketball.
```

Example #3

Here's a more detailed example. Suppose you're searching for a web page displaying the well-known painting *American Gothic*. If you start by just typing **American Gothic** in the search box, you'll generate a huge number of irrelevant hits on a TV show called *American Gothic*. To avoid this, you can refine your search by requesting information on

```
American Gothic -television -TV
```

CAUTION
There are certain small, common words that you can't search for because they show up too often (words such as "is," "and," "the"). These words are sometimes called stop words or buzz words.

(the minus signs instruct your search engine to return pages that *don't* include that word). The results now are a little better, but many pages still mention the TV show, although without using the words TV or television. To further refine your search, you can add a relevant word: painting, for example. To make sure that you don't get pages about gothic-style paintings, you can place quotation marks around "American Gothic." The search

```
"American Gothic" +painting -television -TV
```

doesn't generate an image of the painting, but one of the sites mentions the artist's name, Grant Wood. The final search,

```
"American Gothic" -television -TV +painting +Grant
+Wood
```

generates a number of copies of the image, plus some modern interpretations of the famous couple with the pitchfork, and a page about Anamosa, Iowa—Grant Wood's birthplace.

Searching for Links, Hosts, Applets, or MP3s

Search engines often use special words or commands to search for specific types of information. AltaVista, for example, allows you to search for web documents that contain links to a specific site. This can be invaluable for ego surfing (looking for links to your own web site):

```
link:ezone.org/xian
```

Click the Help button on the main AltaVista page or point your browser directly at **http://www.altavista.com/av/content/help.htm** to see the entire list of special prefixes used to search for anchor text, images, titles, URLs, Java applets, and media files, such as MP3s (see Figure 3.4).

Keyword	Function
anchor:text	Finds pages that contain the specified word or phrase in the text of a hyperlink. **anchor:"Click here to visit AltaVista"** would find pages with "Click here to visit AltaVista" as a link.
applet:class	Finds pages that contain a specified Java applet. Use **applet:morph** to find pages using applets called morph.
domain:domainname	Finds pages within the specified domain. Use **domain:de** to find pages from Germany, or use **domain:org** to find pages from organizations.
host:name	Finds pages on a specific computer. The search **host:altavista.digital.com** would find pages on the AltaVista computer, and **host:dilbert.unitedmedia.com** would find pages on the computer called dilbert at unitedmedia.com.
image:filename	Finds pages with images having a specific filename. Use **image:elvis** to find pages with images called elvis.
link:URLtext	Finds pages with a link to a page with the specified URL text. Use **link:altavista.digital.com** to find all pages linking to AltaVista.

Figure 3.4: AltaVista's Help Page

Good Search Habits

Once you start searching for things on the Net, you'll do it more and more often. You'll begin to rely on searching as a way of navigating this bewildering blob of a network. I recommend bookmarking any search sites you like and possibly even making one your new startup page (as explained in Chapter 2). In general, for important searches you'll want to search more than one site to be sure you haven't missed anything obvious.

Although it's possible to do serious research on the Web, the Net is not as dependable as traditional media, and you can't be sure you'll find what you're looking for even if it is out there.

If you perform a search but don't have time to check out all of the returned sites, you can save the search results page as an HTML document on your computer by selecting File | Save As, specifying a folder and file name, and then clicking the Save button. One problem with this approach is that the links on your search results page may age and become out of date, in which case you'll need to perform the search again. (The Web changes fast.)

A similar method of preserving a search is to bookmark the query itself. If you try several searches and come up with a combination of keywords that seems to ferret out the results you want, you can bookmark the results page. What this really does is bookmark the gibberish in the address box that constitutes your search query (as far as the database you consulted is concerned). Later, if you return to this bookmark, the search will actually be performed anew, with up-to-date references, but using those same keywords from your original query.

Finding Software

Besides looking for information and specific web sites, you may also want to hunt for useful software on the Internet. A lot of software on the Net is free, at least during a trial period when you can consider whether to buy it. Software you eventually have to pay for is called *shareware.* Software you don't have to pay for is called *freeware.* Sample software that includes only a limited set of working features is called *crippleware.* You can hunt for all the different varieties of programs at clnet's Shareware.com site (see Figure 3.5).

If you know the name of the program you're looking for, you can search for it directly by name. You can also search for a shorter word or word fragment that you think appears in the name of the program you want. If you have no clue about the program's name, you can still hunt around the site, looking at things such as the latest additions to the listings or the most popular downloads. If you find what you're looking for, Shareware.com won't actually have the file for you to download. Instead, it will give you a list of the FTP archive sites where the file can be found. All you do is click one of the links to get the file you want.

Finding People and Businesses

Aside from looking for information, you might also want to see if someone you know can be reached by e-mail. As with the rest of the

Figure 3.5:   Searching for software at clnet's Shareware.com site

Net, e-mail addresses exist pretty much in chaos, so there's no single definitive list of e-mail addresses anywhere, but there are several useful sites you can try, including WhoWhere shown in Figure 3.6.

- **WhoWhere (part of Lycos now)** http://whowhere.lycos.com/
- **Yahoo People (formerly Four11)** http://people.yahoo.com/
- **BigBook (for businesses only)** http://www.bigbook.com/

Figure 3.6 shows the results of a search at WhoWhere.

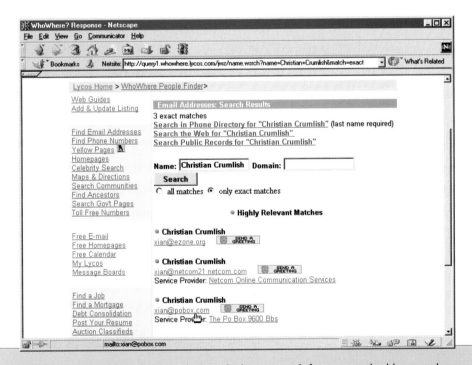

Figure 3.6: WhoWhere lets you choose whether to search for an e-mail address, a phone number, or a web presence. Mail sent to any of these three addresses will get to me.

EXPERT ADVICE

If you're looking for the e-mail address of someone affiliated with a university, try the campus web pages, which may have a list of addresses. This procedure applies to some big corporations as well.

EXPERT ADVICE

At any of these sites, you may want to search for your own e-mail address to see if you are listed. Some permit you to register directly if you wish to be listed. (Some people also register under their maiden names or original home towns in order to be found more easily by old friends.)

Getting Maps and Directions

Portals and other travel or business sites sometimes offer map and direction services. At any of the following sites, you can enter an address in the U.S. and see a map of the locale.

- **Maps on Us (requires registration)** http://www.mapsonus.com/
- **Zip2.com (click Get A Map on the home page)** http://www.zip2.com/
- **Yahoo Maps (from the portal that has everything)** http://maps.yahoo.com/

Most of the maps can be zoomed in or out and most such sites will also offer directions (try to get a second opinion on the directions, as they may not constitute the most direct or convenient route). Figure 3.7 shows a map of the neighborhood around my office in Oakland, California.

How Not to Spam

If you find your name in any of these directories, you might be wondering how it got there. Most likely, your Internet service provider added your e-mail address to one of these directories (or to some more generic resource that the directory maker may have consulted), or the directory obtained your street address from one of the usual sources.

Most of these sites permit people to remove their own listings to protect their privacy. If this is important to you, you should pursue it. Similarly, the sites also all have strict rules against businesses collecting huge lists of e-mail addresses and then sending them all unsolicited

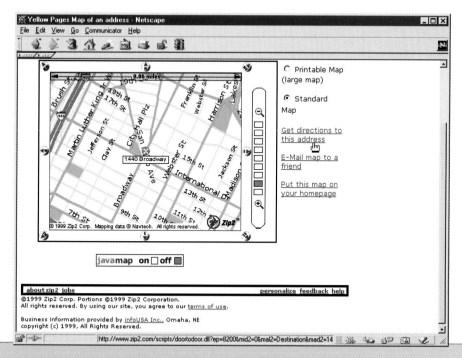

Figure 3.7: Directions to this address from just about anywhere are one click away (well, you have to enter your starting point, too, of course).

junk mail. Scattershot mailings of that sort are usually referred to online as *spam*, and they violate the spirit of the Internet mail system, as well as the letter of the rules of these directory sites.

There's nothing wrong with targeting specific messages to audiences that have expressed some kind of interest in that type of information, but be very careful never to send mailings to large groups of unrelated people. See Chapter 4 for more on mailing lists.

The Importance of Findability

Once you've gotten used to browsing the Net through searching, you'll begin to realize how important it is for businesses and other services that want to gain customers or contacts through the Internet to be found easily. It helps if they have a sensible domain name that anyone could guess, but it's also important for a site to be listed in the major search engines and directories. In Chapter 8, I'll show you how to list your own web site (once you've built it!) at these search sites.

There's More . . .

In the first three chapters, you've learned the basics of browsing the Web and connecting to the Internet, mainly as a passive member of a huge global audience. But there's a lot more to the Internet than reading other people's web pages. A big attraction of the Net is the capacity for connecting to and communicating with people all over the place. The next few chapters explain how to use e-mail, chat-pagers, and mailing lists, and how to stay in contact with your e-mail when on the road.

CHAPTER 4

Keep in Touch with E-Mail

INCLUDES

- Understanding Internet e-mail
- Keeping e-mail under control
- Building an address book
- Sending files via e-mail
- Handling e-mail problems
- Using Microsoft Outlook and other e-mail programs
- Joining mailing lists
- Paging and chatting live

Send Internet E-Mail ➡ p. 99

- If you're on a network, make sure it has an Internet e-mail gateway.
- Enter your recipient's e-mail address on the To: line in the standard Internet format: *their-username@their.Internet.address*.
- Type the topic of your message on the Subject: line.

Keep E-Mail from Taking Over Your Day ➡ p. 100

- Just check your messages a few times a day, instead of staying connected all the time and compulsively checking your messages. (This is one of those "do as I say, not as I do" rules.)

Keep Track of Others' E-Mail Addresses ➡ p. 101

- Save e-mail messages from people as a quick way to store their addresses.
- Create aliases or nicknames for e-mail addresses you use often.
- Set up an address book with names and e-mail addresses.

Attach a File to a Message ➡ pp. 101–102

- In Microsoft Outlook or Outlook Express, click the Insert File button, choose a file, and click Attach.
- In Netscape Messenger, click the Attach File(s) button, click Attach File, choose a file, and click OK twice.
- In Eudora, press CTRL+H, select a file, and click OK.
- In some programs, you can drag a file icon onto a mail message to attach it.

Set Up Your Mail Program ➡ p. 110

- Put your program on the desktop or in the Start or Apple menu for easy access.
- Tell your program your e-mail address and full name.
- Tell your program where to send and pick up your mail.

Protect Your Privacy ➡ pp. 114–115; 118

- Install a stand-alone PGP tool or the Outlook Express plug-in (from **http://www.nai.com/**) to decrypt mail, verify addresses, and add your digital signature to outgoing messages, *or*
- Use the VeriSign Certificate system built into Outlook Express, *or*
- Install the plug-in for Eudora Professional or Light, version 3 or 4, available from **http://www.eudora.com/**.

Sign Up for a Mailing List ➡ pp. 119–123

1. Search for an interesting list at the Publicly Accessible Mailing List site (**http://www.neosoft.com/cgi-bin/paml_search/**).
2. Read the subscription instructions; note the mailing address for subscribing (it's usually different from the address of the list itself), and the information you need to include in the message or subject header in order to subscribe.
3. Send your subscription request (most lists will acknowledge with an automated reply message).

Page Folks for Chat ➡ pp. 128–131

1. Download and install ICQ (**http://www.icq.com/**), AOL Instant Messenger, or another pager program.
2. Search for your friends and add them to your "buddy list."
3. Set ICQ (or your other program) to run in the background whenever you're connected to the Net.
4. Send out chat requests or wait for your friends to page you.

When you get past the hype (and truly exciting developments) of the World Wide Web, you'll notice that what really holds the Internet together is e-mail. In a century that has seen the invention and widespread acceptance of the telephone and television, perhaps we've become all too accommodating to each new communication medium. In some ways, though, I'm surprised that the academics, researchers, and military personnel who originally populated the Internet managed to keep such a useful tool a secret for so long.

Hassle-Free Mail

CAUTION

The act of checking your e-mail can easily become addictive and destroy productivity. Be conscious of how you integrate the use of e-mail into your work (or even home) life, so it doesn't eat up more than its share of your time.

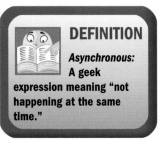

DEFINITION

Asynchronous: A geek expression meaning "not happening at the same time."

The biggest advantage of e-mail is convenience. You don't have to print your message, put it in an envelope, stamp it, and take it to a post office. In comparison to other forms of telecommunication, e-mail has the advantage that it is not immediate. Sure, e-mail travels much more quickly than traditional paper mail (called *snail mail* by e-mailers), but unlike a phone call, an e-mail message does not demand immediate response. So e-mail enables you to schedule some of your communication with others and postpone interruptions until you're ready for them.

Unlike voice mail, which is similarly asynchronous, e-mail enables you to keep a written correspondence. Still, you can't yet assume that your e-mail correspondents will necessarily see and respond to your mail in a timely fashion, so for urgent business matters, it's best to employ additional means of communication.

Compared to other forms of written communication (conventional mail, fax, telex, and so on), e-mail is also relatively cheap. In addition, there's something tangibly more likable about e-mail as compared to other forms of quick communication. Receiving written e-mail messages carries some (if not all) of the appeal of finding letters in your "real" mailbox. Also, unlike in phone conversations, you can make sure you've said precisely what you want to say in exactly the right tone before you click the Send button. But I don't need to convince you about e-mail. If you're reading this book, the wave has caught up with you and you're already on the Net.

In this chapter, I'll give you an overview of e-mail and show you how to use typical e-mail programs. I'll also show you how to find and subscribe to mailing lists and how to page people to "chat" with them live, when e-mail isn't immediate enough for you.

Internet E-Mail Addresses

The Internet provides a common medium for sharing many different types of e-mail. It doesn't matter if you use Outlook in your office and the person you want to send mail to uses America Online. With Internet mail addresses, you can send a message to that person just as if you were both on the same network. The only requirement is that the messages must be formatted the same way, with certain standard headers—which your e-mail program will take care of for you. Ideally, your program will hide most of those headers from you as well.

For now, Internet e-mail is still primarily a plain-text medium, so don't expect your clever use of fonts, boldface, and graphic lines to go over well with your Net correspondents. It may travel across a LAN to an office buddy just fine, but it will not make it through the eye of the needle that is an Internet mail gateway. You'll notice that many people ignore this traditional wisdom and you'll find yourself receiving heavily styled messages when the capabilities of your mail program matches the sender's (and messages with lots of apparent garbage when they do not). Most new e-mail programs can create or interpret HTML formatting, the type used for web pages, but I'm not so sure this is a good thing, given that many e-mail programs out there will "choke" on the HTML and litter your message with distracting, unreadable garbage.

However you look at it, an Internet e-mail address always appears in this form: *username @Internet-address*. The Internet-address portion takes the form host.subdomain.domain, with the host name sometimes optional. To send e-mail to someone via the Internet, make sure to enter the address in this form. Generally, e-mail

The reason you sometimes get e-mail with enormous headers is that the message originated in a different e-mail program.

DEFINITION

Gateway:
A program or computer that regulates communication between two networks, the Internet and a local network, or any two network media.

In many networked e-mail systems, and at online services such as AOL, when you send mail to someone else on the same system, you can specify just the username.

addresses are not case-sensitive (meaning they don't distinguish between uppercase and lowercase letters), although sometimes the username may be.

Here are some typical e-mail addresses:

```
President@whitehouse.gov
billg@microsoft.com
jsoames@uclink4.berkeley.edu
estephen@emf.net
kyrie@engr.sgi.com
BIFF99@aol.com
gelezeau@dmi.ens.fr
```

E-Mail for Busy People

When you are really busy, e-mail can be either a blessing or a curse (or both at the same time). Not having to drop what you're doing to reply to a query can help you organize your own time effectively. But don't let e-mail interrupt you! If you're constantly checking your mail and getting involved in more and more casual online conversations, your productivity may suffer and e-mail may become another black hole that eats up all your free time.

I don't want to make e-mail sound like a drag, though. Most people really enjoy it as a form of communication. Just keep it within reasonable boundaries as part of your work day. The real question is how can you best integrate e-mail into your online existence.

Later in this chapter, I'll explain the details of three popular (and easy-to-get) e-mail programs and give you enough to go on to use any program to read your mail. Here I'll just outline a generic mail session.

EXPERT ADVICE

Tempting as it may be, don't keep your e-mail program running and connected all day long. Try to limit yourself to checking your mail every hour or so (or even two or three times a day, perhaps at the beginning, middle, and end of your work day, if you have Herculean self-control). Of course, how often you should check your mail depends on how much you need to communicate in this manner.

A Typical Mail Session

Here is a summary of a typical mail session:

1. Run your mail program. It will tell you if you have new mail.

2. Select and read mail in your Inbox.

3. Reply to (or forward) messages, quoting from the original if necessary.

4. Save messages you'll need to deal with later and delete as much mail as you can.

5. Compose new mail. (Sometimes, this is the first thing you'll do.)

6. Send all new messages if there are any in your Outbox.

7. Deal with older, saved mail, if the time is ripe.

8. Quit your mail program.

Sending Copies of E-Mail

With e-mail, it's just as easy to send a message to two or more recipients as it is to send it to a single person. To send e-mail to more than one recipient, you can put all of the e-mail addresses in the To: header of the new message and separate each with a special character (such as commas or semicolons, depending on the mail program). You can also enter additional addresses on the Cc: line. (Cc originally stood for carbon copy and is now, since the demise of carbon, assumed to mean "courtesy copy.") Addresses on the Cc: line will receive a copy of the mail and will appear in the message headers seen by recipients.

Some e-mail programs also permit the use of a Bcc: line, which stands for blind courtesy (or carbon) copy. Addresses in the Bcc: header will receive a copy of the mail but will not appear in the message headers seen by recipients.

It's a good idea to keep copies of your own outgoing mail. Some mail programs do this for you as a matter of course or let you choose a setting for this purpose. If your program doesn't work this way, you can still send a copy of each message to your own address.

DEFINITION

Host: The name of a specific machine in a larger domain or subdomain (such as squinky.microsoft.com), but you don't need to know any of this, really.

Domains and Subdomains: Ways of organizing Internet addresses. Domains are large areas divided by purpose (.com for commercial, .edu for education, and so on), and subdomains are smaller areas within those larger domains (ibm.com, princeton.edu, and so on).

DEFINITION

Inbox:
The folder in your mail program that contains incoming mail before it's been deleted or moved to another folder for storage. (Also *in-box, in box.*)

Keeping Your Inbox Under Control

One of the hazards of e-mail is an overflowing Inbox. If you don't keep your e-mail strictly under control, it can easily overwhelm you. To prevent this, you have to develop some good e-mail habits:

- Delete mail as soon as you've read or dealt with it, unless you need it for your records.
- Move messages out of the Inbox and into topical mailboxes, either to deal with the messages later or to store them for future reference.
- Read and answer or deal with your mail as expediently as possible.
- Don't store messages in your Inbox. It should contain only new mail!

That last item is the most difficult to follow. I myself am guilty of leaving lots of undealt-with mail in my Inbox "to remind me." In fact, I have over 700 messages in there right now (and it's only Monday!).

Filtering and Forwarding Mail Automatically

Filtering is absolutely critical if you subscribe to mailing lists (see later in this chapter). Without it, you have to file by hand every message that comes in from the list!

The future of e-mail sees inclusion of intelligent agents that filter and sort incoming mail, perhaps find information for you out on the Net, and even reply automatically to certain messages. For now, some e-mail programs enable you to set up automatic filtering or forwarding. Filtering is sorting messages (based on keywords) as they come in or go out, and either filing them or performing some action on them. The actions you perform can be changing the message's priority, deleting the message entirely, replying automatically, printing the message, and so on.

NETIQUETTE

If you're too busy to respond to e-mail in a timely fashion, consider sending a brief message saying that you did receive the mail and that you'll respond at length when you have the opportunity.

If you set up automatic forwarding, your e-mail program will send some or all of your mail to another address. (The term *to forward* is also applied to the manual task of sending an individual piece of mail on to another address.) Forwarding can be especially useful if you have more than one e-mail address but you want all your mail shunted to one account so you can check it all in one place.

Keeping Track of Other People's Addresses

Once you get online, you'll need to start a collection of other people's e-mail addresses. The low-tech way to save an e-mail address is to keep a message from that sender (stored in a folder, not cluttering your Inbox). You can then reply to that message whenever you want to reach the sender. In the long run though, it's more convenient to create an address book or at least a collection of shorter nicknames (also sometimes called aliases) for your friends' e-mail addresses.

More and more often, people are including their e-mail addresses on business cards (some are including web addresses as well).

Sending Files via E-Mail

Probably the biggest frustration with e-mail these days results from sending files as attachments. Why would you want to do this anyway? Increasingly, when you're working on a file—say a word processor document, a presentation, or a spreadsheet—you'll need to send it to someone else. Sure, you can print it (depending on the type of document it is) and send it by mail or courier. But what if you want your recipient to have access to the electronic file itself, to give them the ability to change or edit the document? Then you have to send the file. Again, you could put the file on a disk, stick it in a cardboard mailer, and entrust it

EXPERT ADVICE

If you need to exchange e-mail addresses with someone who does not remember her address, just ask her to send you mail (give her your address); you'll capture her address in that first message.

DEFINITION

Attachment:
A file that has been encoded as ASCII text and then included as part of an e-mail message. If your mail program can't read the encoding, it will show you the ASCII gibberish at the tail end of your message.

to a delivery service. However, it can be much faster (and easier) to simply send the file attached to a piece of e-mail.

You will have no problem if you are working within a given network or within an online service such as AOL or CompuServe, but the methods used to attach files to Internet e-mail are not yet standard for every type of mail gateway. You may have to ask your recipient, sender, and possibly even tech support to learn what specifically will or won't work. Even if you can send and receive attachments, you'll still have to agree on file formats that both you and your correspondent can use.

Managing Multiple E-Mail Accounts

If you find yourself with multiple e-mail accounts to manage (such as a work address and a personal address), then you'll need to set up your mail program to check mail at each of the addresses (or set up your mail program on your computer at work with one account and your mail program on your computer at home with the other account). If you need to pick up the same mail messages from more than one machine, then you'll want to make sure that at least one of the mail programs automatically leaves the mail messages on the mail server instead of deleting them after retrieving them, so that the same messages will still be available when retrieved by the second machine.

Optional E-Mail Features

Internet e-mail standards are constantly evolving. Here are some useful new features that are not yet widely implemented, but are getting there.

See Appendix A for details on connecting to (and disconnecting from) the Internet.

Reading Mail Offline

Because some forms of Internet connectivity charge you the whole time you're connected, you may want to investigate handling your mail offline. This means connecting briefly to download new mail and then disconnecting. You can then read your mail and compose your replies without being connected and then connect again briefly to reply.

Some programs automate the process of offline mail reading, but with any mail program, you can check your mail, disconnect your Internet connection, and then read and respond to your mail offline. Here's how:

1. Connect to the Internet.

2. Run your mail program (it will check for new mail).

3. Log off from the Internet.

4. Read and respond to your mail at your leisure. (Replies will sit in your Outbox until they can be sent.)

5. Log back on to the Internet.

6. Send your mail.

7. Log off from the Internet again.

Composing Mail Outside of Your Mail Program

If you're not completely comfortable in the space provided for composing messages in your e-mail program, you can also write messages in a word processor and then cut and paste them into your mail program (this is different from attaching files).

You have to watch out for the special typesetting characters that modern word processors are forever inserting into your documents (such as curly quotation marks, long dashes, and special symbols such as ô and Æ), because they will generally appear as garbage characters once the mail has passed over the Internet. Here's the best way to avoid such problems:

1. Write your message in your word processor.

2. Save the document as a plain text file.

3. Close the document. Then open it again.

4. Copy the entire document with the Edit | Copy command.

5. Switch to your e-mail program and start a new message.

6. Paste the document into the message with the Edit | Paste command (or use Edit | Paste Special to insert the selection without any extraneous formatting).

Some programs, such as Eudora, now automatically correct curly quotation marks.

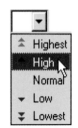

Prioritizing Mail

Most mail programs can assign a priority level to messages—from highest, to normal, to lowest—to tell a recipient whether a message is urgent and requires a quick reply. Use this kind of signaling only when necessary or people will start to assume you're always crying wolf. In crises, though, a priority flag can really help a message stand out in a crowded Inbox.

Confirming Receipt of Mail

Some e-mail programs allow you to specify that you be notified when your recipient has received (or even opened) your mail message. This trick isn't supported everywhere on the Net; for now it works only within specific networks.

Maintaining Security and Privacy

DEFINITION

Encryption: **Mathematical encoding of a message or file in order to keep its contents secure. Decoding such a message is referred to as decryption.**

E-mail pathways are not secure. As your message flits across the Internet to your recipient, it is copied and stored (at least temporarily) on many computers in between. In some ways, e-mail messages are like postcards. Anyone "carrying" the message can read it, even if most would never do so. The only way to put a message in an "envelope" is to encode it with some form of encryption. Although encryption of e-mail is possible, unfortunately none of the popular e-mail programs incorporate an easy way to do this. Therefore, don't send anything by e-mail that could damage you or anyone else if read by the wrong person.

As I'll explain later in this chapter, the most popular mail programs offer one or more privacy or security systems, either built into the software or available as a plug-in. New versions of Eudora come with PGP (Pretty Good Privacy). There's a PGP plug-in for Outlook Express, and a built-in VeriSign certificate system. Netscape can handle VeriSign certificates as well as those vouched for by other certifying agencies. There's no PGP plug-in for Netscape (yet).

See Chapter 5 for how to handle e-mail while on the road.

Some E-Mail Conventions

As a new communication medium, e-mail has developed its own conventions. It's often easy to spot first-time e-mailers, because they tend to borrow from other familiar written styles. An e-mail message is not a postcard, not a letter, not an office memo (but can be similar to all three, naturally).

The headers in an e-mail message (To:, Date:, Subject:, and so on) make it resemble a memo, but most people write e-mail in a more informal style, reminiscent of conversation.

In the next few sections, I'll describe some of the conventions of e-mail communication, so you can get into the swing of things as quickly as possible.

Providing Meaningful Subject Lines

A good Subject: line describes your message without going into too little or too much detail. You shouldn't need more than a dozen words in the Subject: line. If you're asking a question, it's far better to use a specific subject, such as "Need help locating the new Forbin report," rather than "Important!" or "Need Help" or "Here's a question." On the other hand, an ultra-specific Subject: line such as "I still need your 53-word response to the 11/15/99 Janan memo because it's been a week already" is too unwieldy and leaves you little to say in the body of the mail. Better to cut the subject down to "Need your response to the Janan memo ASAP!" and leave the details for the body of the message itself.

When writing to someone you don't know or posting to Usenet newsgroups, don't try to attract attention by giving your message a provocative but irrelevant subject. Many beginners have tried the old trick of "Subject: Sex!" and then begin the message with, "Now that I have your attention." This kind of bait-and-switch technique generates poor results.

After a few replies back and forth, a Subject: line may get stale. For example, the original message to you might have the subject "Office Picnic." But after you reply to the sender and she replies to you, you may put off reading about a message that seems to be about the by-now -past office picnic. So remember to change the Subject: line to reflect the current topic.

Quoting to Provide Context

It is common to quote some of the message you are responding to in a reply, to provide some context to your message, although it's not always necessary. However, as soon as you get a message from someone reading "I'm afraid not" or "Yes, let's do it!" and you can't remember what you said in your original message, you'll understand how helpful it is to include some of the original message in a reply.

CAUTION

When replying to a message, be careful not to excerpt the original message in any way that might change the meaning in its original context. For that matter, you should never edit an original message to alter its meaning.

```
When you wrote:

>If we upsnarch the quince-wimble, I think we'll have the problem
>under control.

I wasn't sure what you meant by "we."

    --xian
```

Most mail programs will automatically include all of the original message (or offer to do so) when you start to reply. Furthermore, you can usually turn this feature on or off. Be sure to trim as much of the quotation as you can so your recipient can save time rereading and to make sure that your reply doesn't get lost in the shuffle. Leave just enough of the original message to provide context. Also, use blank lines (press ENTER) between quoted text and new text so it doesn't all clump together. If you're sending an unrelated message, delete all the quoted text. Change the Subject: line, too, while you're at it.

By the way, the system of quoting using greater-than signs (>) or other characters in front of each line comes from Unix mail programs, which until now have dominated Internet e-mail. Some programs allow you to customize the quotation characters or use different characters, such as a vertical bar (|), colon (:), or even the initials of the person being quoted. If you do customize your program, strive for readability.

Other programs change the color, font, and so on to show quotation. Be careful not to assume that such enhancements will come across correctly on the Internet (as opposed to within your office), where the only common denominator is essentially the standard keyboard characters.

It is considered boorish in some circles to have a signature longer than *four lines.*

Using a Signature

You may notice that all the mail you get from a correspondent ends with the same tag line, or even several lines. Usually, the person isn't typing that information at the end of each message but instead has something called a signature file that the mail program automatically appends to each outgoing message. The text in a signature file is usually referred to as a signature, but signatures are also called sig blocks, sigs, .signature, and .sig (the latter two are Unix terms, pronounced dot-signature and dot-sig, respectively).

So what should you have in your signature, assuming you want one? Well, you'll at least want to include your name and possibly your e-mail address, in case your recipient can't get it from the message automatically. You probably won't want to include your phone number. Some people include favorite or inane sayings or elaborate drawings made of keyboard characters (called ASCII art after the name of the standard computer character set—ASCII).

```
--
E. Stephen Mack (Zeigen)                        estephen@emf.net
Winter Weather, Berkeley, CA           http://www.emf.net/~estephen/

            But who are YOU to tell ME to question authority?
```

Keep the lines of your message well under 80 characters (the maximum for certain text-only computer systems), so quoted messages will still fit on everyone's screen neatly. I find that 75-character lines work fine.

Assuming you use e-mail for work, keep your signature business like. Remember that once you've sent e-mail to anyone, there's a scrap of text with your name attached floating around, and you never know to whom it might be sent or where you might end up seeing yourself quoted.

When you use e-mail for personal correspondence, no one should resend your mail elsewhere without your permission, but it does happen.

Speaking Informally

Do not be offended if you receive e-mail that dispenses with the customary "Dear Sir or Madam"-type of salutation. Although many people will preface a message with "Hi" or anything from "Dear Ms. Higgenbotham" to "Hey Now!", it is completely acceptable to just

It's still a good idea to maintain decorum in business correspondence.

NETIQUETTE

It is inappropriate to post others' private e-mail messages to any public discussion group or to forward messages to third parties without the express permission of the original sender.

plunge directly into a message, in that breathless, late twentieth-century way.

Some e-mail correspondence resembles long, drawn-out (and thought-out) conversations, and written conversations also provide the potential for wordplay, visual puns, even collaborative poems, and so on. So slip off your shoes and relax before beginning your correspondence.

Using Smileys :-)

Of course by now, you know about smileys; those sideways faces made from punctuation characters that are also sometimes called *emoticons*. Because e-mail is said to be a cold medium—conversational, yet lacking the facial, vocal, and body language cues that people use in other forms of communication to smooth out interaction—there is a great danger of misinterpretation, of people taking offense, of arguments.

You may have heard of the practice of "flaming," which essentially means chewing out someone in e-mail or in a discussion group, usually in a vitriolic and sometimes satirically or sarcastically humorous way. Such scurrilous attack messages are referred to as flames. Many flames are provoked through the sort of ambiguity and offense-taking that I just alluded to. Thus the practice arose of appending a smiley, such as the basic one shown here (tilt your head to the left), to the end of anything even mildly controversial. (Certain popular abbreviations, such as IMHO—in my humble opinion—also aim for the same effect.)

CAUTION
Some people abhor the use of smileys and will flame you mercilessly just for using them. Also, keep them out of for-the-record communication.

:-)

;-)

>:-(

There is now an entire vocabulary of smiley faces, many of them silly and rarely used. Semicolons are often substituted for colons to denote winking.

And the mouth character can be changed to indicate frowning (or other less clear expressions).

There are whole books dedicated to this minor semaphore-like communication form, and I encourage you to pick one up if you are really interested (and not too busy).

Spam, Unsolicited Mail, and Other Problems

As e-mail becomes a ubiquitous medium, unsolicited e-mail messages, chain letters, and come-ons have started appearing in mailboxes more and more often, just as unsolicited fax messages have started appearing. While this may not cost you money (unless your service provider charges you for mail), it is still a waste of your time as well as rude.

If you receive an unprompted message, reply to the sender, ask where the person got your address, and tell the person not to send you any more mail (and to take you off any mailing list you may have been put on without your permission). If an unsolicited message continues to be a problem, send a Cc: copy of the message to postmaster@*sender's-address* (use the same details as after the @ sign in the sender's address), so the person knows you mean business and that the person's mail administrator knows what is going on.

Many spammers these days use fake return addresses, so you can't really reply to them. For these sorts of messages, quickly throwing them in the trash and ignoring them is about the best you can do (for now).

Other Problems with Mail

If you get complaints from friends that their mail to you is bouncing (coming back with "recipient unknown"), or if you experience other problems, contact your own mail administrator. If you are on a small network, you probably know the administrator personally. On a larger network, send mail to postmaster or to postmaster@*your-address* and ask the administrator to look into your problem.

If you reply to someone's message and your reply comes bouncing back, check the To: header. It's possible that your correspondent's mail program or system is incorrectly configured and that the address is being garbled. Make sure the address on the message that bounced looks like a correct Internet address, with the form *username @something.something.thing*. If it does not, resend the message after editing the To: header manually.

Choosing a Mail Program

There are a multitude of e-mail programs out there and there's no way I could do them all justice in this chapter (hey, I'm a busy person too!). Depending on how you connect to the Internet and what type of computer setup you have, you may end up using one of many different

Be wary of scams that sound too good to be true. Treat unsolicited commercial e-mail the way you would phone calls at dinner time or traveling salespeople at the door.

Some bounced messages only tell you that a server along the route is still attempting to send the mail. Not every system on the Internet is up and running 24-hours a day.

e-mail programs. Fortunately, aside from the inevitable idiosyncrasies in command names, menu placement, and optional features, most mail programs work essentially the same way. I'll discuss Microsoft's Outlook and Outlook Express, Netscape Messenger, and Qualcomm's Eudora, a popular stand-alone e-mail program.

If you're already set up using a different program, you should still be able to follow most of these instructions, though you may occasionally have to hunt around for the right menu or command. Even if your office still uses, say, cc:Mail for Windows 3.1, you can get any one of these programs and try it out.

Key Setup Information, No Matter What Mail Program You Use

No matter what mail program you use, you'll have to tell it certain things about your e-mail account. If you work in an office, someone there ought to be able to supply the correct information, but you may be able to figure it out for yourself. Most of what you have to enter is based on your username and Internet address. You should only have to set up your mail program once (unless you change service providers).

Setting up Netscape Messenger was covered in Chapter 2.

DEFINITION

POP:
Post Office Protocol; a standard method of storing and retrieving e-mail.

SMTP:
Simple Mail Transport Protocol; the most common method of distributing e-mail on the Internet.

- If you need to supply a POP account, enter your full e-mail address (your provider will tell you if you need to specify a host machine in this address, something like *yourusername@popmailer.yourprovider.com* even if people sending you mail can just use *yourusername@yourprovider.com*).

- For your SMTP server (that's the machine that handles your outgoing mail), you can probably enter that part of your address after the @ sign. (If your service provider requires that you use an address like smtp.*yourprovider.com* or mailer.*yourprovider.com*, they will inform you of this—call your technical support if necessary.)

- For your return address, enter your e-mail address as you give it out to others (such as *yourusername@yourprovider.com*).

Microsoft Outlook and Outlook Express

Microsoft has offered a number of different e-mail programs over the years. The one that now comes with Internet Explorer is called Outlook Express (it is similar to, but different from Outlook, which comes with Microsoft Office). If you have Internet Explorer but not Outlook Express, you can download it by following the Software Updates procedure described in Chapter 2. Windows 98 comes with Outlook Express as well, but you may still be due for an update by the time you read this. While Outlook Express is free, Outlook comes with additional features (mostly contact and scheduling features). I'll discuss Outlook Express first, and then cover the differences in the Outlook section.

Outlook Express

The first time you run Outlook Express, the program will offer to become your default mail program and will offer to connect you to the Net whenever you start the program without first connecting. A wizard will also help you to configure the program. After clicking Next to move past the introductory screen, you'll have to enter your name and full e-mail address.

Now click Next again. You'll need to enter the names of your incoming (POP3) and outgoing (SMTP) mail servers. Hopefully a network administrator or helpful person from your Internet service provider will already have given you these machine names (often the POP3 and SMTP names are identical).

Now we're getting down to the details. Clicking Next leads Outlook Express Configuration to ask you for your e-mail account

---

EXPERT ADVICE

In Outlook, you can create a new mail account at any time by selecting Tools | Accounts, clicking the New button, and then entering the incoming and outgoing mail information and your password.

If you ever want to change your
account information or add a
new Internet e-mail account,
select Tools | Accounts, and then
select an account and click the
Properties button, or just click
the New button. After that, the
procedure is the same as
outlined here.

Press CTRL+R to reply to a
message. Press CTRL+F to
forward a message.

and password. The e-mail account name is the part before the @ in
your e-mail address. If you enter a password here, you won't have to
enter it each time you get your mail; however, this will make your
mail less secure since anyone using your computer will have access to
your private mail. Consider leaving the password blank, so you will be
prompted for it each time you get mail. Click Next when you've filled
in these fields.

Last, you need to indicate what type of connection you use. If
you're part of a corporate network, you should choose the first option,
I Use A LAN Connection. If you want to work offline or have several
different ways you can connect, choose I Connect Manually. If you
use a modem to dial in to your account, choose the third option, I
Use a Modem To Access My Email and then select your dial-up
networking connection from the drop-down list (see Appendix A if
you haven't set up dial-up networking yet).

That's it! Click Finish to begin using Outlook Express.

Reading, Replying to, and Forwarding Mail in Outlook Express

In Outlook Express, new messages appear in boldface. To read a message,
select it, and the message will open in the lower half of the window.

To reply to a message, click Reply To Author (or Reply To All if
you want to reply to an entire list of recipients).

Outlook Express will start a new message in its own window,
supplying the recipient's name in the To: line and quoting the message to
which you're replying. Edit the quoted material if necessary, type your
reply message, and then click the Send button on the toolbar.

To send a reply not to the original sender but to a third party
instead, click the Forward button. Outlook Express will quote the
original message as in a reply but will leave the To: line blank for you
to enter the addressee. Type a recipient's address or click the To:
button and follow the instructions in the section "Sending New
Messages in Outlook Express" later in this chapter.

Saving and Deleting Messages in Outlook Express

To store a message in a folder in Outlook Express (or Outlook), select
Edit | Move To Folder or press CTRL+SHIFT+V. You can even create a

new folder on the fly this way. Just click the New button on the Move Items dialog box.

To view the contents of a folder, choose the folder you want in the left-side pane.

- Any folders you created with the File | Folder | New Folder command will appear in this box.
- The Deleted Items folder contains mail you have deleted.
- The Outbox folder contains any outgoing mail you've prepared, which will be sent when you click the Send And Receive button.
- The Sent Items folder stores a copy of mail that has been sent.

To delete a message in Outlook Express, click the Delete button on the toolbar. The message will be moved to the Deleted Items folder.

To permanently get rid of messages, just delete them from the Deleted Items folder. Outlook Express will warn you that these will be permanently deleted.

J ust press DELETE to delete a message or a number of selected messages.

Sending New Messages in Outlook Express

To send a new message in Outlook Express, click the New Mail button (in Outlook, the New Mail Message button) on the toolbar. A New Message window will appear. Type an address in the To: box or click the little phone-file card icon to bring up the Select Recipients dialog box, which allows you to select names from your address book.

In the Select Recipients dialog box, choose a name from the list in the left window and click the To: button to add it to the recipient list, or click the New Contact button to create a new entry in the address book. This brings up the Properties dialog box.

EXPERT ADVICE

In Outlook (not Outlook Express), you can enter a recipient's name directly in the To box, and Outlook will use the correct address if the name is among your contacts, or underline it with a squiggly red line if it is not. Right-click on an unidentified name to choose a recipient or create a new contact entry.

If you consider your message to be very important, click the stamp (in the upper right of the window) and choose High Priority from the menu.

Enter the new name, e-mail address, and any other information you want to add and then click OK. (*Then* click the To: button to add it to the recipient list.) Repeat this process if you want to add other recipients. Then click OK again to add the recipient(s) to the message.

Tab down to or click the Subject: box and type a subject line. Then press TAB again or click the message area and type your message. When you're done, click the Send button.

To attach a file in Outlook Express, click the Insert File button on the toolbar. In the Insert Attachment dialog box that appears, select the file you want to include and then click Attach. You can look in any drive or folder for the file you want to attach. The file will appear as an icon in a pane at the bottom of your message window.

When you "send" a message in Outlook Express, it's placed in your Outbox folder. Messages in the folder are not actually sent until you deliver them. To do so, click the Send/Receive button (or press CTRL+M or COMMAND+M).

Protecting Your Privacy with Outlook Express

Outlook Express features a built-in security system similar to that used by PGP, referred to as a Digital ID. To use it, you first have to get your own digital ID. Select Tools | Accounts, select your e-mail account, and then click the Properties button. In the Mail Properties dialog box that appears, click the Security tag. To read up on exactly how these ID's work, click the More Info button. To get your own Digital ID, click the Get Digital ID button.

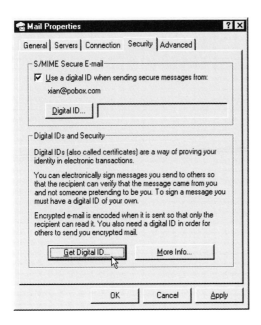

If you would prefer to use the PGP system, visit the PGP web site at **http://www.pgp.com/** or the Network Associates site at **http://www.nai.com/** and download the free plug-in for Outlook Express there.

Netscape Messenger

Another mail program you might consider using is Netscape Messenger, which is actually a module of Netscape Navigator. It's still limited in some ways compared to full-fledged mail programs, but if you have Netscape, you have this module already. (Some offices have standardized on Netscape Messenger, so you may not have a choice.)

You can start Netscape Messenger several ways: by selecting Communicator | Messenger Mailbox in Netscape, by clicking the envelope icon in the lower-right corner of the Navigator window, or the usual way, from an icon or menu item.

If you downloaded just Netscape Navigator (the stand-alone browser), then you'll have to get the Netscape Messenger module (or the entire Communicator suite) from the Netscape web site by choosing the Program Updates feature explained in Chapter 2.

Reading, Replying to, and Forwarding Mail in Netscape Messenger

Folders appear in the upper-left pane of the Netscape Messenger window, and message subjects appear in the upper-right pane. To read a message, select it. The message will open in the lower pane (see Figure 4.1).

Press CTRL+R or COMMAND+R to reply to a message.

To reply to a message, click the Reply button (or click Reply To All if you want to reply to an entire list of recipients). Netscape Messenger will start a new message (in its own window), supplying the recipient's name in the To: box, and quoting the message to which you're replying. Edit the quoted material if necessary, type your reply message, and then click the Send button on the toolbar.

Press CTRL+L or COMMAND+L to forward a message.

To send a reply to a third party instead of the original sender, click the Forward button. Netscape Messenger will quote the original message as in a reply but will leave the To: line blank for you to enter

Create a new message.

Reply to the selected message.

Get new mail.

Your messages are listed here (unread ones appear in boldface), sorted by Sender, Subject, or Date.

Your selected e-mail appears here.

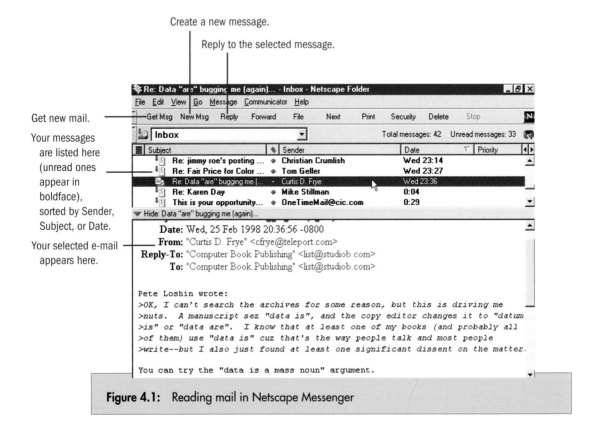

Figure 4.1: Reading mail in Netscape Messenger

the addressee. Type a recipient's address or click the To: button and
follow the instructions in the section "Sending a New Message in
Netscape Messenger" later in this chapter.

Saving and Deleting Messages in Netscape Messenger

To store a message in a folder in Netscape Messenger,
you first have to create the folder:

Message	
New Message	Ctrl+M
Reply	▶
Forward	Ctrl+L
Forward Quoted	Ctrl+Shift+L
Add to Address Book	▶
File Message	▶
Copy Message	▶
Mark	▶
Flag	
Unflag	
Ignore Thread	K
Watch Thread	W

0 Inbox	▶
1 Unsent Messages	
2 Drafts	
3 Sent	
4 Trash	
5 Studio B	

1. Select File | New Folder.

2. In the dialog box that appears, type a name
   for the folder.

3. Choose Local Mail from the drop-down
   Create As Subfolder Of list box.

4. Click OK.
   Then you can store it:

5. Select Message | File Message | *folder name.*

To view the contents of a folder, just click the folder you want in
the drop-down list box on the Location toolbar.

To delete a message in Netscape Messenger, click the Delete button
on the toolbar.

Just press DELETE to delete a
message or a number of
selected messages.

Sending a New Message in Netscape Messenger

To send a new message in Netscape Messenger, select File | New
Message, click the New Msg button on the toolbar, or press CTRL+M
(or COMMAND+M). A New Message window will appear. Type an
address in the To: box. Tab down to or click the Subject: box and
type a subject line. Then press TAB again or click the message area and
type your message. When you're done, click the Send button.

Attaching a File

To attach a file in Netscape Messenger, click the Attach File(s) button
on the toolbar. In the Attachments dialog box that appears, click

Attach File. In the "Enter file to attach" dialog box that then pops up, select the file you want to include and click Open. Then click OK.

Protecting Your Privacy with Netscape Messenger

To protect your mail from snoops, select Communicator | Security Info. In the Security Info dialog box that appears, click the Yours category. To get a certificate with which you can sign your messages and enable your correspondents to encrypt messages in a way that you can decrypt and read them, click the Get A Certificate button. This will connect you to the Netscape web site where you can select a certificate agency, follow the instructions to obtain a unique certificate, and make up a PIN (password) for future use with the certificate.

To encrypt outgoing messages, select the Messenger category of the Security Info dialog box. Then check Encrypt Mail Messages, When It Is Possible. You can also check Sign Mail Messages, When It Is Possible if you wish. Then click OK.

To look into alternative security plug-ins available, select Help | Security. You can also visit the PGP web site (**http://www.pgp.com/**) or the Network associates site (**http://www.nai.com/**) to purchase a stand-alone version of PGP.

Eudora (Light and Professional)

Eudora was designed specifically for Internet e-mail and early versions of it were distributed for free on the Internet. More recent versions of it are made by Qualcomm in two "flavors": Light and Professional. The Light version is freeware, but always lags behind the professional version in terms of features. The Professional version must be purchased.

Pegasus Mail is another pretty good and free e-mail program that you might want to try. You can download it from *http://www.pegasus.usa.com/*.

To get the freeware version of Eudora, point your web browser at **http://www.eudora.com/** and find the link for Eudora Light. Click Download Eudora Light and PGP, answer Yes to all the questions regarding U.S. export control (assuming you are in the U.S.), give them your e-mail address, and then choose your platform. The

Qualcomm web site will then automatically transfer the installation file to your computer (in a folder you specify). When it has fully arrived, double-click the downloaded file and then run the Setup program to install Eudora.

The steps for evaluating the Pro version for 30 days are very similar after you click the appropriate link on the main Eudora page.

To send a message in Eudora, select Message | New Message. Eudora will start a message for you in a new window.

These days, Eudora seems most popular among those who try to minimize their use of Microsoft products. When virus writers are targeting Outlook's capability of opening file attachments automatically with Office macro viruses and worse, Eudora is blissfully immune to such attacks.

DEFINITION

Freeware: Software that's free to download and use, as opposed to shareware, which is free to download, but for which you are expected to pay a licensing fee if you continue to use it after a trial period.

Mailing Lists

A mailing list, often referred to simply as a list, is made up of e-mail addresses, usually with a single e-mail address set up that forwards all messages sent to it to every address on the list. This facilitates a group conversation in which anyone on the list can participate and which can potentially spawn various threads from a single original post.

Lists do have their downsides as well, especially for a busy person. A high-traffic mailing list will flood your Inbox in no time. It's natural to join and quit (subscribe to and unsubscribe from) mailing lists freely, as your interests wax and wane or as the traffic on a list changes. If you're too busy for any kind of conversational lists, you may still be interested in some announcement-only lists, which essentially broadcast information without providing a forum for discussion.

A mailing list is an actual e-mail address associated with a list of addresses. When the mail server of the main address receives incoming mail, it automatically forwards it to every address on the list. Such mailing lists are maintained either by human volunteers or by robotic mailing list programs (controlled by e-mail commands).

The main thing you need to know before subscribing to a list is whether it is administered by a human or a robot. With human-administered lists, you send plain English messages to the administrator

DEFINITION

Post: A message sent to a public forum of any kind, such as a mailing list or Usenet newsgroup (from the analogy of posting a message to a bulletin board). Also called an article.

Thread: An ongoing conversation on a single topic or theme, usually with each message under the same subject.

when you want to join the list, quit it, inquire about it, or change your status on the list. With robot-administered lists, you send carefully worded messages that include commands for the program that controls the list.

Digests

Some mailing lists can also be subscribed to in a "digestified" form, meaning that a group of messages (from that day or week, or every ten or so messages) are lumped into a single digest and sent out. Digests can help reduce the number of messages appearing in your Inbox for a high-traffic list. Digests often have the feel of a newsletter—often a very democratic newsletter in which anyone can participate and there is no editor. A digest will have a subscription address separate from the main mailing list from which it's derived. If you subscribe to a list and then realize it's too busy for you, subscribe to the digest, and then unsubscribe from the primary list, once you're sure you're receiving the collected messages.

Moderated Lists

Some mailing lists have a moderator, a volunteer who screens messages sent to the list and posts only those that are on-topic (directly related to the topic of the list) and noninflammatory. Moderated lists tend to have fewer posts, which can make them more appealing to busy people.

Finding Mailing Lists That Interest You

Because mailing lists are being formed (or dying out) every day, it would be a full-time job to keep up with the entire set of lists. Fortunately, the Internet community includes many people who voluntarily maintain references to exactly that kind of information. You just have to know where to look.

Probably the definitive source of mailing lists is a document called, naturally enough, Publicly Accessible Mailing Lists, currently in 20 parts and containing descriptions of over 1,500 mailing lists. Point your Web browser at **http://www.neosoft.com/internet/paml/** to go to the Publicly Accessible Mailing Lists (PAML) web site (see Figure 4.2).

DEFINITION

Robot: On the Internet, usually refers to an automated process that may or may not behave like a real person (as opposed to a mobile tin can in a science fiction movie). Also called bots or agents.

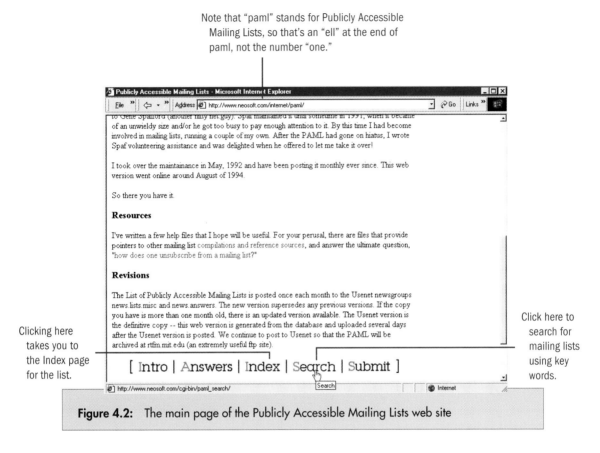

Note that "paml" stands for Publicly Accessible Mailing Lists, so that's an "ell" at the end of paml, not the number "one."

Clicking here takes you to the Index page for the list.

Click here to search for mailing lists using key words.

Figure 4.2: The main page of the Publicly Accessible Mailing Lists web site

Read the main page and then click the Search link. You'll be able to search for lists using key words (see Figure 4.3).

If you have any trouble connecting to the PAML site, you can find the same information (in a less structured form) at **http://www.cis.ohio-state.edu/hypertext/faq/usenet/mail/ mailing-lists/top.html**. It lists the parts of the PAML document in the form that it's posted to Usenet newsgroups. Or you can try directly accessing the archive site where the posted documents are stored at **ftp:// rtfm.mit.edu/pub/usenet-by-group/news.answers/mail/ mailing-lists/**.

If you don't find what you need in PAML and you want to look for other lists of mailing lists, try Yahoo!'s big central listing at **http://www.yahoo.com/Computers_and_Internet/Internet/ Mailing_Lists/**.

CAUTION

The RTFM site is frequently busy and difficult to connect to. Try the wee hours of the morning for an easy connection.

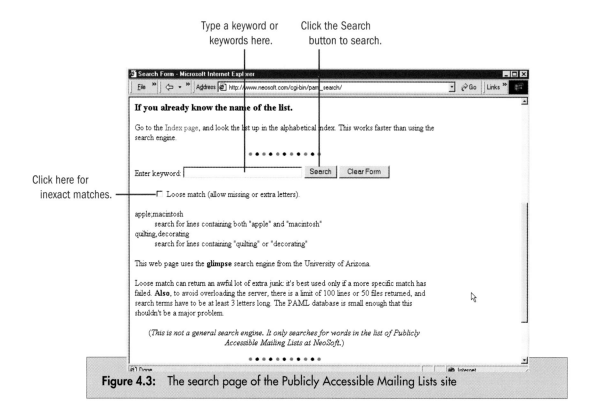

Figure 4.3:   The search page of the Publicly Accessible Mailing Lists site

Another mailing list site you might want to check out is Liszt.com (**http://www.liszt.com/**), which is searchable and has over 66,000 lists.

If you're still having no luck, try some general web searches (as explained in Chapter 3) and add the words +list or +"mailing list" to your search terms. Web searching and browsing will often lead you to web sites associated with list communities or sites that offer links to related resources, frequently including mailing lists.

How to Subscribe to a Mailing List

Subscribing to a list means requesting that your e-mail address be added to the list so that a copy of each post to the list is sent to you. The methods for subscribing vary, depending on whether the list is human-administered or robot-administered.

NETIQUETTE

Be very careful not to send a subscription request to the list itself. There is always a separate mailing address for such administrative matters.

Generally, though, they involve sending a brief message to an administrative address, often of the form

```
subscribe listname
```

Some mailing list programs require that you also include your own name on that line.

So, for example, to subscribe to the Busy People mailing list hosted at Tiedrich.com, you send a message to **majordomo@lists.tiedrich.com** with the following contents:

```
subscribe busypeep
```

To unsubscribe from a list, you generally send a message to the same address reading **unsubscribe** *listname* or **signoff** *listname*.

When you join a list, you're usually sent a welcome message, a set of instructions for unsubscribing, and other useful information. Save this message. Create a special folder for it in your mail program and add similar messages you get from other lists when you join them. Eventually, they'll come in handy.

Starting Off on a List by Lurking

Mailing lists (and newsgroups) usually have many more readers than participants. It is considered totally normal (and is actually recommended) that you read a list for a while before you post for the first time. This is called lurking. Despite the sinister sound of the term, lurking is good netiquette and restrains new people from jumping into the middle of old conversations without understanding the background and ideas that have led up to the current point. Once you get the hang of the topic threads and have a feel for who's who, you can contribute more intelligently and with less likelihood of stepping on toes.

NETIQUETTE

Keep your posts to a mailing list on-topic. It's natural for threads to occasionally drift from the main purpose of the list, but take your conversations to private e-mail as soon as they're obviously out of the scope of the list.

Frequently Asked Questions

DEFINITION

RTF: Also called RTFAQ; it stands for "read the FAQ" and is a generic answer to frequently asked questions in a mailing list or Usenet newsgroup. (This is roughly the equivalent of responding, when asked the spelling of a word, "look it up in the dictionary.") Not to be confused with RTFM, which stands for "read the *mumblin'* manual."

For every list, there are certain questions that are frequently asked, especially by new contributors (also called newbies). The questions themselves may be perfectly reasonable, but after you've been on a list for a while, it gets tedious to keep seeing (or answering) the same questions. Because of this, a tradition has arisen on the Net for lists and other discussion groups to assemble Frequently Asked Question lists, usually referred to as FAQs (pronounced "facks"). FAQs often evolve as a collective effort, though usually one person must take responsibility for maintaining the document.

When you join a list, wait or ask for the FAQ to be posted so you can get answers to the most common questions before piping up with your own. Some FAQs are posted regularly to Usenet and archived at sites accessible from the Web. People on the list will tell you where to look (they'll appreciate your finding the answers to those questions yourself rather than bothering them).

Contributing to a List

To contribute to a mailing list, all you have to do is send mail to a list address. If you're responding to a previous post, you can usually just reply in your mailer. If you want to reply to the entire list, make sure that the To: address is the mailing list and not the individual who posted—how you can reply depends on how the list is set up. As with any mail, trim off as much of the quoted material as you can, but retain enough to make the context of your reply clear.

EXPERT ADVICE

Any time you're replying to a list post, check the To: line of your e-mail message to make sure you're sending the mail where you think you are.

Responding Privately

As a general rule, err on the side of replying to individuals instead of to the list as a whole. There's nothing wrong with posting to the list, but some conversations naturally spawn side chats that really have nothing to do with the list. Before you post to a list, ask yourself if you're really just talking to the previous poster. If so, send the mail directly to her or him.

Some lists are set up so that your mail program's Reply command automatically posts back to the list. Others are set up so that your reply goes automatically to the individual poster. Here's how to make sure you respond to the right recipient:

1. Select the e-mail address of the sender and copy it (CTRL+C).

2. Press CTRL+R (or use your mail program's Reply command).

3. Check the address in the To: line.

If the address is that of the original poster, leave it alone. If the address is to that of the list, delete it and replace it with the address of the original poster as shown in Figure 4.4.

Avoiding Flame Wars

Probably because the communication is not face to face, e-mail makes it easy for people to lose their tempers and send insulting mail to each other. Such messages are called flames, and when they're sent to a mailing list they can engender a long series of flames and counterflames, known collectively as a flame war. It may be tempting to get in there and mix it

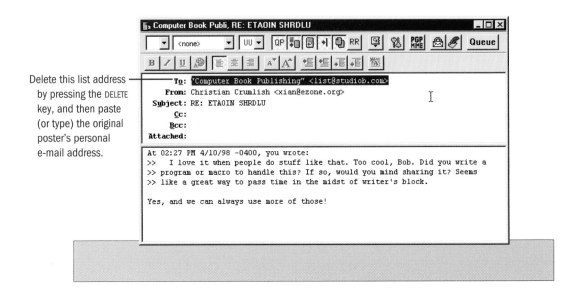

Delete this list address by pressing the DELETE key, and then paste (or type) the original poster's personal e-mail address.

up with everyone, especially the first time you see this happening, but it's really a waste of everyone's time. Often the original offense was simply a poorly worded message that a reader construed as an insult. Stay out of flame wars and don't fan the fire.

Some people like flaming so much that they post deliberately inflammatory messages, called flamebait. If you read something that fills you with the urge to immediately reply in terms as scathing as possible, pause for a moment and think about whether that is precisely how the writer hoped you would respond. Don't give the writer the satisfaction.

If someone misinterprets something you wrote and takes offense, just apologize. No harm will be done, and you may make a new friend. Many a flame war has been headed off by a timely apology. Later, think about what you wrote and be more careful in the future about how you put things.

EXPERT ADVICE

The Internet offers many other types of forums besides mailing lists, including the famous Usenet newsgroup system, also known as Netnews. For more background on Usenet, check out a highly informative document called the Usenet Info Center FAQ, available on the Web at *http://sunsite.unc.edu/usenet-i/info-center-faq.html*.

Going on Vacation

If you'll be away from your e-mail for a while, you may want to temporarily unsubscribe from your mailing lists. For most mailing lists, you'll have to send an unsubscribe message as described earlier: mail to the list-request address (not the list itself!) with an empty subject, and usually the word **unsubscribe** followed by the name of the list.

Starting Your Own List

What if you want to start your own list? Well, you may be able to. First of all, check with the administrator of the network you're on, or with the features offered by your Internet service provider (see Appendix A for more about shopping for providers). It may be that there's an existing majordomo program running on your system and that you can create a new mailing list with it, or even have someone more technically adept do it for you.

Failing that, you may consider paying for an easy-to-administer mailing list. A company called ICG offers some reasonably priced mailing list alternatives—the cheapest option is $8/month—at their Listbox.com site (see Figure 4.5). Listbox also offers an easy, password- and forms-based interface for majordomo, called Webdomo, through its web site. Visit **http://www.listbox.com/** to read more about the options for yourself. (Another such list provider is Onelist at **http://www.onelist.com/**.)

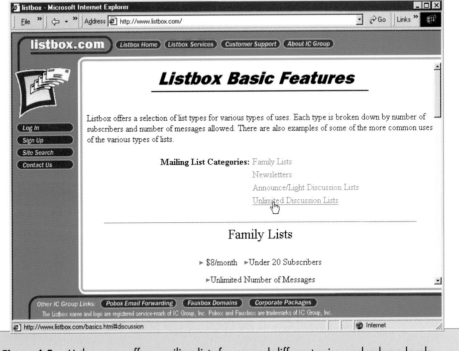

Figure 4.5: Listbox.com offers mailing lists for several different price and volume levels.

Page Your Friends

Besides the post office and bulletin board methods of communicating, the Internet also has the capability of supporting real-time interactive conversation. First there was a program called Talk that enabled two users to carry on sentence-by-sentence conversations. Next came chat, which enabled multiple users to communicate in this way. Then came IRC, which stands for Internet relay chat. As with many other Internet facilities, IRC is a client-server system in which individuals run client programs to connect to centralized servers (and thence to other users).

There are also a number of newer technologies that incorporate more than just text in real-time transmissions. Many of these programs, such as Internet Phone, actually take advantage of the IRC protocols. The demands of fast-paced business today sometimes require *virtual* conferences, linking participants all over the globe in real-time meetings and strategy sessions. Besides enabling participants to talk to and possibly see each other, some of the new conferencing programs allow people to collaborate over the Net and even to share software.

At this moment, by far the most popular new chat programs are those referred to as "buddy lists" or pagers (or both). The features vary from program to program, but most of them enable you to create a list of friends who are on the system. The pager, such as ICQ (the most popular such program at the moment), notifies you of who's online and tells your friends when you're available. You can page friends or leave them messages for when they do connect.

Meanwhile, the live chat model has mutated and spread to the Web (where a number of web-based, non-IRC chat systems reside) and to imaginary three-dimensional virtual worlds. Oh, to be young and have free time again!

ICQ (I Seek You)

Lately, many Internet regulars have started using "buddy list" software that keeps track of your Net-connected friends, shows you who's online (also shows them when you are), enables you to page your friends, and notifies you when they page you. The most popular tool (by far), at least at this moment, is called ICQ ("I seek you"), and you can download it quickly and install it from the ICQ web site (**http://www.icq.com/**).

ICQ is easy to set up (the dialog boxes walk you through everything), and you can search for your friends on the Net by e-mail address, name, ICQ nickname, or ICQ number. You can even have ICQ keep a look-out for friends who may join the ICQ network in the future (or send them mail encouraging them to join).

At any time you can click the Add/Find Users button to search out specific friends or people with various interests (see Figure 4.6).

Whenever you run ICQ (and it's easy to have it running in the background all the time), it tells you which of the people on your buddy list are online and which are offline. Double-click a nickname to have the person paged.

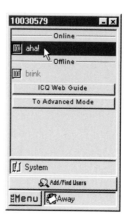

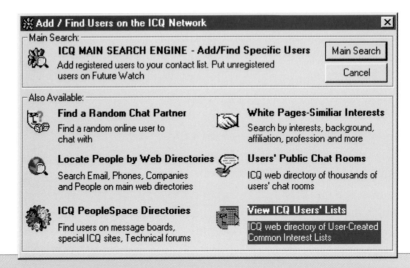

Figure 4.6: ICQ's Add/Find Users dialog box offers several different approaches to getting your chats started. (Some choices take you to pages at the ICQ web site.)

At this time, Mac users can only send messages back and forth in separate windows (which disappear once you send). Windows users can carry on conversations in an IRC format or in a split-screen mode. In any ongoing conversation, you can click the Message Dialog button to bring up the entire sequence so far, as illustrated here:

IS THIS FOR ME?

Chat fits into a busy person's routine only if used to pass brief urgent messages or to conduct written conversations that need to be turned around in real time (live). All the various forms of chat programs are perfect, however, if you're a college student, unemployed, or depressed. Then again, some of my high-pressure colleagues report that ICQ has enabled them to carry on brief important conversations without the social entanglements of the telephone. As they say on the Net, YMMV (your mileage may vary).

When someone pages you, simply double-click the flashing icon to accept the transmission.

AOL Instant Messenger

Other popular buddy-list pagers include AOL Instant Messenger (which comes with the full Netscape installation), Ding, and ichat Pager. To download these or other popular programs, try starting at **http://shareware.com/**, as explained in Chapter 3.

Other Methods for Chatting and Conferencing

Pager software is only the latest and most popular form of typed, live chatting software on the Internet. There are other types of chat programs, web sites with chat modules, and even ways to add sound and video, for that full-on 2001 effect.

IRC (Internet Relay Chat)

Free-wheeling discussions take place around the clock on the Internet's IRC networks. For more background information on IRC, start at the IRC Help page on the Web (**http://www.irchelp.org/**).

Microsoft Chat and NetMeeting

Microsoft offers its own chat software downloadable from the Software Updates page where you can also get other Internet Explorer modules. Microsoft NetMeeting, another module you can download for free, helps facilitate business meetings by adding a shared whiteboard and the ability to send and receive files (which you can also do with pager programs such as ICQ).

Web Chat Sites

Many web sites offer live discussion or chat facilities focused on the topics of the sites in the hopes of attracting a community. Other sites offer chat only, with a wide range of topics covered. These latter "generic" chat sites include iChat, at **http://www.ichat.com/**, Wired's Talk.com, Talkcity.com, Chatting.com (**http://www.chatting.com/**), and the WebChat Broadcasting System (**http://chat.go.com/**).

Voice and Video Chatting

For people with microphones or video cameras plugged into their computers, there are all kinds of new variations on the IRC model for multimedia communication, including Internet Phone (for voice) and CU-SeeMe (for video), and their many competitors. For more information on Internet Phone (IPhone), go to VocalTec's Internet Phone home page at **http://www.vocaltec.com/iphone4/ip4.htm**. To get more information on CU-SeeMe, visit the CU-SeeMe Welcome Page at **http://cu-seeme.cornell.edu/**.

There's More . . .

You may come to rely on your e-mail to get work done, as more and more business is done over that medium. In fact, you may find that next time you travel somewhere on business, you'll need to receive your e-mail while on the road. In Chapter 5, I'll tell you how to prepare for the trip and how to stay connected while traveling. After that, it's back to the Web, as you learn about what financial management resources are available online in Chapter 6, and how to make and publish web sites in Chapters 7 and 8.

Stay Connected on the Road

INCLUDES

- Finding local access numbers on the road

- Connecting to the Net from a hotel (or an airplane)

- Keeping your mail available on the server

- Copying yourself on mail sent from the road

- Getting a free "webmail" account

- Managing multiple e-mail accounts

Connect to the Net While Traveling ➡ pp. 135–142

1. Before you go, find a local dial-up number for your ISP in your remote location (and make sure you pack important documents in your laptop or on diskettes).
2. Set up the new phone number and location in your dialer.
3. Browse the Web and check your mail.

Copy Yourself on Important E-Mail ➡ pp. 143–144

1. Avoid returning home or to work to realize that you don't have copies of important messages by using the Cc: or Bcc: line in your outgoing messages while traveling to send copies of your messages to yourself.
2. Set up a filter on your remote machine (and when you return) to archive mail from yourself outside of your Inbox.

Get a Free Webmail Account ➡ pp. 145–148

1. Sign up for free e-mail at one of the portal sites.
2. Check your messages from any Internet-connected device.
3. Send and receive file attachments, no problem.

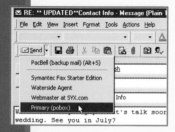

Juggle Multiple E-mail Addresses ➡ pp. 148–151

1. Set up a separate account or personality in your mail program for each address you use.
2. Decide which accounts should be checked automatically when you send and receive mail.
3. Be careful to reply to a message using the return address you prefer your recipient to use (especially if you check one or more of your addresses infrequently).

The Internet as a mass medium is out of its infancy but still toddling along with the occasional stumble. Nearly everyone, from your grandma to your auto mechanic, has an e-mail address (and maybe even a web site), and more plans and business deals are made via the Net today than ever before. When you go on vacation, you'll probably want to avoid getting your e-mail (though I remember checking my mail every week or so in cyber cafés in the U.K. during a vacation nearly three years ago), but you *will* want to be able to check your mail when you travel on business, to conferences, in emergencies, and so on. In this chapter, I'll help you set yourself up to get access to the Internet when traveling and to check your mail while on the road. I'll also introduce you to the most portable form of e-mail account yet: the free webmail account, and I'll finish up by giving you some tips about managing multiple e-mail accounts without driving yourself batty.

　　First things first; you have to ensure your Internet connection before you can browse the Web or check your e-mail.

Mobile Access to the Internet

If you need to connect to the Net while traveling, then you'll need an account with an ISP (even if you normally connect to the Net through a free work or school account), one that has a local access number where you're going (and preferably most everywhere else). Then you'll need to set up your laptop computer's dialer to connect to the account in the remote location (or, if you don't have a portable computer, write down your connection information in case you get access to a computer when traveling). When you arrive at your destination, you should be able to connect for no more than the charge for a local call and start browsing the Web and/or checking your e-mail immediately.

Before You Go

For both your Net connection and your e-mail account(s), there are a few steps you should take before you leave for your trip. For the connecting side of things, you need to make sure you've got an ISP that has local access numbers at your remote destinations, and you need to know what those numbers are.

Getting an ISP with Reach

See Appendix A for more information about signing up with an ISP.

Even if you benefit from an apparently free connection (someone is paying for it, of course), to gain mobile access you'll need your own ISP account (unless you want to pay for hotel long-distance charges to your office). If you already have an ISP, you're all set, assuming your provider has a local access number at your destination. If it doesn't (I'll explain how to look up access numbers in the next section), you'll need to get a new or additional ISP.

Providers that have local access numbers blanketing the U.S. include the large online services (America Online, CompuServe, MSN, Prodigy), and some of the independent ISPs that have built up large customer bases over the last few years (such as Mindspring.com, Earthlink.net, and many others).

Finding Local Access Numbers

Your ISP will make it easy to get local access numbers:

1. Go to your provider's home page.
2. Click the link for access numbers (or phone numbers, or dial-up).
3. Jot down any numbers for locations on your itinerary.

EXPERT ADVICE

If you travel abroad, you'll probably want an account with an online service that has an international presence, such as CompuServe).

EXPERT ADVICE

CompuServe offers an 800 number you can dial for access, but you're charged a per-minute premium for using it, so a local access number is still preferable. Of course, the 800- (and now, 888-) number system works only in the United States.

Figure 5.1 shows the web page listing local New York City access numbers from Concentric.net, the provider I use to connect to the Internet via modem at home.

If you end up forgetting to bring your access numbers, you may have to make one long-distance call to connect to your usual dial-up number in your home area, connect to the Web, visit your provider's home page, and get a number in your new location.

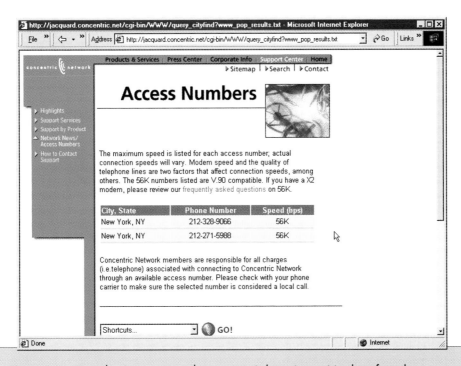

Figure 5.1: From the Concentric.net home page, I chose Access Numbers from the shortcut menu, entered the Manhattan area code (212), and got these two choices for my trip next month.

Setting Up a Dialer in a Hotel Room

If you equip yourself with some key information (your username and password for your ISP, the mail server information I explained in Chapter 4, the remote "local" access number, and any calling-card numbers and passcodes you plan to use), then you can get yourself set up with minimal hassle on arrival at your destination. You can set up the dialer before you go, but you might want to check with the hotel (if you'll be staying in one) to find out the number you dial to get an outside line.

Windows Setup

In Windows, select Start | Programs | Accessories | Communications | Internet Connection Wizard (or just Connection Wizard) to create a new dial-up number.

1. Select the third option, I Want To Set Up My Internet Connection Manually, and click Next >.

2. Click Next > again to confirm that you will be using a modem.

3. Type the area code and phone number for your ISP's local dial-up number in the remote location and click Next >.

4. Enter your username and password (for the ISP) and click Next >.

5. Type a name for the connection to help you recognize it (such as **Concentric in New York**), and click Next >.

6. Click Next > to set up your e-mail account.

EXPERT ADVICE

It's a very good idea to call ahead to speak with a concierge about your hotel's phone system. Depending on the "modernity" of the wiring, you may need special tools, such as an acoustic coupler. There are several competing hardware kits for dealing with such "road warrior" conditions.

7. If you've already set up this computer in the past to get your mail in your home area code, then select the existing e-mail account and click Next > (otherwise, click Create A New Internet Mail Account, click Next >, and enter your e-mail username, password, and incoming and outgoing mail servers, as explained in Chapter 4).

8. If the mail settings look right, click Next > (otherwise, click Change Settings and then click Next >.

9. Then click Finish to connect to the Net (or uncheck the Connect To The Internet Immediately option and then click Finish to connect later).

To put an icon for the new connection on your desktop, select Start | Programs | Accessories | Communications | Dial-Up Networking, right-click on the icon for the account you just created, drag it to the desktop, and select Create Shortcut(s) Here.

Finally, you've got to tell your dialer where you're calling from today. Double-click the new connection icon you just created and click the Dial Properties button. In the Dial Properties dialog box that appears, click the New button (see Figure 5.2).

EXPERT ADVICE

Drag that icon to the taskbar to make another convenient shortcut.

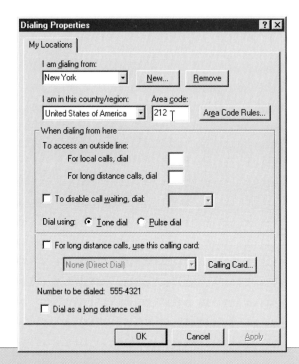

Figure 5.2: Create a new location so Windows will know where you're dialing from.

Click OK, type a name for the location (such as **New York**), and enter the local area code (so the dialer can recognize the remote number as local to your current location). Based on the phone system at your hotel (or wherever you're staying), you may also need to enter a number for dialing an outside line. (If you're charging all your calls to a calling card, click the Calling Card button, enter all the numbers you need in the Calling Card dialog box that appears, and then click OK.) Click OK. The number should now be listed in the Connect To dialog box without an area code.

EXPERT ADVICE

Put a few commas after the number you dial for an outside line or your calling card number to make the dialer pause before starting into the real number.

Macintosh Setup

On the Mac, find and run the Internet Setup Assistant.

1. Click the Update button.

2. Click the right arrow twice.

3. Type a name for the new connection (such as **Concentric in New York**) and click the right arrow twice.

4. Type the remote phone number (without area code), press TAB, type your dial-up username, press TAB, type your dial-up password, and click the right arrow twice.

5. Enter the IP addresses of your domain-name servers (your ISP should be able to provide these), and click the right arrow.

6. Enter your e-mail address and password, and click the right arrow.

7. Enter your incoming and outgoing mail servers (as explained in Chapter 4), and click the right arrow twice.

8. Click the Go Ahead button.

9. Then click Quit.

Browsing the Web

Once you've successfully connected to the Net, you can browse the Web as you would ordinarily. However, when you encounter a web page whose address you want to save for future reference, you should consider e-mailing yourself the page or its URL instead of bookmarking it, since your bookmarks will not be consistent from one computer to the next (that is, unless the laptop computer you're using for the trip is your usual primary—or only—computer).

EXPERT ADVICE

When you return from your trip, restore the original dial-up account.

EXPERT ADVICE

Be sure to connect to the Net manually before running your web browser, so that the browser doesn't automatically dial long-distance to connect to your ISP.

On the off chance that your office is standardized on Netscape and is running a Roaming Access server, you can select Edit | Preferences in Netscape, choose the Server Information category under Roaming Access, and enter the requested information about your LDAP and HTTP servers (ask your system administrator). You can then choose to have Netscape retrieve such useful information as your bookmarks and address book in the Item Selection category (see Figure 5.3). When you're done, click OK.

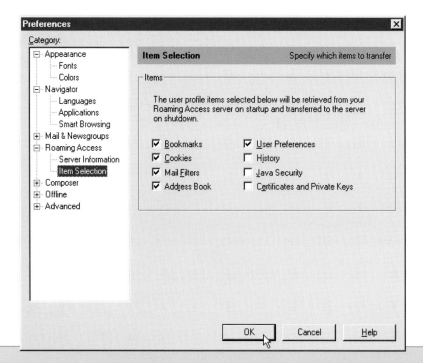

Figure 5.3: If you've got a Roaming Access server available, you can take your bookmarks and address book with you.

Getting Your E-Mail on the Road

Just as with your Internet connection, there are a few things you should do before you leave on your trip. Primarily, it's important that you set up your mail program to leave mail on your server, both on the laptop you'll be taking with you (if you have one) and at your regular computer, at least the last day or so before you go (so that mail that comes in just before you leave town will still be available for you when you arrive at your destination). It can also help to download mail onto your laptop several days in advance, so that you have the recent history on your active mail conversations.

Before You Go: Leaving Mail on Your Server

To make sure that the mail you read while traveling will still be available to you when you return, you should set your mail program to leave your mail on the server. In Outlook, select Tools | Accounts. Select your mail account, click the Properties button, and then click the Advanced tab. In the Delivery area at the bottom of the tab, click Leave A Copy Of Messages On Server (see Figure 5.4). Then click OK.

Copying Yourself on Messages

When working with e-mail at one stable location, you can choose to keep copies of all the messages you send in your Sent Messages mailbox (or the equivalent), in case you ever need to double-check some information or obligation to which you've committed yourself. However, when you're traveling, messages you send will only stay in the Sent Messages mailbox of the mail program on your laptop or the remote computer you're using. Therefore, to make sure that you end up with all your messages in order when you return, make a point of including your own e-mail address on the Cc: or Bcc: line of any important messages you send while traveling.

Both on the road and back home you'll then probably want to set up a filter (or Rule, as Outlook calls it), to automatically sort any messages that come from you into your Sent Messages mailbox.

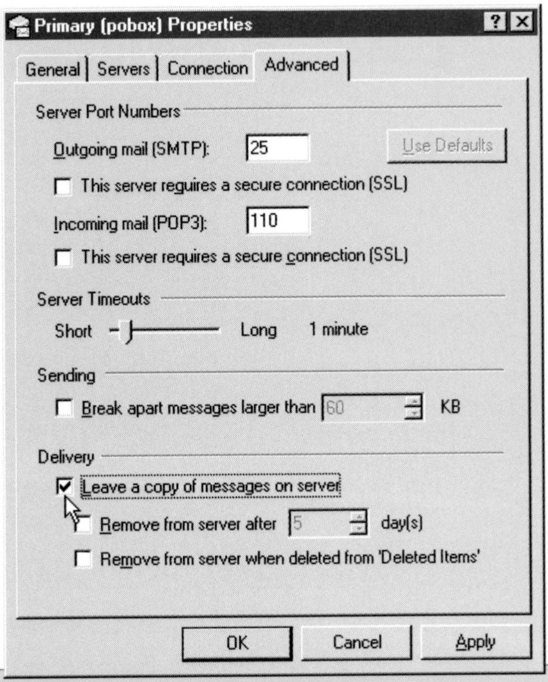

Figure 5.4: Leave messages on your server till you return.

EXPERT ADVICE

Eudora's Reply To All command automatically includes the sender's e-mail address among the recipients.

Using a Free Webmail Account for Roaming Access

Another approach to remote e-mail is to a get a free e-mail account that you can access via the Web ("webmail") from any functioning Internet connection. This doesn't solve the remote ISP problem, as you still need to be able to connect, although a cyber café may take care of that problem (or a friend with a network or ISP connection you can borrow). All the portal sites and many other commercial web sites offer free e-mail accounts as a way of registering you as part of their online community. You're not obligated to attend any sing-alongs, though.

Table 5.1 shows some of the more prominent free webmail providers of the moment.

The service called Juno doesn't require separate ISP access.

Setting Up a Free Webmail Account

To set up a webmail account, visit the provider's home page and choose the mail link (or go directly to one of the URLs listed in Table 5.1), and then sign up for an account. First you'll have to read the provider's terms of service and agree to them. Then, you'll be asked for your name and other information about yourself, as well as your preferred username (which will most likely be already taken, so be prepared to become bob974 or whatever). The provider will also try to collect some demographic information from you (see Figure 5.5). Don't sweat over the perfect answer too long.

The provider may ask you for more information about your location, in order to customize your home page, and might offer you any number of free alert or information services delivered directly to your Inbox.

CAUTION

Read carefully to see whether the webmail provider gives you the option of not receiving announcements and solicitations and of not permitting your address to be given out to advertisers. Be sure to opt out of any mail or marketing you don't want to receive.

Webmail Provider	Web Address to Sign Up	E-Mail Address Format
Altavista Email	http://altavista.iname.com/	*you*@altavista.net (or many other vanity addresses)
Deja.com	http://www.my-deja.com/	*you*@my-deja.com
Eudora Web-Mail	http://www.eudoramail.com/	*you*@eudoramail.com
Excite.com	http://mail.excite.com/	*you*@mailexcite.com
Hotbot.com	http://members.hotbot.com/	*you*@hotbot.com
Juno	http://www.juno.com	*you*@juno.com
Mailcity	http://www.mailcity.lycos.com/	*you*@mailcity.com
MSN Hotmail	http://www.hotmail.com	*you*@hotmail.com
Netscape Webmail	http://webmail.netscape.com/	*you*@netscape.net
Yahoo! Mail	http://mail.yahoo.com/	*you*@yahoo.com

Table 5.1: Some of the many free webmail service providers

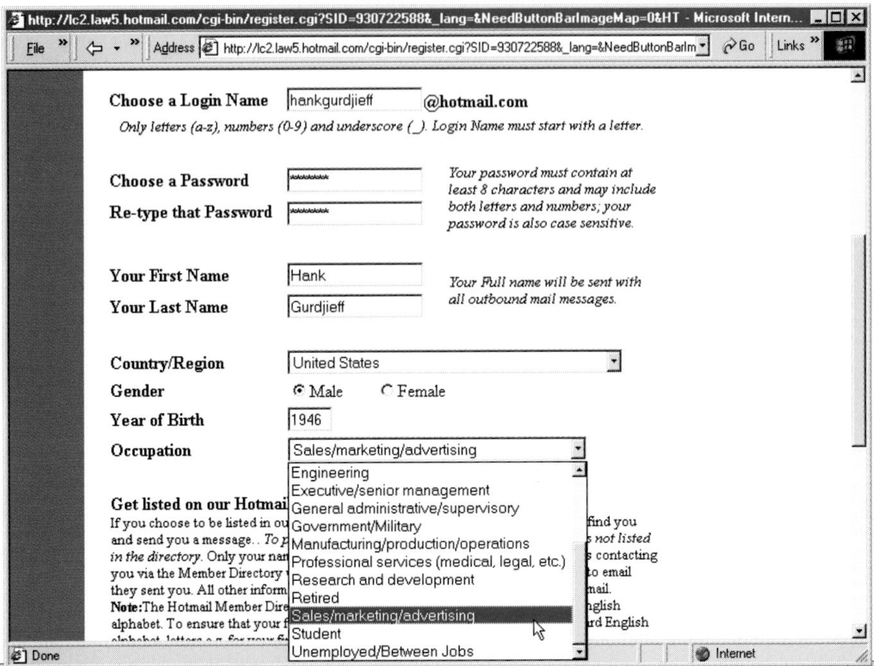

Figure 5.5: The Rocketmail questionnaire isn't *too* intrusive.

Some free webmail accounts, but not all, can also download your ordinary mail into your webmail Inbox. If you choose to look at your pre-existing mail stream this way, be sure to leave the mail on the server (see Figure 5.6).

Webmail accounts become more sophisticated all the time, and most of them already offer filters to help you keep your mail flow under control and sorted into mailboxes (as explained in Chapter 4), as well as other advanced mail features.

Accessing Free E-Mail

To check your webmail or to compose and send new messages from the free account, first point your web browser at the service's home

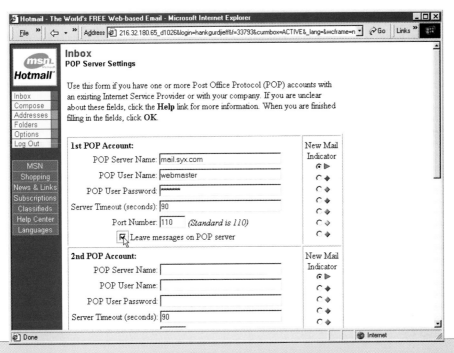

Figure 5.6: If you're going to pick up your POP (regular) mail through a webmail account, be sure also to leave the mail on the server.

page so you can log in. Then choose Check Mail (or Check POP Mail or Check External Mail) or something similar. The terminology varies from provider to provider, but the functions are all the same. The mail server will show you what mail you have in your Inbox, if any (see Figure 5.7).

To open and read a message, click on its subject. To reply to the message, click Reply or Reply All. To send a new message, click Compose (or New Message). While the interface is entirely based in the Web, you should find the procedures familiar, as they are modeled on conventional mail programs such as Outlook or Eudora.

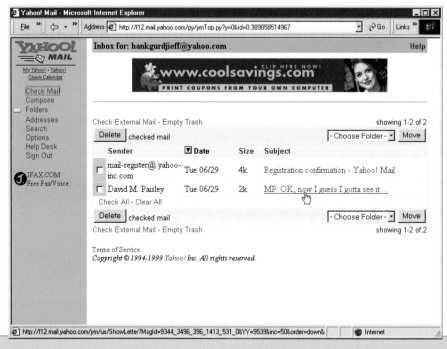

Figure 5.7:   There are two messages in the Inbox: the welcome message that was sent automatically when I set up the account, and a message that's come in from one of my POP accounts.

Managing Multiple E-Mail Accounts

If you end up with multiple e-mail accounts from home, work, or webmail accounts, then you'll need to take some steps to keep your mail under control, to avoid either losing important messages or receiving duplicate copies or messages you don't need (such as work messages at home or vice versa).

Setting Up Web Access to Any POP Account

As with the free webmail accounts I mentioned in the previous section, you can actually set up a web front-end for any POP account at a

service like MailStart (**http://www.mailstart.com/**). Figure 5.8 shows
a message to me from a music-related mailing list, viewed through
MailStart's web site.

Forwarding Mail Automatically

There are two ways to handle multiple accounts. You can have your
mail program check each account separately, as explained in the next
section, or you can arrange to have one or more of the mail servers
automatically forward mail to a single address. Another use for
forwarding is to have duplicate messages sent to an extra account, as a
backup system. For example, I use Pobox.com for a permanent e-mail
address that won't have to change even if I change my primary e-mail
account. Pobox is just a forwarding service, not a POP mail provider,
so I don't pick up mail directly from Pobox.com. Instead, the Pobox
address is set up to automatically forward mail to the account I'm

CAUTION

**Because of the
nature of the
POP3 protocol, checking
your mail over the web is
not completely secure,
meaning that your password
is conceivably vulnerable if
someone is trying to break
into your mail feed. To
preserve security, you may
choose to avoid using any
kind of webmail front-end
for your POP account(s)
or you can change your
password from time to time.**

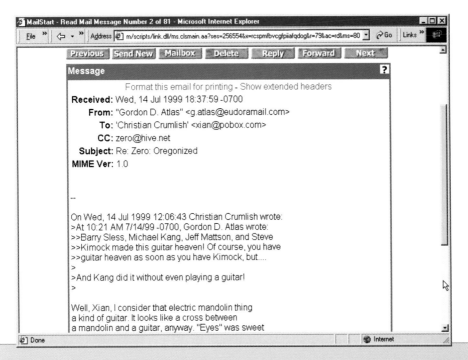

Figure 5.8: Gordon's right, of course—Kang's instrument is some weird kind of mando-tar.

currently using as my primary incoming e-mail server. As a precaution, I also have that mail forwarded to the Pacbell e-mail address that came for free with my work ISP account.

Checking Multiple Accounts

All the popular mail programs can be set up to check multiple mail accounts. In Outlook, select Tools | Accounts, select the account you want to include when checking mail, and make sure that Include This Account When Receiving Mail is checked (see Figure 5.9). Or uncheck that option for accounts you don't currently want to check.

In Eudora, select Tools | Options, and then click the Personalities category. For each personality (separate return address), you can select or deselect Check Mail, depending on whether you want

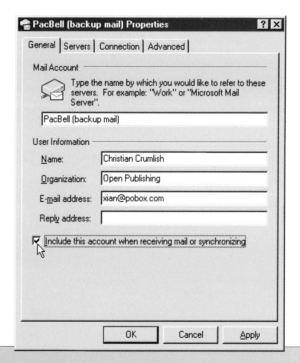

Figure 5.9: I have duplicates of important mail sent to my Pacbell account, so I'm setting up Outlook to check that account.

Eudora to get mail from that account automatically whenever you check (or send) messages.

Sending and Replying with the Correct Return Address

If you've got mail all coming into the same server, then you must be careful when sending mail that you specify the correct return address. When replying to messages, your mail program will take care of this for you by automatically using the address to which the message was sent as the return address on your reply. However, when you compose a new message, the mail program will use your default or primary return address unless you specify otherwise. Even when replying, you may still want to change the return address, as when you are trying to encourage correspondents to start using a new address for you.

In Outlook and Outlook Express, you can specify the return address from which you are sending by clicking the little button to the right of the Send button and then selecting the account from which you mean to send.

In Eudora, hold down SHIFT while starting a new message or replying to choose a personality (mail account) on the fly. In versions 4.0 and later of Eudora Pro, you can choose the personality to use for your return address directly on the From line of a new message.

There's More . . .

Well, now you've covered the basics. You know how to browse the Web, how to send and receive e-mail (at home and abroad) and communicate with other people on the Net in other ways. For the rest of the book, I'm going to shift your focus back to the Web. In Chapter 6, I'll help you get oriented in the brave new world of personal-finance management online. In Chapter 7, you'll learn how to create your own web pages, and in Chapter 8 I'll show you how to go live on the Web with your own site.

CHAPTER 6

Manage Your Finances Online

INCLUDES

- Finding financial web sites
- Doing your banking online
- Shopping for the best rates for loans or insurance
- Getting help with financial planning
- Researching and tracking investments on the Web
- Choosing an appropriate investment strategy for the Net
- Investing directly online (and working with brokers)

FAST FORWARD

Start at a Financial Portal Site ➜ pp. 158–159

Cover many of your basic financial research needs from all-purpose financial web sites such as:

- **Quicken.com** http://www.quicken.com/
- **Yahoo! Finance** http://finance.yahoo.com/
- **Microsoft Money Central** http://moneycentral.msn.com/

Find General, Specialty, and Niche Financial Sites ➜ pp. 159–161

Search for financial sites at directories such as:

- **Yahoo! Finance and Investment** http://dir.yahoo.com/Business_and_Economy/ Finance_and_Investment/
- **Investor Home** http://www.investorhome.com/
- **Investor Guide** http://www.investorguide.com/
- **InvestingSites** http://www.investingsites.com/

Test Financial Plans and Scenarios ➜ p. 167

- **Smart Money** http://www.smartmoney.com/si/tools/oneasset/
- **S&P Personal Wealth** http://www.personalwealth.com/
- **Smith Barney's Asset** http://www.smithbarney.com/.

Choose an Investment Strategy ➜ pp. 170–176

1. Go the traditional route by delegating your financial decisions to a broker.
2. Share the decision-making with a professional or financial advisor.
3. Do it all yourself (with discount brokerages).

The last year has seen an explosion of people investing directly on the Net. According to some sources, there are roughly 60 million traditional brokerage accounts today and nearly 8 million online brokerage accounts. That number is expected to more than double in the coming year. An analyst from BankBoston estimates that the number of online brokerage accounts will reach 25 million by the year 2003. Even now, 25 million of the 60 million people mentioned above monitor their traditional brokerage accounts on the Internet. And while the average size of a conventionally traded portfolio is $50,000, the average size of an online traded portfolio is $350,000!

Stepping back from investments (let alone day-trading), financial industries and markets in general are more tightly integrated with electronic networks today than ever before. A wide range of financial activities has become accessible to you as an individual using the Web. You can do your banking online; you can research loans, insurance, and investments on the Web; and, of course, you can buy and sell stocks and other financial instruments online.

Dante Had Virgil—I've Got Bill Valentine

To properly guide you through this monied thicket requires expertise beyond my own as a humble starving writer. The decisions you make will have real consequences, and the immediacy of the Web can make important choices almost *too* easy to make without sufficient reflection. So, in order to give you a handle on what's available and how to approach it, I've enlisted the advice of William L. Valentine IV, CFA, an investment manager for high-worth individuals (his site is at **http://www.valentineventures.com/**) introduced to me by my editor. Bill writes several weekly columns, including his own InvestMentor column (which you may sign up to receive by e-mail for free at **http://www.valentineventures.com/freeVIL.htm**).

The first thing Bill told me was that when he started his own investment firm, he set out to determine whether he could replicate the information beamed to the Bloomberg device (a dedicated computer hooked up to the Bloomberg financial news wire service) sitting on the desktop of every institutional investor in the world. He found that, with a lot of hunting and sorting, he could do so—in the form of a series of web site bookmarks (many of which you'll encounter here in this chapter). Bill tells me he has six hours worth of new information to read every day. His job, in essence, is to know where to get information and how to make sense of it. Information in and of itself is not valuable without the ability to interpret it (in fact, a *little* information is a dangerous thing).

Online Brain Surgery

To drive home this point of caution, Bill drew a medical analogy for me: Being your own investment manager is a bit like being your own doctor. Even if you can access the entire medical library at Stanford, you should still probably not perform brain surgery—particularly not on yourself.

In this chapter, we'll tell you what financial and investment resources are currently available on the Web, how to make use of them, and how to decide what and what not to do online. We can't tell you what stocks to buy (obviously), and we can't even tell you exhaustively how to go about picking a stock, but we will give you a rough outline of the steps you'll need to research and execute any investment decision. Before you go to your computer, ask yourself what role you want to play in managing your own finances. Once you start looking around on the Web, you'll be awash in information and resources, and it will help if you have a clear idea of what you're trying to accomplish.

We'll try to introduce you to what you can learn and do on the Web so *you* can make a more informed decision about what you want to do or what you should do. You know best how much time you have available, what sort of risks you can afford, how sophisticated you are about financial matters, and what your own personality is like.

Financial Resources on the Web

Web resources range from bank account sites that enable individuals to watch their checking and savings accounts to sites one can use to run a multimillion-dollar investment portfolio. There are quite a few financial portals or what Bill calls "supermalls" that should be more than adequate for many casual financial researchers or investors. Most people choose one and stick with it, because it's a pain to reenter your financial information at a new site or track and update the same information at several sites.

Then there is a seemingly unlimited number of niche financial web sites that offer some specific service or type of information. In the strange new ecology of the Web, some financial portal sites inevitably acquire some of the more innovative new niche sites and incorporate them into their full-service spread. Some of the most valuable stuff out there, though, can only be found at the quirkiest spots. A site that does one single thing really well—provides the freshest data about one specific thing—can prove to be more valuable at times than a site that does everything pretty well.

You need a mix of sites that offer pure data and sites that feature opinion and commentary. Bill explained it to me this way: You can think of financial web sites as ranging from totally general raw data at one extreme to solid opinion at the other. For pure raw data, the real value such a site can bring is the organization (such as a charting site showing historical data on a stock that you can manipulate eight ways to Sunday). Opinionated sites offer the other side of the coin, instead of pure numbers, interpretation of data. It's the great mystery of finance, some people make better use of data than others.

Another type of financial portal site is a directory that links to other resources, from portal to niche sites, and keeps itself up to date, so you don't have to go hunting all over for the latest, newest sites.

Many sites fall somewhere in between. TheStreet.com (**http://www.thestreet.com/**), for instance, doesn't have half the tools or functions of a portal site, but it has 20 to 30 writers with strong opinions and free rein to express themselves. Everyone's dying for content because, eventually, if you can envision all of these tools gravitating toward the portal concept, the distinguishing point of each site will end up being its own proprietary content.

On the investment side of the equation, the transacting of financial products has become a cottage industry. For example, Quicken.com (**http://www.quicken.com/**) is a portal, partnered with several hundred vendors of insurance and mortgages. They'd like it, for instance, if you would shop your mortgage online at the site.

At one point, not all sites had the same information. Quicken.com, for example, once had the muscle to get exclusives. But now, mortgages are becoming commodity product, so you get same quotes everywhere. This should drive down margins in time, as people shop.

Full-Service Financial Portals

You'll probably want to choose one of the comprehensive financial portals as a home base for your personal finance needs. There's a "portal war" of sorts going on in this field as multiple contenders for your attention co-opt niche sites and incorporate their services into an ever-expanding menu of options. A full-service financial portal site might offer most or all of the following services:

- Financial news
- Compatibility with personal finance software
- Financial planning tools (such as tools for calculating eventual retirement benefits or college costs)
- Tools for screening and selecting mutual funds or stocks
- Research and opinion articles on the market and individual stocks or funds
- Customized investment portfolio watch lists and e-mail alerts (to tell you when certain prices become available)
- Online collaboration with broker and/or electronic trading with low commissions

Leading portals today include Quicken.com (shown in Figure 6.1), Yahoo! Finance (**http://finance.yahoo.com/**), Microsoft Money Central (**http://moneycentral.msn.com**), CBS Marketwatch (**http://www.marketwatch.com/**), FinanCenter (**http://www.financenter.com/**), Wall Street City (**http://www.wallstreetcity.com/**), and the Motley Fool (**http://www.fool.com/**).

Directories of Personal Finance Sites

Another type of central jumping-off web site for financial matters is a directory, a site whose sole purpose is to provide you with an organized list of links, by topic, to all the other personal finance sites out there. Such a directory site is not full-service, so you probably won't want to use it as your home base; but it can still be a helpful

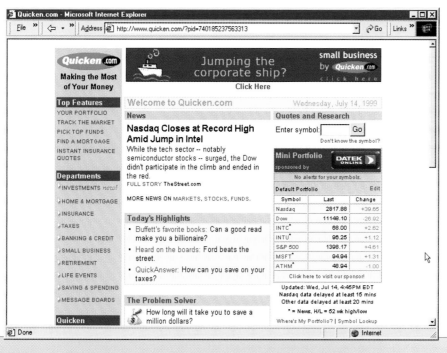

Figure 6.1:   Quicken.com is one of the most popular financial portal sites.

resource, saving you valuable research time hunting around the Net for this or that financial site. A directory should cull out the less useful sites and not just list them all. Perhaps more importantly, it should organize sites by subtopics so that you can find them easily, even when you don't know the name of the site you're looking for, but only its purpose.

A directory site works hard to keep its listings up to date, so you don't have to. Consequently, you should revisit directories regularly to see what's new. Directories can also help you find specialty and niche sites.

Directory sites include Yahoo! Finance and Investment (**http://dir.yahoo.com/Business_and_Economy/Finance_and_ Investment/**), Investor Home (**http://www.investorhome.com/**), Investor Guide (**http://www.investorguide.com/**) and InvestingSites (**http://www.investingsites.com/**), shown in Figure 6.2.

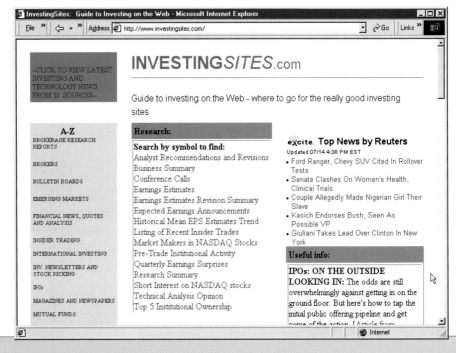

Figure 6.2: InvestingSites is a directory of—you guessed it—investing sites.

Specialty and Niche Web Sites

By definition, it would be impossible to name every type of specialty
and niche financial web site out there. Even if it were possible, someone
will launch a quirky new site next week (or the week after this book
is sent to the printers) and we'd still be behind the eight ball. In the
broadest sense, though, a specialty personal finance web site is one
whose function is specific to a single topic, such as:

- Stock charts
- Blue-book values for automobiles
- The Federal Reserve's economic data
- Lots of other stuff

For the most part, you can use directory sites to find out about new
or interesting niche sites, or find them yourself while surfing. Figure 6.3
shows a site dedicated entirely to charts.

Figure 6.3: If you like charts, you'll love BigCharts.

I've included here one of Bill Valentine's *InvestMentor* columns on predicting the direction of the economy.

Predicting the Economy

Can't be done. Predicting the economy, that is. Professional economists have the same forecasting ability as weathermen and astrologers. But hey, that means that after reading this primer, your predictions will be right up there with the best of them. The rule of thumb about data on the economy is "Less is more." The government tracks thousands of statistics every month, but you only need to concern yourself with seven measures (my "Big 7"). I've listed them below. Each of them differs by what it measures and by how much it impacts the stock market. While no one of these works perfectly, when taken collectively, they create a portentous mosaic.

Following each description, I provide you with the web address that will take you to the data. Most are part of a site at the University of Alabama (**http://bos.business.uab.edu/browse/**). In those cases, you'll need to chart the data by clicking GIF Chart Of This Data. Be sure to select the radio button on the bottom of the chart that says Percent Change From Same Period Last Year and then the Make Chart button. The dates of upcoming economic announcements can be tracked at **http://www.leggmason.com**.

1.   GROSS DOMESTIC PRODUCT (GDP)   GDP is the total value of all goods and services produced in a year by a given country. What matters as an indicator is the annual percentage change. This figure is reported quarterly. The GDP is the broadest measure of the economy. The definition of a recession is two consecutive quarters of negative annual percent change in GDP. The announcement of GDP each quarter has some impact on the stock market, but typically only when the number is a surprise to investors. As evidenced by the Third Quarter 1998 growth rate of 3.4 percent, the economy at the time of this writing, according to GDP, is quite strong.

- **http://bos.business.uab.edu/charts/cgi-bin/data.exe/OKfedstl/gdpc92+1**

2.   INFLATION RATE   The inflation rate is the change in the prices of goods and services in an economy. A small amount of inflation is a good thing, and is part of the Federal Reserve's (or, in other countries, the central bank's) mandate. Too much inflation is bad because it erodes the value of your currency. Disinflation is worse, because falling prices mean companies have to sell their goods for less in the future but incur costs in the present. That eats into margins and earnings and results in a recession.

My favorite ways to gauge inflation are the Consumer Price Index (CPI), which measures a basket of typical consumer purchases, the Employment Cost Index (ECI), which measures changes in salaries and benefits, and the GDP Price Deflator, which is a statistic used to adjust the GDP for inflation.

Inflation, like porridge, needs to be not-too-hot and not-too-cold—sudden changes in "temperature" spook the stock market.

- **http://bos.business.uab.edu/charts/cgi-bin/data.exe/OKfeddal/pgdpcw** (GDP Deflator)
- **http://bos.business.uab.edu/charts/cgi-bin/data.exe/fedstl/cpiaucsl+1** (CPI)
- **http://bos.business.uab.edu/charts/cgi-bin/data.exe/OKfeddal/ecicp** (ECI)

3. INTEREST RATES

Interest rates represent the cost of borrowing money. The Federal Reserve sets interest rates on overnight borrowing (Fed Funds and Discount Rate), and all other interest rates ultimately conform to the direction the Fed sets. Low interest rates encourage borrowing, which stimulates growth—but if too much growth occurs, inflation accelerates and spoils the party. High interest rates make it expensive to do business, but they also cool off overheating inflation.

Interest rates differ by the length of term of borrowing. When they are arrayed by term and rate, you have a yield curve. Usually, the longer the term of the borrowing, the higher interest rates will be, thus the curve should slope upward moving left to right (from short-term to long). In addition to the direction of all rates, note the relationship between the "long" end of the curve and the "short" end of the curve. If short-rates exceed long-rates (creating an inverted slope), that's a very bad thing. When investors have concerns about the short-term, they prefer to lend "long," and that drives long rates down. This forces companies to pay high rates for borrowing in the short term and erodes margins and earnings. Only once in the last 45 years has an inverted curve not led to a recession. Recently the United States economy came close to inverting before the Fed dropped short-term rates in September, 1998 (creating a positive slope).

- **http://www.bloomberg.com/markets/C13.html**

4. LEADING INDICATORS

The Leading Indicators is a composite index (tracked by the Department of Commerce) made up of 11 spot measures of the economy (including some of my Big 7) that should "lead" GDP by a few months. Examples are: length of average work week, housing starts, and changes in inventories. The index works reasonably well, but the stock market pays little attention to the Leading Indicators.

- **http://bos.business.uab.edu/charts/cgi-bin/data.exe/OKfeddal/jlead**

5. UNEMPLOYMENT RATE   The unemployment rate is the percentage of the work force without jobs. The two things to watch are the absolute levels of unemployment and the rate-change from the prior year. Historically, the unemployment rate rarely dips below 3 percent or rises above 10 percent. Whenever unemployment has risen by 1 percent from the prior year, the economy has been in recession. Thus, when the annual change inches towards 1 percent, watch out. Market analysts and investors keep their eyes on unemployment data when it's rising.

- **http://bos.business.uab.edu/charts/cgi-bin/data.exe/fedstl/unrate+2**

6. MONEY SUPPLY   Money supply is a measure of how much money is in the system at any given time. In the United States, the Federal Reserve controls this by buying and selling Treasury bonds. To increase money supply, it buys Treasuries (putting money into the system); to decrease the supply, it sells them. A growing money supply is necessary for a growing economy. When an economy heats up on the back of expanding money supply, the risk is inflation (too much money chasing too few goods); thus the Fed tightens the supply. If the Fed tightens too much, it chokes off the growth. The stock market doesn't pay much attention to the announcement of money supply (…anymore—it used to).

The measures of supply (the "money aggregates") are M1, M2, and M3. I watch for the annual changes in M1 (all currency, checking deposits) and M2 (M1 plus bank deposits below $100K and money market funds).

- **http://bos.business.uab.edu/charts/cgi-bin/data.exe/fedstl/m1sl+1**
- **http://bos.business.uab.edu/charts/cgi-bin/data.exe/fedstl/m2sl+1**

7. STOCK MARKET   The stock market is a discounting mechanism for the future directions of earnings because stock price behavior is based on the short-term operating expectations of investors. Half of all bear markets immediately precede recessions.

- **http://www.bigcharts.com** (click on "Indexes")

What Can You Do?

I know, I know, you're eager to talk about investing, specifically getting in on this runaway bull market before it tops out, but let's not overlook the other sorts of personal finance services offered online.

Banking on the Web

Depending on your bank account, you may already be able to log onto a web site and see and manipulate your account information (or pay bills directly). Wells Fargo offers just such a service at **http://banking.wellsfargo.com/** (see Figure 6.4).

EXPERT ADVICE

Depending on your bank, it's also possible to simply use a checking program such as Quicken with an Internet connection to automatically interact with your account electronically.

Financial Planning

Financial planning is ultimately a very personal activity, and the task can be made easier with tools that help you project the effects of

Figure 6.4: I'm not a Wells Fargo customer, but even if I were, I wouldn't publish my checking account balance in a book!

CAUTION

No mechanical calculation can substitute for professional advice regarding your personal information.

investment decisions into the future and web-based templates that help you work backward from your investment goals. Portal sites such as Quicken.com and Microsoft Money Central offer these sorts of forms-driven financial planning tools to help you determine, for instance, whether you are going to meet your retirement goals with your current savings-and-investment plan.

I've included here one of Bill Valentine's *InvestMentor* columns with some advice about financial planning.

Asset Allocation (How Not to Screw It Up)

News flash: The most important investment decision you'll make is not how many dot-com stocks you buy!

The thing you need to do right is to choose the appropriate percentage of your investment portfolio to invest in stocks versus bonds versus cash versus other assets. The big thinkers within investment circles will tell you that *roughly 90 percent of your investment results* will be determined by how you had your money divided among asset classes (the other 10 percent being attributed to security selection). This is ironic when you consider that we often spend 90 percent of our time talking about securities.

In dealing with hundreds of investors over the years, I've found that most cannot articulate what their asset-allocation strategy is, and therefore end up with improper allocations. Some use overly simplistic formulas ("subtract your age from 100 and put that percentage into stocks"). Worse still, some actually let their market prognostications influence their asset allocation (aided by the brokerage firm knuckleheads who go on TV and the Web to generate trades). The decision to invest among classes should be neither arbitrary, nor dynamic. Below are the five most important asset allocation considerations.

1.   TIME HORIZON BETWEEN NOW AND WITHDRAWAL
The time you have before you need to access your money is your most important consideration. Stocks (and real estate) provide the best long-run average rates of return, but they fluctuate in the short/intermediate term. Any assets that you won't need for ten or more years needs to be in stocks, period (even some of a retiree's portfolio needs to last over ten years). Under ten years, you want to introduce the lower-return asset classes like bonds and cash. Money needed within a year should be all bonds/cash. It's possible to have two time horizons, however. Your IRA/401(k) is long-term (stocks), but you might need your savings for a down payment within the next year (bonds/cash).

2. THE NEED TO DRAW INCOME OUT OF THE PORTFOLIO

Bonds are not to be used for "diversification" and have no place in a long-term portfolio. Their long-term real rate of return is half that of stocks, so bonds amount to an opportunity cost over time. But bonds do two things better than stocks. They preserve capital and can provide an income yield. If you need to withdraw a certain amount from your portfolio per month, let bond interest meet those needs. Thus, the amount of bonds you hold is primarily related to the amount of income you need.

3. THE NEED TO PRESERVE CAPITAL/MINIMIZE VOLATILITY

As I just mentioned, bonds preserve capital (when held to maturity). The only asset class that does that better is cash (money market funds). If you cannot afford to have your portfolio lose value (because you may need to liquidate an amount), you need to have bonds/cash. This means you'll give up return, though.

4. THE NEED TO HAVE THE INVESTMENTS IN LIQUID ASSETS

Should you need to withdraw some of your investments, you want them to be in cash or something that converts to cash easily. Virtually all mutual funds, large/mid cap stocks, money market funds, and Treasury bonds fit this description. Beware of real estate, illiquid stocks, and bonds.

5. THE TAXABILITY OF THE INVESTMENT ACCOUNT

Today there are a lot of tax-sensible investment options (municipal bonds, tax-efficient funds). They don't belong in your tax-deferred accounts such as IRAs, 401(k)s, etc., but could make a lot of sense in a taxable savings pool. There are ways to determine which vehicles deserve to be there.

To tie these considerations into an asset allocation, you'll want to use financial-planning resources. Do-it-yourselfers should use Quicken's tool. Those who want a warm body to help develop a plan they will implement themselves need a financial planner. Those who don't want the hassle should use a money manager. Whatever the case, a deliberate allocation is the first step toward success.

Other sites that offer financial-planning tools include Smart Money (**http://www.smartmoney.com/si/tools/oneasset/**), S&P Personal Wealth (**http://www.personalwealth.com/**), American Century (**http://www.americancentury.com/**), and Smith Barney's Assess (**http://www.smithbarney.com/**), shown in Figure 6.5.

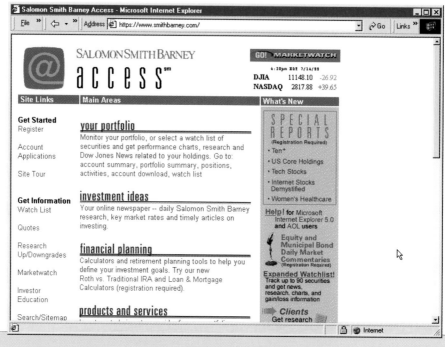

Figure 6.5: Smith Barney's Assess site offers financial planning tools.

Shopping for Loans or Insurance

One way to make sure you're getting the best possible rates for loans or insurance is to shop around. You can do this online at any of a number of web sites. Whether it's mortgages or insurance, you can shop them one of two ways. You can check out terms individually at the financial institutions, or you can use an online "shopping center" to compare different companies to each other.

Researching and Tracking Investments Online

To invest responsibly, you must research your decisions carefully in advance, seek advice, weigh various opinions, and use whatever information you can obtain as widely as possible. Start by keeping up with financial news. The dominant news sites include NewsAlert (**http://www.newsalert.com/**), Business Week Online (**http://www.businessweek.com/**), CBS MarketWatch (**http://www.cbsmarketwatch.com/**), the *Wall Street Journal* (**http://www.wsj.com/**), and Cents Financial Journal (**http://lp-llc.com/cents/**).

But there's more to research than keeping up with news and the opinions of columnists. You'll probably begin your search using a "screening tool" that allows you to filter stocks or funds by your desired criteria. Most of the portals have screening tools, such as the one shown in Figure 6.6 at **http://www.stockpoint.com/leftnav/pages/stockfinderpro.asp**.

Once you've identified a list of prospective stocks or funds, you'll want to use all of the research tools that are ubiquitous to the portals, including company news, SEC filings, historical financials, and so on (see Figure 6.7).

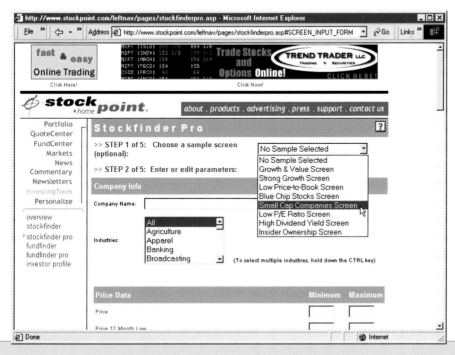

Figure 6.6: StockPoint.com's screening tool

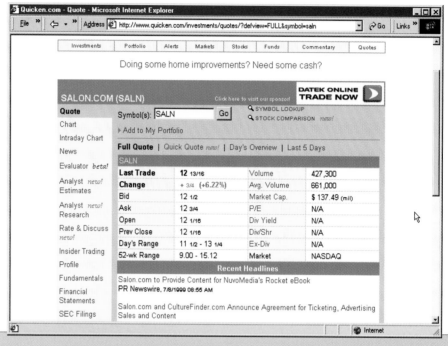

Figure 6.7:   I got information on Salon.com by entering **SALN** in the search box at http://www.quicken.com/investments/quotes/

Investing on the Web

Most of the buzz about personal finances and the Web these days surrounds the idea of investing directly—literally buying and selling stocks and other financial products through the Internet. The rest of this chapter will address the different aspects of this subject.

Strategies for Different Types of Investors

The Internet has put investing directly in the hands of more individuals than ever before, but there are different levels of service available and tradeoffs to be made between paying a premium for professional advice and economizing on the brokerage fees while going it alone. Just because you *can* go it alone, though, do you really want to? Ask yourself that first. There are different types of investors, ranging in independence, and you'll need to determine what sort of investor you are—or intend to be—to make wise use of the services offered online. People at different stages of their lives or with different financial wherewithal will require different investment strategies. If we offered exactly the same advice to students, people who've just graduated from school and are starting out in life, young couples, families with two full-time workers, retirees, and so on, we would be doing all of them a disservice. Instead of trying to determine every possible sociological variable that may affect a reader's needs, we'd instead like to focus on your level of independence, which is to say your degree of confidence in making financial decisions yourself.

How Involved Do You Want to Be? (How Much Control Do You Want?)

In the following sections we'll address three types of investors, differing primarily in their degree of independence:

1. **Delegators** People who take responsibility for decisions but hand most of their financial matters over to a professional (whether because of a lack of time, interest, experience, or for any other of a whole variety of reasons).

2. **Co-Pilots** People who like to play a role in the decision making but need or prefer to have someone with experience looking over their shoulders.

3. **Independents** People who like to do everything—as much as possible—themselves.

First, though, we'll mention a few resources that would be important for investors in every category.

Everybody

Investor sites that everybody should make use of include the portals mentioned earlier, the directories, and the financial news sites. Bill suggests that although the *Wall Street Journal* Interactive Edition is not free, it's well worth the cost (and for that fee, you also get *Barron's* and SmartMoney.com) and about the only site worth paying for.

I've included here one of Bill Valentine's *InvestMentor* columns about his top seven favorite personal-finance sites.

Bill Valentine's Top Seven Personal-Finance Web Sites

Once upon a time, I managed money at a big firm with deep pockets. The Internet, for all practical purposes, hadn't been "invented" yet. Lacking that resource, we bought the necessary information needed to make investment decisions. As recently as just a few years ago, access to the following information would have cost the same as a small island in the Pacific (or a house in Northern California). I've listed my favorite seven sites for you to bookmark on your browser. Collectively, they provide you enough information to handle all of your investment and financial decisions.

There are two kinds of web sites with which investors should concern themselves. First of all, there are "comprehensive" sites. These are the hubs where you can go to get most of the information you need. There are hundreds of these, but you really only need one. And there's no better hub than Quicken.com.

- **Quicken.com** Aside from its outstanding roster of contributors (sitting up a little taller, clearing my throat), the site gives you 90 percent of what you need to actively manage your own finances. The key features are news, quotes, and portfolio tracking.

The second kind of web sites are what I call "data sites." They are places where you can go for specific information on one or more aspects of investing. My top choices are:

- **ADR.com** The most critical mistake investors will make over the next five years will be having too little exposure to non-U.S. securities. As a country, our geocentric asset allocation is rearward looking and the avoidance of foreign stocks dramatically limits the opportunity set of potential investments. One argument against foreign stocks used to be that you couldn't obtain enough information about the companies. That is no longer the case, thanks to sites like ADR.com. ADRs are stock certificates that trade on U.S. markets but that represent shares in foreign companies. You can use this site to look up all sorts of information on foreign companies. One very interesting, notable tool is the Institutional Holdings list. For any foreign stock, you can see which mutual funds and institutional managers own shares, along with how much they own and whether they've been buying or selling recently. Cool.

- **Morningstar.net** If you want to research mutual funds, this is the best place I've found on the Internet—and it even has stock stuff. It contains the entire Morningstar database of fund ratings, which they sell in book form. If you register on-site, the cost is a big goose egg! This is a perfect example of the inefficiency in data pricing caused by the Internet. Don't buy any mutual funds without looking at this site.

- **The *Wall Street Journal* Interactive**   This site is not only the online version of the *Wall Street Journal*, but it is chock full of tools and data. Access to some of the site is free, but to get the full edition of the *Wall Street Journal*, you must subscribe. With a subscription, you get every version of the Journal (each one of the five U.S. regional versions and the Asian and European editions) plus a free link and subscription to the online publications of *Barron's* and *Smart Money*. This is one of the only sites you should ever pay for.

- **Bigcharts.com**   They're not just big charts; they're big, juicy charts. This site allows you to create charts of any stock or index in the United States. You can create most of the classical technical indicators such as moving averages, RSI, and volume. They've recently added a feature that allows you to chart a stock intra-day using data points for every minute of trading. Whoa! Good stuff.

- **University of Alabama at Birmingham**   In an earlier sidebar, I wrote about how to predict the economy using seven measures. The University of Alabama at Birmingham site allows you to track most of the seven measures by providing a charting tool for use with the otherwise unintelligible data sets provided by, and imported from, the Federal Reserve. You'll need to chart the data by clicking GIF Chart Of This Data; then be sure to select the radio button on the bottom of the chart that says Percent Change From Same Period Last Year and then the Make Chart button. Bookmark this site after reading my primer on tracking the economy.

- **The Ohio State University Fisher College of Business**   This site was the first investment site I ever saw on the Internet. The main site itself is Ohio State University's. The address above takes you to just one part of OSU's web site and allows you access to the deep recesses of the finance department. It is a comprehensive site that links you to endless resources. Go to the site and poke around—it's amazing. The Financial Data Finder (**http://www.cob.ohio-state.edu/~fin/osudata.htm**) section is my single favorite page on the Internet. It has an alphabetical listing of investment data providers (of course they're linked) with a description of each.

Delegator

Even delegators may want to use the Web to follow financial news, check their accounts, and to keep up with opinion. They also may want to pay bills online, seek out resources such as financial advisors, or buy insurance or a mortgage. Delegators rely on the help of accountants or financial planners.

Some sites specialize in broker comparison, which help you pick the right broker for your needs. These sites include Expert Online Investment Advocates (**http://www.xolia.com/**), Gomez Advisors' Internet Broker Scorecard (**http://www.gomez.com/**), KeyNote Systems' Online Brokerage Index (**http://www.keynote.com/**), The Motley Fool Brokerage Center (**http://www.fool.com/**), and Market Guide Investor (**http://www.marketguide.com/**).

Co-Pilot

For those interested in directing their finances with the help of outsiders, there are a lot more sites available. In a fundamental sense, the Web is more appealing to these people because they enjoy playing a role in the decision-making.

Co-pilots tend to operate in one of two ways. The first is when they seek external assistance in developing a financial plan, but implement the plan themselves, using mutual funds. Morningstar.net is the most comprehensive web site for mutual fund information, of interest to virtually anyone with a mutual fund, 401(k), or savings account. A co-pilot needs access to an online brokerage, whether it's one of the new brokers that has emerged on the Web or a traditional broker now going online, as Merrill-Lynch did in early 1999 after swearing not to less than eight months earlier. Co-pilots might venture into buying mutual funds online as a conservative step up the chain and then perhaps buying a stock or two online (a whole new universe).

The second way co-pilots work is through a traditional brokerage relationship. In the traditional relationship, the broker does not have authority to trade without your consent. However, the broker executes the trade. The co-pilot will have a retail brokerage account and may access it online. Discover (**http://www.discover-brokerage.com/**) offers access to Morgan Stanley research for a fee. Figure 6.8 shows Sure Trade (**http://www.suretrade.com/**), the budget version of Quick & Reilly.

The brokerage industry used to be the only conduit to owning the equity. In 1942 you *had* to call a broker. The trend is moving away from the traditional approach that relied so heavily on the authority of the broker, as it gets squeezed between fee-based advisors (who, not being brokers, have no possible conflict of interest) and the do-it-yourself approach.

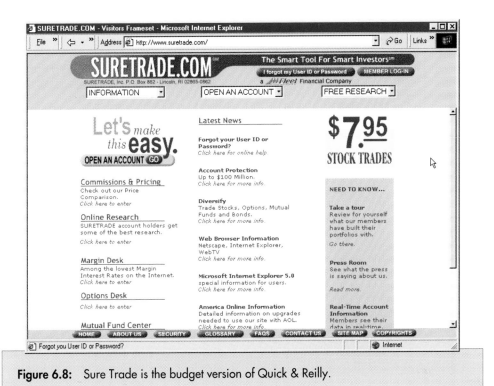

Figure 6.8: Sure Trade is the budget version of Quick & Reilly.

Independent

Web sites useful specifically for independent investors are mainly the niche sites. The trick, says Bill, is winnowing them down (he's got more than 100 in his bookmarks). Independents are generally more interested in the community sites, such as those offering live chatting, bulletin boards, or newsgroups, where they can hash out their ideas in the company of other investors. The Motley Fool site offers this sort of community appeal. You should use such forms of research as only one of many sources for a balanced mixture of advice, opinion, and raw data.

Independents like to buy and sells stocks. There are 7,000 actively traded U.S. stocks today. Portals all give you tools for evaluating stocks. Microsoft sells some of the content at its site. Most of what is sold (as opposed to given away for free) is geared toward the very independent investor—the same kind of stuff brokers and analysts pay

CAUTION

Stock manipulation is all too easy in this electronic age, so be careful not to take a stranger's tips or touts literally without independent confirmation. It's the same old false information game, but now with a 24-hour captive audience. Any Joe Schmoe can commit this sort of crime with great leverage and minimal accountability.

attention to. Multex (**http://www.multex.com/**) sells the brokerage research of all the brokerage firms.

Online discount brokerage accounts include: E*Trade (**http://www. etrade.com/**), Ameritrade.com (**http://www.ameritrade.com/**), Datek.com (**http://www.datek.com/**), Waterhouse.com (**http://www. waterhouse.com/**), and ESchwab.com (**http://www.eschwab.com/**).

Day Trader

Day traders are the extremes of the independents. They get in and out of stocks in a single day, counting up their profits (or losses) each day. Bill believes that with the costs of transactions and taxability it makes day trading a zero sum game. There's an inverse relationship between the amount of time you spend trading and the return on your investment. The ugly lesson of the '90s will be demonstrated by the people who blew a lot of money day trading. In a raging bull market you're losing only relatively (that is, you may be making money, but you're making it more slowly than the market average), but when the bear market comes, day traders will suffer more obvious losses. "There will be a lot of angry spouses and children," says Bill. "It's institutionalized gambling with a Wall Street gloss."

Where do you draw the line between active investment and day-trading? First off, for day trading, you have to have the whole day free to watch the charts tick-by-tick and pounce. It's another thing entirely (and well within the bounds of reasonable independent behavior) to choose a stock move at night and implement it the next morning.

Yes, But How Do You Pick a Stock?

There's no way you're going to learn all you need to know to pick your own stocks from one chapter in this book, but in the broadest outline, you have to choose a strategy, screen stocks that might fit the strategy, and then research the stocks that pass your initial screening. Choosing a strategy is your business, but once you've got a strategy, web sites can shorten your screening and research time. There's a screening tool at Quicken.com. Standard & Poor's Personal Wealth (**http://www.personalwealth.com/**) offers screening services as well.

CAUTION

Screening alone is not adequate for picking stocks. It's merely a first step to separating the stocks you might want to choose from those that clearly don't meet your criteria.

I've included here excerpts from a three-part series of Bill Valentine's *InvestMentor* columns on how to pick a stock. To read the entire articles, visit his site at **http://www.valentineventures.com/** and choose the InvestMentor link.

Some Advice on How to Pick a Stock

My investment selection process works from the "top down." I decide first what country to invest in, then what sector, and what industry. Lest I be accused of slimy practices, I'll note that I purchased the stock that came out of this process some time before the final decision was published in my three-part series of columns. Further, I would not recommend that anyone else necessarily follow suit. The important part of what I'm describing is the process, not the outcome. The best way to get a general sense of which sectors and industries are growing quickly is to read a lot of business news. I take many of my technology cues from the daily articles in the "Tech Center" section of the *Wall Street Journal* and web sites like InternetNews.com. For example, I've recently developed an interest in "broadband fixed wireless" telecommunication companies. Broadband transmissions are those with very large amounts of data, voice, or video (including the kinds that dominate the Internet). Fixed wireless refers to companies that send out voice, data, and video signals from radio towers using high-frequency microwaves.

I began by trying to dig up articles on "broadband wireless" and "fixed wireless." I used the search engines (Excite, Yahoo!, etc.), the article archives at the *Wall Street Journal*'s online edition, and the search feature at InternetNews.com. Six names were mentioned in two specific articles. I ran these tickers through a search for brokerage reports at Multex.com. (Multex sells brokerage research on their site on a per-report basis, as well as through partnership with folks like Quicken.com). Many of the same industry reports came up for each of these companies.

Finally, I ran the tickers through Quicken.com's comparison screen, usually a good source of competitors, especially in industries with fewer companies.

The subsequent screening of the six companies did not yield any additional competitors. At this point, I had a sufficient familiarity with the names so that I could eliminate three from consideration.

Next, I took a look at the quantitative features of these three companies. This inexact process combines art and science, and is not always pretty to watch. In fact, I'd add my stock selection process to "laws," "love," and "sausage," on the list of "Things you don't want to see being made."

In order to compile the figures you'll need for quantitative analysis, I recommend three sources:

1. Quicken.com (or other major financial online "super-site")

2. Each company's own web site

3. Multex.com (or any site like Quicken.com that carries their reports).

I use Quicken.com to cull financial statistics from the income statement and balance sheet. This data is typically listed on a quarterly basis in the "Financials" section, but where there are holes, I will look in the "News" section for recent earnings announcements (and accompanying financial tables) or in the SEC filings section for annual (10K) and quarterly (10Q) SEC filings. I go to company web sites because they almost always have an "Investor Relations" section that contains either financial tables or all past press releases, which include the aforementioned earnings announcements. Finally, I use Multex for access to reports from the brokerage community whose analysts do a rigorous gathering of statistics including many not found at any of the other sources.

In every analysis, I seek measures of valuation, measures of growth, and measures of financial strength. In the case of these three companies, the answer doesn't lie in the earnings (or cash flow) because they're negative for all three. Telecommunication infrastructure is a capital-intensive business. Companies invest heavily while building out a network and don't expect to see earnings for several years. The key for these companies is to avoid overextending themselves when raising capital, so that they can rapidly increase revenue that eventually translates into earnings.

Qualitative analysis is about "what the numbers don't tell you." Because none of the three companies I chose had consistently attractive financial figures, I needed to look elsewhere for clues. There are several sources that combine to create a mosaic of each company. Collectively, they allow for my qualitative analysis.

I begin by printing out the "Business Description" of each company found in the most recent 10K SEC filing. They can be lengthy but do the best job of describing the company (the descriptions you find in the Annual Report tends to be Pollyanna-ish). I also read the footnotes of the financial statements, where there are often nuggets of information hidden. Finally, I read the section about the business and investment risks associated with the company. Most of this information is self-evident, but occasionally it can tip you off to something you might have overlooked.

I also search the recent news on the company. This includes press releases as well as news wire articles that mention the company. Additionally, I use the Quicken.com article archive to search trade publications for articles that do not normally appear among those listed in the "News" section.

Increasingly, company web sites are a revealing source of information. If things about the company are not clear to me, I'll e-mail or call their Investor Relations department.

From there, I go to the Multex reports (reports written by brokerage analysts). I try to find two or three broad industry reports that include references to the companies I'm considering. Additionally,

I like to print out at least two company-specific reports for each candidate, written by brokerage analysts. For the most part, these reports have a "promoting" bias (in that analysts generally don't write extensive reports about why they don't like a particular company). Therefore, you're left to form your own opinion. This requires a certain amount of familiarity with the industry in question, but, by the time I get to this point in the process, I've done a fair amount of reading on the sector.

Finally, I look at the price chart of the stock to get a sense of its short-term direction. My belief about the cyclical nature of stocks is that all stocks are subject to momentum and mean-reversion from time to time. I want to hold off buying a stock that has been experiencing momentum for several months because I want to avoid participating in the slide as it inevitably reverts to the mean price-appreciation trend. Also, I don't like buying a stock when it's in the middle of an uninterrupted price depreciation. Further, I don't like to see a historic pattern of dramatic volatility. A nice, upwardly trending chart of a stock that is at least 15 percent below its all time high is the ideal.

There is no magical formula for how I tie all this information into a decision to buy a stock. Look at enough companies and you'll begin to develop your own sense of what feels good versus what doesn't. In the final analysis, all three of these companies are sexy. The likeliness is high that all three could be taken over at any time as they would be a valuable asset in any tele-conglomerate's portfolio.

To invest your money with any less due diligence would be fool hardy.

Last Words of Opinionated Advice

Bill left me with these words of advice: "You don't have to pay for anything on the Internet (except for the *Wall Street Journal*), and you can be a great investor with a great portfolio." Information that used to be available only to those with a $200,000 research budget is now essentially free.

I've also included here Bill Valentine's *InvestMentor* column on the top five mistakes made by investors. Be sure to visit his site if you want more of his advice (such as how to pick a mutual fund, whether to pay down debts before investing, whether taxes might actually be a good thing, and so on).

The Top Five Mistakes Made by Investors

Investing is not like fly-fishing. I had to learn how to do both, and let me tell you, while it's awkward to be a bad fly-fisherman, it beats losing money. A bad fly-fisherman runs the risk of looking like an idiot as he defoliates both sides of a stream. It's harder to picture what bad investing looks like because it often manifests itself in the form of "opportunity cost"—and you rarely hear investors talk about "the one that got away." Yet while less visible, bad investing can be catastrophic. We all make mistakes (and moreso at first) but the key is learning from them.

In today's market, there are millions of first-time investors, many of whom have chosen to go it alone. As uncomfortable as it is in the start, everybody's a beginner the first time. While some investors are best served by investment advisors (like large investors or those with complex situations), everyone stands to benefit from learning the fundamentals. The key to how quickly you develop a graceful investing form is how quickly you learn from your mistakes.

Here are five I see all the time:

1. IMPROPER ASSET ALLOCATION

"Asset allocation" is the term for how much you put into each of the asset classes (stocks, bonds, cash,) and styles (domestic securities versus international, "value" versus "growth," aggressive versus conservative). Several studies have shown that roughly 90 percent of investment return is determined by asset allocation and only about 10 percent comes from security selection. It often seems like we apportion our concentration in the opposite amounts. Your asset allocation should be determined by your specific circumstances. No factor is more important than your time horizon as the longer you have until you need to withdraw your investment, the higher your volatility tolerance. Additionally, consideration needs to be given to:

- The amount of income you require your investments to produce
- Your tax situation (and how you want your gains handled)
- The need to have some or all of your assets readily available (liquid)
- Your emotional ability to deal with uncertainty
- Your long-term return objective

One way people end up with an improper asset allocation is by letting "market predictions" interfere with what should be an otherwise static asset allocation, also known as "market timing." Anyone who makes large shifts between asset classes is playing with fire. Another common mistake some folks make is in confusing their personality with the "personality" of different investments. For example, I often hear, "I'm a conservative investor, so I want to be in bonds because they're conservative, right?" Investors who have all bonds—and a long-term investment horizon—have increased their risk, not reduced it, because bonds are a poor hedge against the most important long-term consideration: inflation. Determining the proper asset allocation is not difficult, but it is the single most important decision you'll make as an investor, so it should be done right.

2. TRADING TOO OFTEN   The second biggest mistake I see is unnecessary security trading. Forget for a minute that it costs at least 1 percent of the investment just to get in and out of a stock (even when trading online). The main reason that you want to trade less frequently is that most cycles in the market are several years long. This means that it's very difficult to truly assess the success or failure of an investment in the short run. It is as much our nature to be attracted to investments that we don't own and that are performing well as it is to be disappointed with ones that we *do* own that are performing poorly. The retail brokerage industry has spent the last hundred years trying to convince you that you need to trade more often than is in your best interest. Why else would they be giving their research away on the Net? It's so that you'll be able to see all the weaknesses of your current investments, as well as all of the great ideas that you should be switching to. Performance chasing ensures that you buy at the top and sell at the bottom. Everyone pays lip service to "long-term," but few run their portfolio that way.

3. PAYING TOO MUCH IN FEES   The investment industry, more than most, has an inordinate number of bloodsuckers. There is a limited, reasonable amount of expense that should be borne by the investor in the process of intelligent investing. However, Wall Street has cast a veil of mystery over their profession so as to keep you paying for access to the "gurus" that hold the keys to the mystery of making money. Here are examples of the things you should avoid because their result does not justify their cost.

- Loaded mutual funds (as well as any fund that has high operating expenses or 12b-1 fees). There are thousands of great no-load funds with low operating expenses, especially index funds.
- Retail brokerage relationships (that are commission-based). There should be only three types of relationships: none at all, fee-based financial planning, or fee-based advisory.
- Variable annuities (and many types of Whole Life). Don't confuse insurance with investment.
- Long-term care insurance. An attractive idea, but a cost-prohibitive solution. Save on your own.
- Wrap fee advisory relationships. In a wrap-fee arrangement, offered by retail brokerages to wealthy clients, the stock broker sets up a brokerage account that invests with outside management firms for a fixed annual fee including brokerage commission. Wrap fees have traditionally run between 2-5 percent, but the arrangement is becoming extinct, and you should *never pay more than 1.5 percent per year for an advisory relationship.*

4. OVER-DIVERSIFICATION   Being diversified across asset classes and investment styles serves to lower the volatility of your portfolio as well as reduce the likeliness of permanent loss from any single investment. But there is such a thing as over-diversification. Too much of anything is a bad thing. I see it often when prospective clients share their portfolio with me—too many mutual funds have made their way into the portfolio. When you consider that the average mutual fund holds over 100 securities, it's not hard to find yourself invested in thousands of stocks by owning a dozen funds. In a simple sense, the more stocks you own, the more you tend to mirror the results of the broad market. If that's your goal, own an index fund—it's cheaper than an actively managed fund and it guarantees full market participation. No one should own more than 30 stocks—or more than seven mutual funds—under any circumstance.

5. NO PHILOSOPHICAL BASIS FOR INVESTING   As someone who constantly challenges investors to articulate their philosophies, I'm critical of those who can't. Lacking a philosophy, you're left without a basis for your investment decisions and selections. That puts you at the whim of the external forces that cause you to make the four mistakes listed above. I've written at length about forming an investment philosophy, but will be the first to concede that your philosophy can be very different from mine—and we can still both do well. Any philosophy consistently adhered to will beat a random set of choices. Give some thought to what types of investments best suit your style and how you will measure their results. Invest for the long term and continue to learn and refine along the way.

When the bear market arrives—and arrive it will—the punishment for poor investing will be more severe than it is today. In a market where most investments are rising quickly, even bad choices make money. Take this opportunity to hone your craft—for it's best to have your ducks in a row to avoid giving back your hard-earned gains.

And when you feel confident that you've built your skills up, might I suggest that you try fly-fishing?

There's More . . .

To take a step beyond consuming information on the Web and start publishing your own web pages or developing your own web site, see Chapter 7 for how to create web pages and Chapter 8 for how to publish on the Web and how to maintain and promote a web site.

CHAPTER 7

Make Web Pages with Ease

INCLUDES

- Understanding web publishing
- Planning a web site
- Creating web pages
- Understanding HTML codes
- Editing web pages with FrontPage Express, Netscape, or Word
- Formatting web pages
- Inserting hypertext links
- Advanced web design

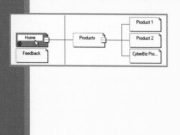

Plan a Web Site ➡ pp. 187–188

1. Organize your source documents.
2. Consider possible interlinks.
3. Create a folder hierarchy.
4. Design your home page.
5. Plan for future growth.

Create HTML Documents ➡ pp. 189–190

All HTML documents

- Start with <HTML>
- Have a head that starts with <HEAD>, which has a title enclosed between <TITLE> and </TITLE>, and ends with </HEAD>
- Have a body that starts with <BODY> and ends with </BODY>
- End with </HTML>

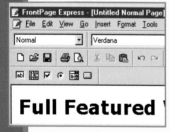

Create Web Documents with
Microsoft FrontPage Express ➡ pp. 197–200

1. Select Help | Product Updates to download the FrontPage Express program if you have only Internet Explorer installed.
2. Create a new file (click the New Page button).
3. Type (or paste in) text.
4. Format your text with buttons from the toolbars.
5. Insert images and links.
6. Save and publish the document.

Create Web Documents
with Netscape Composer ➡ pp. 200–206

1. Select Help | Software Updates to download the Composer module if you have only Navigator installed (if you have Netscape Communicator, you can skip this step).
2. Click the New button and then click New Blank Page.
3. Type (or paste in) text.
4. Format your text with buttons from the toolbars.
5. Insert images and links.
6. Save and publish the document.

Create Web Documents
with Microsoft Word ➡ pp. 206–209

1. If you're working with a version older than Word 97, download and install Internet Assistant from **http://www.microsoft.com/word/internet/ia/**.

2. Start a new web page with File | New. Choose the Web Pages tab and double-click one of the predesigned page templates or the New Web Page (you may also create any type of Word document and later just save it in HTML format).

3. Choose the File | Properties command to assign a title.

4. Assign heading levels with the drop-down Style list on the Formatting toolbar.

5. Format text with any of the normal formatting buttons that remain on the toolbars.

6. Click the Insert Picture button to insert a picture.

7. Click the Insert Hyperlink button to insert a hypertext link.

Just when you've gotten yourself an e-mail address and have begun to explore the World Wide Web, you learn that there's another level of status on the Internet these days—having your own home page. The best-known open secret on the Net is that creating a home page is easy. It's just a matter of putting together a text file and adding a few tags.

Meanwhile everybody and their brother, and their brother's companies, are setting up sites on the Web, ranging from flimsy storefront mail drops to complex interactive worlds. You may be too busy to design and build a complicated web site, but you'd be surprised how easy it is to put together a few simple pages to make information from your department available to everyone within your company, or to promote a project.

An Overview of Web Publishing

I can't go into the details of installing and running a web server in this short space. Fortunately, there are a lot of alternatives to maintaining your own server. See Chapter 8 for information on how to publish your pages on the Web (or on an intranet).

Suddenly, the World Wide Web has opened up an entirely new avenue of publishing, one that avoids much of the costly overhead of print publishing and which is open to anyone—or at least anyone with access to a web server. A web server is a program that delivers requested pages to web client programs (browsers).

A web site consists of a home page, all the web pages that are linked from the home page, all the pages linked from *those* pages, and so on. You should always be able to return to a site's home page from any page at the site. Not every page need be linked directly from the home

---

IS THIS FOR ME?

It's possible to get a lot of value out of the Internet without ever publishing your own content there, but the time you take to learn the basics of web publishing might pay off in the development of an intranet web site for your workplace, a personal home page, or even a web presence for a large-scale enterprise.

page, but the essence of a well-designed web publication is the organization of the links.

There are two major steps in web publishing: (1) designing and creating the pages, and (2) publishing the site. In this chapter, I'll tell you how to go about creating web documents. You don't need to worry at first how to make your pages available to the public (or to your colleagues). Instead, you can build your pages in a staging area—most likely a folder on your own hard disk. Chapter 8 will tell you how to get your pages out there when you've finished creating them (as well as how to maintain them and how to promote your site once it's published).

Planning a Web Site

Here are the steps to follow in designing a web site:

'll cover just the basics of web site creation in this chapter—but enough for a busy person!

1. Clarify the relationships among documents and organize a structure for the pages at the web site.
2. Design, write, and format the documents in a staging area.
3. Weave together related pages with hyperlinks.
4. Publish the site (go live from the staging area).
5. Promote the web site to its intended audience.
6. Maintain the site with regular updates.

If you are basing a web site on existing documents or a mixture of existing documents and newly created ones, assemble all your source documents and plan a folder hierarchy that reflects their relationships to one other.

Think carefully about how you want your documents to link to each other. This is likely the part of web design with which you are

EXPERT ADVICE

If you organize your documents and folders with a little forethought, you'll find it easier to maintain and update the site in the future.

least familiar. Linking documents in sequence is often a good place to start, but don't overlook the potential for creative and flexible cross-linking of documents. Often a single document will refer to several others. Each of those references can be an active link. You can link to specific parts of documents, too.

Try to plan for potential future growth of your site. The Web is not a static medium. An orphaned site quickly becomes stale and out of date. Think about what areas of the site might end up being expanded upon or replaced. If you anticipate future changes, such as updated statistics or newer publications, they'll be much easier to implement when the time comes.

Web Pages Explained

I n a multiple-frame view, make sure to first select the frame whose source you want to view, or you may end up viewing the content-free source for the frameset document.

So what exactly is a web page? It's an HTML document, with the extension .html (.htm on some older Windows computers). But what's an HTML document? It's really just a plain text document with special tags, each of which starts and ends with an angle bracket. Look at an HTML file and you'll be <I>surprised</I> how easy it is to read.

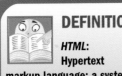

DEFINITION

HTML: Hypertext markup language; a system of tags used to describe hypertext documents that consist mainly of text, formatting instructions, and hypertext links.

A Little HTML Never Hurt Anyone

In most browsers, it's very easy to take a look at the underlying HTML document that is the source for the displayed web page. In Netscape and most other web browsers, the command is View | Document Source (or, for pages with frames, View | Frame Source) or something similar. The HTML source document will appear in a new window or in a text editor such as Notepad (in Windows) or SimpleText (on a Mac). You can select and copy sample HTML from such a window and paste it into a new file.

It used to be that the fastest way to learn about HTML was to look at the source files of interesting pages, but most commercial pages have become so encrusted with scripting code for advertisement and interactivity purposes that it's much more difficult now to learn HTML simply by scanning the code of a well designed page.

How to Create HTML Documents

I'll explain the basics of HTML here, but you don't have to read about HTML if you don't want to. There are more and more tools appearing on the Net that enable users to create web documents without having to know much about the underlying HTML tags. Generally, they let you create and format a document normally and then perform a conversion for you. At the very least, they can automate the insertion of tags and hypertext links.

I'll explain three such tools, Microsoft FrontPage Express, Netscape Composer, and Word 2000, later in this chapter.

HTML Document Layout

All HTML documents must start with <HTML> and end with </HTML>. Between those codes are two sections, the head and the body, marked at beginning and end by <HEAD></HEAD> and <BODY></BODY>, respectively. The only tag inside the head of the document that you need to know about is the title tag (<TITLE>*the title goes here*</TITLE>). Figure 7.1 shows a diagram of a basic web document.

Figure 7.2 shows the document interpreted and displayed by a web browser.

What's New with HTML?

The latest version of HTML, version 4.0, attempts to reconcile and standardize most of the innovative tags introduced by Microsoft and Netscape in their ongoing browser war. Meanwhile, the latest versions of the browsers are testing out new, incompatible variations of style sheets and DHTML (dynamic HTML). Of course, this is driving web

To see the source of a web page in Internet Explorer, right-click an empty part of the document in the window and select View Source from the menu that pops up, or use the View | Source command.

CAUTION

Just because someone else has used HTML in a certain way on the Web doesn't mean it's correct. So you may be incorporating erroneous coding into your pages if you merely copy from other's people's published pages.

EXPERT ADVICE

Since all HTML documents have the same basic tags, there's no need to retype them again and again. Create a template.html document that has the basic tags, along with your name and e-mail address at the bottom. Then you can copy this file and rename it whenever you create a new HTML document.

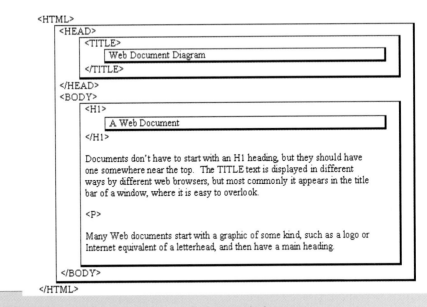

```
<HTML>
    <HEAD>
        <TITLE>
            Web Document Diagram
        </TITLE>
    </HEAD>
    <BODY>
        <H1>
            A Web Document
        </H1>

        Documents don't have to start with an H1 heading, but they should have
        one somewhere near the top. The TITLE text is displayed in different
        ways by different web browsers, but most commonly it appears in the title
        bar of a window, where it is easy to overlook.

        <P>

        Many Web documents start with a graphic of some kind, such as a logo or
        Internet equivalent of a letterhead, and then have a main heading.
    </BODY>
</HTML>
```

Figure 7.1: A conceptual diagram of a basic web document

designers crazy as they attempt to make interactive web sites that work, or at least don't crash, on several different versions of two competing browsers, and on multiple platforms.

Meanwhile, the Web is gearing up for the introduction of XML, a new markup language that will complement HTML and help separate out the different goals of structuring documents, identifying the nature of their contents, and controlling how they are displayed in various media (on the screen, when printed, and so on).

Fortunately for you, none of this stuff is working well yet, and you can't be expected to keep up with it until it's way more standardized. All the HTML and web-design techniques I'm going to show you in this chapter are dead basic. They'll enable you to create coherent documents for display on the Web that will work just fine on any browser. By the time dynamic HTML, XML, and HTML 5 or whatever are sorted out, ordinary web editors such as those described later in this chapter will have grown the ability to take advantage of the emerging standards.

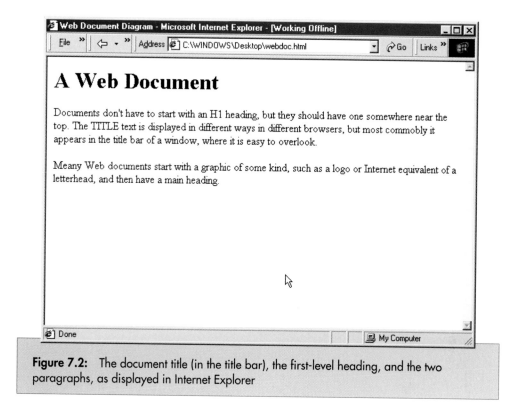

Figure 7.2: The document title (in the title bar), the first-level heading, and the two paragraphs, as displayed in Internet Explorer

Online HTML Reference Material

If you want to learn more about HTML, visit some of the reference sites on the Web shown in Table 7.1.

Choosing a Web Editing Tool

There are so many different ways to create web documents that it's hard to know where to start. The three broad categories of tools are

- Plain-text editors
- HTML tag editors
- WYSIWYG (what you see is what you get) editors

Reference	Web Address (URL)
A Beginner's Guide to HTML	http://www.ncsa.uiuc.edu/General/Internet/WWW/HTMLPrimer.html
Netscape's HTML Reference Guide	http://developer.netscape.com/library/documentation/htmlguid/index.htm
An Example Page That Makes Sense	http://www.dcn.davis.ca.us/~csandvig/ip/example.html
Hypertext Markup Language (HTML)	http://www.w3.org/hypertext/WWW/MarkUp/
HTML Quick Reference	http://www.cc.ukans.edu/~acs/docs/other/HTML_quick.shtml
Style Guide for Online Hypertext	http://www.w3.org/hypertext/WWW/Provider/Style/Overview.html
How Do They Do That with HTML?	http://www.nashville.net/~carl/htmlguide/index.html
Yahoo!'s HTML listing	http://dir.yahoo.com/Computers_and_Internet/Information_and_Documentation/Data_Formats/HTML/
Composing Good HTML	http://www.cs.cmu.edu/~tilt/cgh/

Table 7.1: Online HTML References

If you use a plain-text editor, you must type everything yourself, the content *and* the tags. HTML tag editors are similar to plain-text editors but have special commands and shortcuts for inserting the necessary HTML code. They help automate the process and show you what you're working with. The leading such tool is Allaire's HomeSite (**http://www.allaire.com/**).

WYSIWYG editors hide the details of the HTML from you and function much like word processors (in fact, some of them are word processors that have learned to speak HTML). I'll explain three useful tools in this chapter, FrontPage Express, Netscape Composer, and Word. Other good web publishing tools include Adobe GoLive. Most people new to web publishing use some sort of WYSIWYG editor, but I'll also explain how to type the tags yourself, so you at least know what's going on under the surface.

BOOKMARK

There are many different HTML editors that can help you create a web page. To download software in this category, check the HTML Editors sections at TUCOWS *(http://www.tucows.com/)* and Stroud's *(http://www.stroud.com/)*. Anything given five stars (or five cows in the case of TUCOWS) is probably worth downloading.

Creating Web Pages with a Text Editor

This section explains how to create web pages with one of the following simple, raw text editors: Notepad or WordPad (for Windows); TeachText, SimpleText, or BB Edit (on the Macintosh); vi (in Unix); or Pe (in the BeOS).

Converting Old Documents

If you plan to reuse or adapt existing documents, most word processing programs can now save documents in HTML format. You may need to clean up the files a little in an editor, especially if the page layout is tricky. If you can't convert your documents directly to HTML, you'll need to save them as text files or as RTF (rich text format) files. If you save them as plain text (ASCII) files, you'll have to insert all the HTML tags manually. If you convert them to RTF, you can then use an RTF to HTML converter to get at least some of the formatting converted to HTML.

For an RTF converter, point your web browser at **http:// www. sunpack.com/RTF/**, the rtftohtml home page (rtftohtml is a free filter you can download from the Web).

Whenever possible, try to reuse existing web documents, copying them and rewriting them, to save yourself the tedium of entering the basic tags over and over.

DEFINITION

RTF: Rich text format; a Microsoft text-based format designed to retain formatting information for file transfers between incompatible systems or formats.

Writing the Text

A big part of the job, as with the creation of any document, is the writing of the text. Do it in a word processor and save it as a text file with line breaks; or type it in your text editor if you prefer. As with any formal document, do the writing and the formatting in different stages, so that each job is done thoroughly.

Because web browsers ignore line breaks in HTML documents, press ENTER any time you want to make your HTML document clear and easy to read or edit.

Numbered and bulleted lists can be nested, one inside of another, to create subordinate list levels, but be careful not to cross the tags.

Formatting a Web Page

All the formatting tags you incorporate into your document will go between the <BODY> and </BODY> tags. Most tags go before and after the text they affect, in pairs. Table 7.2 shows a basic set of tags you'll probably want to use. For elaborate documents, consult an HTML designer. Putting together a graceful document is harder than it looks. At the very least, pick up a simple design reference.

Inserting Graphic Images

Don't overlook the mixed-media potential of the World Wide Web. A big part of the sudden popularity of the Internet is the Web and the simple fact that web pages can display pictures (on most web browsers). Web sites with illustrations and effective use of graphics are much more

Purpose	Tag
First- through sixth-level heading	<H1></H1>,...,<H6></H6>
New paragraph	<P>
Line break, same paragraph	
Horizontal line	<HR>
Bold, italics, underlining	<B></B>,<I></I>,<U></U>
Emphasis, strong emphasis	<EM></EM>,<STRONG></STRONG>
Equal-width text (as made by a typewriter)	<TT></TT>
Start or end of numbered list	<OL></OL>
Numbered list item (don't type the number)	<LI>
Start or end of bulleted list	<UL></UL>
Bulleted list item	<LI>
Start or end of definition list	<DL></DL>
Definition term	<DT>
Definition	<DD>

Table 7.2: Some Common Formatting Tags

inviting and communicative than the text-only world that the Internet has only recently emerged from.

The two widely recognized graphics image file formats on the Web are GIF (with the extension .gif, for graphics interchange format) and JPEG (with the extension .jpg, the Internet standard promulgated by the Joint Photographics Experts Group). JPEGs can be compressed to much smaller sizes than GIFs (although there are trade-offs in image quality), and JPEGs are much better suited for photographs and other continuous-tone images. GIFs are perfectly adequate for images with solid blocks of color, and they can also include transparent backgrounds and animation, neither of which can be done with JPEGs.

A new file format, PNG (with the extension .png, for portable network graphics format), combines some of the advantages of both other formats, and is supported by the latest versions of both major browsers, but there are still inconsistencies in the implementation from one browser to the next, so the time for this format has still not quite yet come.

The basic tag for inserting a figure is <IMG SRC="*filename*" ALT="*text*">, where *text* is alternative text to be displayed by nongraphical browsers and browsers with image loading turned off. To learn more about the <IMG> tag, view the source of some pages that use illustrations in ways that appeal to you.

CAUTION
Pictures take longer to download than text and consume more hard-disk space, so use them judiciously. Keep art small and reuse graphical elements so they'll have to be downloaded only once.

Inserting Hypertext Links

The bottom line of the Web is its hypertext nature. The real genius of hypertext is that it hides the baroque Internet addressing protocols that are so clumsy to discuss and learn about. Sure, you still have to type some URLs, but even those are getting easier. (For example, you can visit my web site by just typing **syx.com** in Internet Explorer or Netscape.) Most of the time, though, navigating the Internet can be as simple as pointing to the name of something you want to see or hear, and clicking your mouse.

There's the rub. To make your own web site, it's up to you to plan and insert the hypertext links. The HTML tag used for hypertext links is <A>, the anchor tag; you can use it in any of the ways shown in Table 7.3.

Link Element	Anchor Tag
Clickable hypertext link pointing to another HTML document or other type of file (such as a sound or movie file)	<A HREF="*filename*">***active-text***</A>
Hypertext link pointing to a named anchor in this same document	<A HREF="*#name*">***active-text***</A>
Link pointing to a named anchor in another HTML document	<A HREF="*filename#name*">***active-text***</A>
Named anchor point	<A NAME="*name*">***active-text***</A>
Combined link and anchor	<A HREF="*filename*" NAME="*name*">***active-text***</A>
Clickable image link	<A HREF="*filename*"><IMG SRC="*button-graphic*"></A>

Table 7.3: Hypertext Link Anchor Tags

Make sure documents are in the same hierarchical relationship where you're creating them as they will be when and if they are moved.

Files in the same directory don't have to be identified by a full pathname. In your index.html file, you can link to a file called dogs.html with just the tag <A HREF="dogs.html">*active-text-about-dogs*</A>. If you have subdirectories (a good way of organizing your site), indicate directory levels with a forward slash (as in Unix; not a backslash as in Windows). For example, if you move dogs.html into the pets subdirectory, the tag would be <A HREF="pets/dogs.html">. The parent directory can be indicated with two dots (..), so, for example, the dogs.html file can link back to the index with <A HREF="../index.html">.

These shorter versions of pathnames are called relative addresses; files on a different computer would need to refer to your pages with the full URL, including the path—for example, **http://www.yoursystem.com/~yourname/pets/dogs.html**.

Finishing the Web Document

When you're finished working on your document (for now), save it with a one-word file name (ending in .html).

CAUTION

If you want to save a text file in Windows 98 with an extension besides .txt, you have to reveal file extensions. To do so, choose View | Options in any folder window and uncheck "Hide MS-DOS File Extensions For File Types That Are Registered."

EXPERT ADVICE

Most web servers will treat a file named index.html as the default file in a directory (meaning the one that is shown if no file is specified). For this reason, the root, or home page, of a site is often named index.html. Microsoft servers (and web editing tools) prefer default.htm.

Creating Web Pages with Microsoft FrontPage Express

Your installation of Microsoft Internet Explorer may already include FrontPage Express, in which case you can get started right away. Otherwise, run Internet Explorer, select Help | Product Updates, and download the FrontPage Express module.

Microsoft FrontPage Express has some of the editing features of Microsoft FrontPage (which can be bought singly or as part of a Microsoft Office package), but none of the site-management features. If you have FrontPage installed, then Internet Explorer will prefer it to FrontPage Express by default.

Creating a Web Document from Scratch

If you are creating a file from scratch, select File | New. This brings up the New Page dialog box:

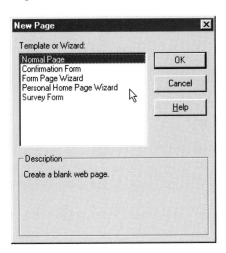

To create a blank document, select Normal Page and click OK. To base your document on one of FrontPage Express's templates, select one of the other four choices and click OK. For everything but the Normal Page option, a wizard will walk you through a questionnaire and then assemble a basic page for you. After that, you can edit it just as you would your own work.

Editing Existing Files with FrontPage Express

You can work with any page that's out there on the Web. Just browse until the page is displayed and then click the Edit button to launch your default editor (or click the drop-down button next to it to see your choice of editors).

You can also run FrontPage Express directly, select File | Open, click From Location, and then type the URL of the document you want to work with to open a file for editing. To pick up a page from your hard drive, select File | Open, and then type the path and file name, or click the Browse button, find the file, and click Open. Either way, click OK to load up the page.

If you base your work on someone else's on the Web, communicate with them and make sure that you don't plagiarize their content.

Formatting the Web Page

Microsoft FrontPage Express works more or less like Word or any other simple word processor with a few specific web features built in. Most of the useful editing and formatting commands are available on the toolbars at the top of the window (see Figure 7.3). You can tell

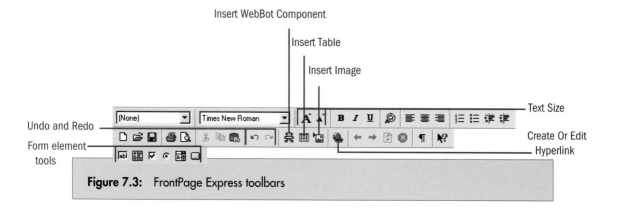

Figure 7.3:   FrontPage Express toolbars

what most of the buttons do by their names (just point to a button and a ToolTip appears).

You should give your document a new, real title before you save it for the first time. The document's title is what will show up in search engines, so give it something specific and descriptive. Once you've done that, you can forget about the title. To give your document a title, select File | Page Properties, type a title in the Title box, and click OK. You can select text by clicking and dragging. (You can select horizontal rules and images just as easily.) To delete selections, just press the DELETE key. To cut a selection so you can move it elsewhere, click the Cut button (or right-click and select Cut).

Creating headings is easy to do with the drop-down Change Style list box on the Paragraph toolbar. Just select the text you want to make into a heading (or put the insertion point where you want to start typing your new heading), click the Change Style list, and select the heading level you want.

Inserting Graphic Images

The basic method of inserting an image is to move to the point where the image is to appear and then use the Insert Image button. This assumes that the image already exists; you can create images with a number of different programs, or get (non-copyrighted!) images from public-domain icon and image libraries.

Inserting Hypertext Links

The usual approach to creating hyperlinks is to type the text (or insert the graphics) into the document first and *then* select the salient text (or image) and associate a link with it. With Microsoft FrontPage Express, inserting hyperlinks is simply a matter of selecting text and then clicking the Create Or Edit Hyperlink button. Once you've filled in the required link information, click OK. The text that activates the link will appear underlined and blue (as is typical of links when displayed in web browsers).

Finishing the Web Document

When the document is completed, select File | Save (for now). You can then save the file locally on your hard drive. To make it available over the Internet, however, you'll have to publish it. To publish a document means transferring it to your web server and making it accessible for Internet users. Publishing your pages (using FrontPage Express and other methods) is explained in Chapter 8.

Creating Web Pages with Netscape Composer

Netscape Communicator includes the Composer module. If you have just Netscape Navigator installed, select Help | Software Update, and download Composer.

With Netscape Composer, you can create a web document in a few simple steps:

1. Create or edit the document.
2. Type or paste in your text, or edit existing text.
3. Format the document.
4. Save the document.
5. Publish the document.

Creating a Web Document from Scratch

If you are creating a file from scratch, you have three choices: you can use Netscape's Page Wizard to help you through the process, you can use a template, or you can start with a blank page. To make your choice, select File | New and then choose Blank Page, Page From Template, or Page From Wizard.

Netscape's Page Wizard

The easiest way to crank out a simple page is with Netscape's Page Wizard. When you start a document based on the Page Wizard, Navigator connects you to a site where you can read some instructions and then start picking and choosing elements for your page. When you've finished filling out the Page Wizard form, the wizard generates your page for you, suitable for downloading.

From this point on, the procedure is the same as for saving any document from the Web to your local computer (for editing with Netscape Composer). The instructions for that procedure follow in the section "Editing Existing Files with Netscape."

Netscape Templates

Netscape also provides some document templates for specific purposes. These contain recommended layout and structure, as well as boilerplate text you can replace with your own specifics. This is a great way to get your documents started; you can edit them into shape later.

To start a web document using a Netscape template, first select File | New | Page From Template. This brings up the New Page From Template dialog box.

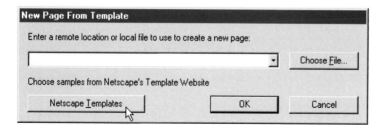

Click the Netscape Template button. This connects you to the Netscape Web Page Templates page. Read the couple of screenfuls of introductory material at the top of the page. Then read the overview of steps for using a template. Select and click a template name. Navigator will take you to the template.

From there, the procedure is once again the same as for saving any document from the Web to your local computer (for editing with Netscape Composer). The instructions for that procedure follow in the section "Editing Existing Files with Netscape."

Starting with a Blank Document

It *is* possible to face up to that proverbial blank white page and just write your own web document, without cribbing other people's ideas or boilerplate. To do so, select File | New | Blank Document. Netscape Composer will create a new document named Untitled and let you have at it.

Once you've started a new page, you have to fill it with information, format it, and link it to other pages. The next few sections will help you do just that.

Editing Existing Files with Netscape

To open a web page from your hard drive, open with File | Open File. You can also work with any page that's out there on the Web. Just browse until the page (or template or wizard result) is displayed and then use the File | Edit Page (or Edit Frame) command; Netscape will prompt you on how to save the file locally. Be sure you're not infringing on anyone's copyrights! (It's best to communicate with anyone whose work you're drawing upon heavily.)

To save the page to your computer, follow these steps:

1. Click the Edit button. This brings up the Save Remote Document dialog box.

2. Click the Save button. Netscape will warn you against stealing other people's artwork. (Good advice! Use art you either own or have permission to use. For that matter, hands off anyone else's text without their permission.)

3. Click OK. The Save As dialog box will appear.

4. Select a folder in which to save this document (and maybe your entire site). Type a file name for the document and click OK.

Formatting the Web Page

If you've ever used a word processor, or even a text editor, then Netscape Composer should be very easy for you to learn. The idea is about the same: You see what you're typing in the main window, and you give commands by choosing them from menus or clicking shortcut buttons. Most of the useful editing and formatting commands are available on the two toolbars at the top of the window (see Figure 7.4). You can tell what

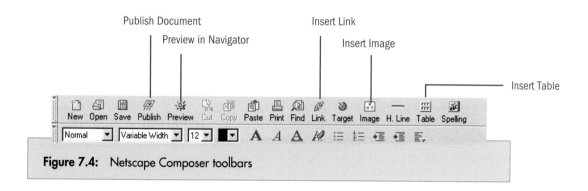

Figure 7.4:   Netscape Composer toolbars

most of the buttons do by their names (just point to a button and a
ToolTip appears).

You should give your document a new, real title before you save it
for the first time. Once you've done that, you can forget about the
title. To give your document a title, select Properties | Document to
bring up the Document Properties dialog box. Type a title in the Title
box and click OK.

You can select text by clicking and dragging. (You can select
horizontal rules and images just as easily.) To delete selections, just
press the DELETE key. To cut a selection so you can move it elsewhere,
click the Cut button (or right-click and select Cut).

Creating headings is easy to do with the drop-down Paragraph Style
list box on the Paragraph toolbar. Just select the text you want to make
into a heading (or put the insertion point where you want to start typing
your new heading), click the Paragraph Style list, and select the heading
level you want.

Netscape Composer makes it very easy to format characters and align
text in different ways. It's usually just a matter of selecting text and then
clicking a button, choosing an item from a drop-down list or menu,
or—at its most complicated—selecting an item from a dialog box. To
make existing text bold, for example, select the text and then click the
Bold button. To type new boldface text, position the insertion point,
click the Bold button, and then start typing. The button will appear to
be pushed in. When you want to continue typing in regular (unbold)
text, click the button again and keep going.

There are a few formatting effects you can apply to entire paragraphs (as well as to headings and other kinds of text). Among them are indentation, alignment, block quotes, and addresses.

When you want to see how your current document will look in the Netscape browser window, save it. Then click the View in Browser button. Netscape will open a new browser window with your current document in it.

Inserting Graphic Images

The basic method of inserting an image is to move to the point where the image is to appear and then click the Insert Image button. This assumes that the image already exists; you can create images with a number of different programs, or get (non-copyrighted!) images from public-domain icon and image libraries. Figure 7.5 shows the Image Properties dialog box that appears.

Inserting Hypertext Links

The usual approach to creating hyperlinks is to type the text (or insert the graphics) into the document first and *then* select the salient text (or image) and associate a link with it. With Netscape Composer, inserting hyperlinks is simply a matter of selecting text and then clicking the Make Link button, or dragging a link (or a local document) directly into the web document you're working on.

Once you've filled in the required link information, click OK. The text that activates the link will appear underlined and blue (as is typical of links when displayed in web browsers).

There are two different broad categories of links, by the way, usually referred to as internal and external links. Internal links connect to

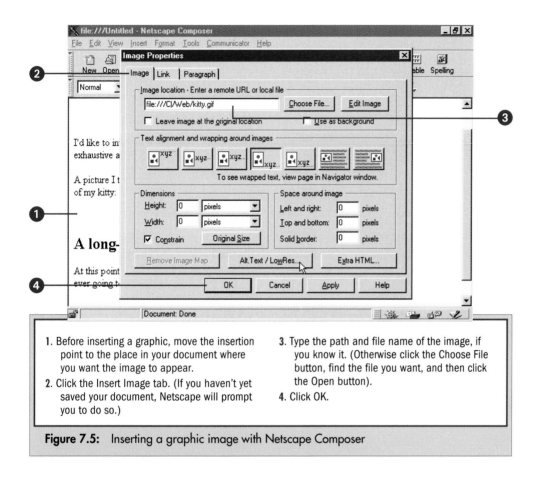

1. Before inserting a graphic, move the insertion point to the place in your document where you want the image to appear.
2. Click the Insert Image tab. (If you haven't yet saved your document, Netscape will prompt you to do so.)
3. Type the path and file name of the image, if you know it. (Otherwise click the Choose File button, find the file you want, and then click the Open button).
4. Click OK.

Figure 7.5: Inserting a graphic image with Netscape Composer

documents (or objects) located on the same computer (server) as the document that contains the link. External links connect to documents or objects located somewhere else on the Net. These are also sometimes referred to, respectively, as relative and absolute links, because internal links are referred to relative to the location of the starting document, whereas external links are referred to by complete web addresses (URLs).

BOOKMARK

For information on how to form web addresses (URLs), see Chapter 1 or the official documents at the W3 headquarters (*http:www.w3.org/pub/WWW/Addressing*).

Finishing the Web Document

When the document is completed, select File | Save (for now). This will save the file locally on your hard drive. To make it available over the Internet, however, you'll have to publish it. To publish a document means transferring it to your web server and making it accessible for Internet users. Publishing your pages (using Netscape and other methods) is explained in Chapter 8.

Creating Web Pages with Microsoft Word

Microsoft Word 2000 can convert HTML documents to Word documents and vice versa. It also has a bunch of toolbar items and menu choices useful for web page design.

You can also use Word's basic File | Save As command and then simply specify HTML as the file format.

Converting Old Documents

If you plan to base a web page on an existing document, first open the document. Then select File | Save as HTML. Give the document a one-word name (no spaces).

If you're using an earlier version of Word (older than Word 97) with Internet Assistant, you won't have the wizard template.

Creating a Web Document from Scratch

Starting a web document even without a model Word document is also simple. Select File | New.

In the New dialog box that appears, you have the choice of making an ordinary (Normal) Word document and later converting it to HTML, or clicking the Web Pages tab, and choosing from a number of predesigned web-page templates as well as a web-page wizard (see Figure 7.6).

Formatting the Web Page

Type the text of the document as you normally would. You won't be inserting HTML tags directly. Instead, you'll use Word's normal formatting commands, such as the Bold, Italic, and Underline buttons on the Formatting toolbar, and styles that are equivalent to HTML tags.

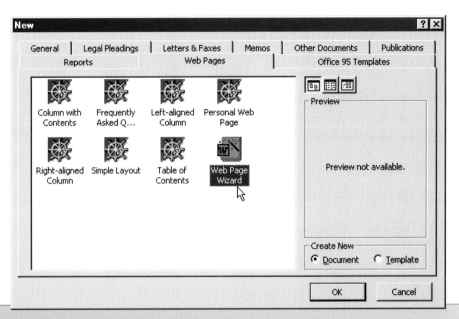

Figure 7.6: If you want a leg up creating your web page, start with the wizard or one of the templates on the Web Pages tab of Word's New dialog box.

For example, to make a line of text into a first-level heading, select the text and then select the Heading 1 style in the drop-down Style list box on the Formatting toolbar. Impose HTML formatting for which Word has direct equivalents, such as numbered and bulleted lists, with the normal Word toolbar or menu commands.

This is technically not part of formatting, but to assign the document's title (usually displayed in a web browser's title bar), use the File | Properties command, type a title, and click OK.

Inserting Graphic Images

To insert a picture into a web document, first place all your graphics files in a single folder. Move your cursor to the location where the image should appear. Then click the Picture button and select a picture from the dialog box that appears. Then click Insert.

Inserting Hypertext Links

Word takes the tedium out of inserting links. First, select the word (or graphic) you want to use as the launching point to the linked destination. Then click the Insert Hyperlink button. This brings up the Insert HyperLink dialog box (see Figure 7.7).

If you want to link to a local document, type it in the Link To File Or URL box. You can click the top Browse button and choose a file from the dialog box; this box lists both .doc and .html files. If you link to a regular Word file, only people using Word as a web browser will be able to read it.

To link to an address on the Web, click the Link To File Or URL box. Then type the address in the box or select it from a list of URLs you've visited. Be sure to type URLs exactly to link to another document on the Web (Word will remember all the URLs you type and allow you to reuse them easily).

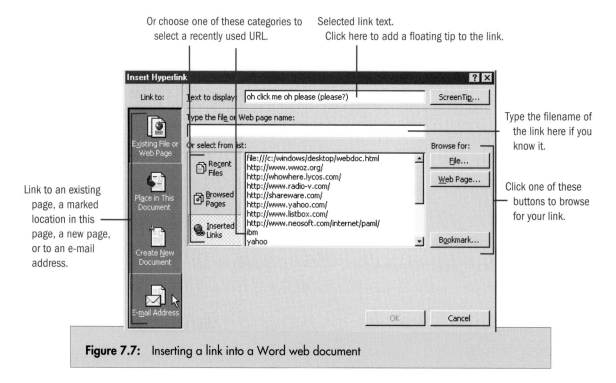

Figure 7.7: Inserting a link into a Word web document

EXPERT ADVICE

If you plan to link to a bookmark within a document, make sure the bookmark exists (or create it) before you try to link it. (Use the Insert | Bookmark command.)

To link to a specific section of a document, choose the "Named Location In File" box and choose a document and bookmark name.

Then click OK. The text that activates the link will appear underlined and blue (as is typical of links when displayed in web browsers).

Finishing the Web Document

When the document is completed (for now), save it. Word automatically displays the View | Online Layout view, so you can see how the page will look on the Web (more or less). If you want to view your page in a browser, click the Web Page Preview button. You can also test the links from within Word, now that Word doubles as a clunky web browser.

Clicking any link should take you to the linked document or bookmark. Use the Back and Forward buttons on the toolbar to retrace your path.

Advanced Web Design

There are more possibilities in web design, although not all of the latest advances have yet been implemented in standard HTML rules or in most browsers. Some advanced elements have become almost commonplace. It's a full-time job keeping up with web design developments, so focus on content first, presentation second, and embellishment last. Here's a list of advanced web design features you might want to explore: alignment commands, tables, borderless figures, gutter space around figures, transparent figure backgrounds, interlaced images that appear to load quickly, background patterns on pages, background colors on pages, customized text colors, variably sized text, style sheets with recommended settings, counters, and frames.

See Chapter 8 for how to publish web documents on the Web and on intranets, using Word 2000 and other methods.

Once the basic site has been laid down, the hierarchy planned, the central pages created, and the details and art filled in, you have two choices. You can publish the pages immediately and work to improve and jazz them up in later revisions, or you can add embellishments, showing off your mastery of sophisticated web design and interactive features, and *then* publish the pages. Either way, once you've published your site, you must think of it as an ongoing commitment, or it will atrophy and become useless in the long run.

If you've learned all the basic techniques of web publishing—creating, editing, and formatting HTML documents; inserting graphic images into web pages; and weaving related pages together into a coherent web site with hyperlinks—and your pages still don't look and feel the way you want them to, then you might want to invest some time (your own) or money (to pay someone else) toward adding advanced features to your developing web site.

I'll explain some of the more popular web design tricks, show you some examples, and point you toward a few online sources for additional information, if you have time to implement advanced features, including:

In Chapter 8, I'll briefly touch on web embellishments that require cooperation from the server side (including image maps, forms, and scripts).

- Colors and background graphics
- Tables
- Multimedia
- Frames

Colors and Background Graphics

Customizing the colors (text, links, and background colors, that is) or slipping background graphics into your web pages is pretty easy, especially if you're using a web editing tool such as Word or Netscape

Composer. Even if you're typing your HTML by hand, the tags are fairly straightforward and easy to learn.

In HTML, you control general color selections for an entire web page, and insert a background graphic if you wish, by typing the following attributes into the BODY tag:

<BODY BACKGROUND="*filename.gif|jpg*"
BGCOLOR="*color*"
TEXT="*color*" LINK="*color*" VLINK="*color*" ALINK="*color*">

Here, LINK specifies the color of an unvisited link, VLINK the color of a visited link, and ALINK the color of an active link (a link being clicked). The *color* assignment can be a hexadecimal RGB (red, green, blue) value, such as #FF0000 (red, because this value indicates maximum red, minimum green, minimum blue); or it can be one of a limited (but growing) set of named colors, currently including Aqua, Black, Blue, Fuchsia, Gray, Green, Lime, Maroon, Navy, Olive, Purple, Red, Silver, Teal, White, and Yellow.

Background patterns have to be the same kinds of files as inline images (that is, GIFs and JPEGs). FrontPage Express, Netscape Composer, and Word all offer dialog boxes for selecting colors and color combinations, and for defining custom colors (by choosing from a color wheel), as well as for inserting background graphics.

Tables

Creating, editing, and formatting tables by hand, unlike color selection, can be very difficult and frustrating. Tables themselves are wonderful and are more often used to structure the layout of a page than they are as tables of data labeled as such. (This is possible because you can set table borders to zero, hiding the invisible grid underlying your page.) The basic table tags are not too difficult to understand (see Table 7.4), but trying to do anything complicated with them is not so easy.

If you want to include tables in your page designs, I heartily recommend using a good web editing tool. With a good web editor, inserting and editing tables can be done on the screen in a much more intuitive fashion than wrestling with tags.

You can also color any specific stretch of text by preceding it with a <FONT COLOR="color"> tag and following it with </FONT>.

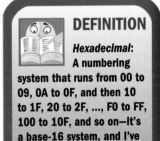

DEFINITION

Hexadecimal: A numbering system that runs from 00 to 09, 0A to 0F, and then 10 to 1F, 20 to 2F, ..., F0 to FF, 100 to 10F, and so on—it's a base-16 system, and I've already told you more than you want to know about it.

Notice that there are no HTML tags for columns in a table. Instead, everything is formatted in terms of rows (and the cells within rows).

Element	Starts With	Ends With
The entire table	<TABLE>	</TABLE>
A row	<TR>	</TR>
A cell	<TD>	</TD>
A header row	<TH>	</TH>

Table 7.4: Basic HTML Table Tags

One environment very well suited for multimedia web content is an intranet, especially one that is not strung out over a large area and reliant on the same sorts of phone lines that the public Internet uses.

Multimedia

Because the Web can deliver any type of file to your computer over the Internet, it's not limited to flat web pages and still pictures. In principle, you can embed or link any type of multimedia file (that is, videos, sounds, animation, formatted documents, interactive programs, and even 3D worlds) into a web site to enhance its presentation values. There are a few drawbacks in reality, though. One is that the multimedia content takes time and money to develop (whether you teach yourself to do it or hire an expert), and the other is that for most people, the Internet terminates in a fairly slow modem connection, and users will end up waiting all day for your infomercial to download.

Be thoughtful about your audience:

- Figure out a maximum practical file size for downloads and stick to it.
- Warn your audience when a link connects to a large file (anything over 50K or so).
- Use extra media elements only when they serve a definite purpose.

EXPERT ADVICE

Consider farming out the things you can't do well yourself, especially while you're learning. There's too much to the Web to be just a good-enough generalist.

The actual techniques for inserting multimedia objects into web pages are simple. You can either link to an object directly (as you would to any document), or you can embed the object either as an image (for some types of animations), with the <OBJECT> tag or with the <EMBED> tag.

Some of the more popular multimedia formats are listed here:

- **Adobe Portable Document Format (PDF)** An efficient way of delivering formatted documents.
- **Sounds** WAV, au, AIFF, and RealAudio files.
- **Movies and animations** QuickTime, MPEG, AVI, GIF89a, and RealPlayer files.
- **Macromedia Director Shockwave files** Small self-running applications that integrate multiple media and can be interactive (with user controls such as buttons and "hot," clickable areas). Many designers these days swear by Shockwave's Flash plug-in.

CAUTION

You can't assume your readers will have the right type of plug-in to play your multimedia content. To deal with this, you can include links from your pages to web sites from which they can download the tools they need. Bear in mind, however, that many will forego the extra steps necessary and miss out on the extra content. Even if you're certain your audience is equipped to appreciate your multimedia presentation, avoid overloading your pages with too many plugged-in bells and whistles.

Frames

If you've ever worked with a spreadsheet program that allowed the screen to be broken into panes, or if you've ever split the screen of a word processor, then you already have an inkling of what frames look like and how they function in web pages. Frames are subdivided regions of the screen. Each frame can behave more or less as a separate web document, so a group of frames is not just a fancy type of table. Frames can also contain links that point to other frames, so that

BOOKMARKS

For more information about Adobe Acrobat and the PDF format, visit *http://www.adobe.com/* or *http://www.pdfzone.com/*. RealAudio and RealPlayer are at *http://www.real.com/*. To create your own GIF animations in Windows, download the GIF Construction Set (*http://www.mindworkshop.com/alchemy/alchemy.html*). For the Macintosh, try GifBuilder (http://www.pascal.com/mirrors/gifbuilder/). 'Visit Macromedia (*http://www.macromedia.com/*) for more info about Director, Shockwave, and Flash.

clicking in one frame (such as a navigation area across one side of the screen) can result in a change in another frame (perhaps in the large, primary area).

Problems with frames can range from minor to severe. Truth be told, not all browsers recognize them (frames have a built-in way of offering substitute pages to browsers that don't "do" frames). Compounding this problem is the nuisance that the standards are still in flux, with Microsoft and Netscape, typically, tossing around changes. Finally, there are the more fundamental issues of whether frames are worth the bother, or even just plain ugly (not to mention wasteful of precious screen real estate).

The ultimate problem with frames is that the coding can be quite tricky, depending on what behavior you want, and poorly coded frame pages can cause unreadable pages that may even crash a user's browser. With that in mind, we'll leave it up to you to decide whether you're too busy to tackle the project yourself.

If you plan to create frames yourself, remember that you can view the document source (for the main page) or the frame source (for any subsidiary frame) to see how frames are put together. If you want to copy any coding literally, cut and paste it from the view windows.

Pages with frames actually consist of several different web documents: a main document containing the frame coding and the alternative coding (for nonframe users); and additional documents, one for each frame.

There's More . . .

You're now ready to go beyond passive involvement in the Web. If you have something to say to the world or a product to promote or a report to circulate, you can now create documents in a format that the entire wired world can read. Chapter 8 will tell you how to go about publishing your web pages both on the World Wide Web and on local intranets.

CHAPTER 8

Establish Your Presence on the Web

INCLUDES

- Shopping carts and other server-side web magic
- Finding a host for your site
- Setting up your own domain
- Publishing your pages on the Web
- Publishing on an intranet
- Promoting your web site
- Maintaining and updating your web site

Publish a Web Document ➡ pp. 230–235

- With Word 2000, select File | Save As, choose a Web Folder or select Internet Locations (FTP) in the drop-down Save In list box, and then save the file directly to your site.
- With Microsoft FrontPage (or Netscape Composer, or most other web design and web site management programs), click the Publish button.
- Upload the file to your site with any FTP program.

When you click on "Suggest a Site" in the appropriate category, you'll see an online form asking for information about your site. (In the "category" space on the form, you'll see the name

Promote Your Web Site ➡ pp. 235–239

- Submit announcements to major search engines and directories (listed in Chapter 3).
- Announce your site on mailing lists and Usenet.
- Communicate with the creators of similar or like-minded web sites and offer to exchange hyperlinks.

Maintain Your Web Site ➡ pp. 239–240

- Assign someone to regularly monitor traffic to and from the site.
- Make frequent updates and changes to your site.
- Consider investing in a site-management program, such as Microsoft FrontPage, Macromedia Dreamweaver, Allaire ColdFusion, Macromedia Drumbeat 2000, or Adobe GoLive (among others).

In the last chapter, I showed you how to create web pages and weave them together with hyperlinks. To make your pages available to the public or to the other users of your intranet, you have to post the pages on a server to which your audience has access. This is what is meant by "going live" with your web site. You'll want to take the time to carefully develop and test your site, but when you have done so, it's time to publish.

Technically, publishing your pages is easy. It's generally done with file-transfer programs or with the built-in publishing features of web-site management tools or web-page design programs. The tricky part is figuring out *where* to publish your site. To publish on the Web, you'll need access to a web server on an Internet host. Publishing on an intranet is relatively easier to arrange, but you'll still need to coordinate with the administrator of the network, who may have a preference about which file server you store your pages on.

If you've been able to create the pages you want to publish from what you learned in Chapter 7, then you can skip directly to "Publishing Your Web Site." If you want to incorporate some site features that require cooperation from the web server, you can start with the first section of this chapter, "Server-Side Web Elements." You can also come back to read that section when you're ready for it.

Server-Side Web Elements

A few of the more advanced web-design elements require cooperation from the web server to work, including the following:

- **Shopping carts**   Programs that enable your web site to fulfill sales orders (commonly referred to as e-commerce).
- **Forms**   The server has to handle the incoming data and generate a response or store the information in a database.

- **Database connections**   The only way to produce a truly dynamic and responsive web site is to build it with a database at the back end. Even busy sites that have largely static (unchanging) content might have some pages served up from a database.

E-Commerce (Shopping Cart) Solutions

Despite the tulip-mania feel of the current Internet boom, the fact remains that few web sites have made money directly for their creators or investors (yet), and the jury is still out on what the viable business models are. The portal race tends towards a winner-take-all monolith site, which seems to miss the point of the Internet entirely. The first wave of commercial web sites borrowed television and radio's advertising-underwritten approach.

But advertising is only one way, and possibly not the most efficient way, to make money on the Net. For years now, many new ventures have sought to make use of the Web as a means of selling products, taking credit card charges, concluding transactions. Even if Amazon.com really does lose money on each book sale as a loss-leader to build their audience portal, it still requires what's commonly called a *shopping cart*—a way for users to purchase the products they've chosen.

It's no longer necessary to create your own shopping cart/credit card interface from scratch. There are literally thousands of competing "e-commerce" or "shopping cart" solutions vying for your business. Some are available as shareware so you can test them before paying. Some come bundled or are designed to work with a specific web-design tool (such as Microsoft FrontPage or Elemental Drumbeat) or web server.

If you're looking for a shopping cart solution appropriate to the scope of your site, consider dropping by the E-Commerce Directory

EXPERT ADVICE

Programs like FrontPage come with simple ad-banner managers, and companies like NetGravity (*http://www.netgravity.com/*) provide comprehensive advertising solutions to large-scale, popular, busy sites.

at **http://www.onlineorders.net/links/** (it includes categories such as Free, FrontPage, and even Auctions, the gold rush of the moment). Let me caution you, however, that many of the free solutions require at least a complicated installation, if not a rudimentary familiarity with scripting or compiling program code. If you have to hire someone to set up the free solution for you, then it ceases to be free (or is that obvious?). Portal sites such as Yahoo! and Netscape offer further directories of shopping cart products. (Netscape's page, for example, is currently at **http://directory.netscape.com/Computers/ Internet/Commercial_Services/E-Commerce/Shopping_Carts**, but it's easy enough to drill down to it from the main page.)

Interactive Forms

To really make your site grab your reader, you should include interactive pages—pages that either request input or involvement from the user or that change or respond to the user's actions. However, livening up web documents in this way is no cup of tea. It requires at least some basic scripting abilities, and depending on the level of your ambition, it can require full-fledged programming work.

The most basic kind of interactive page is a form. If you've bought anything on the web, downloaded any shareware, or used a search engine, you've already filled out a form. Remember typing your name and maybe your credit-card information and then clicking a Submit button? That's a form.

It's one thing to learn the coding that makes forms look good on the screen. Although it's a little tedious, it's not too hard, and if you've become accustomed to working with dialog boxes, then you'll recognize the different types of doodads that make up a form. However, it's another thing entirely to get the forms working on the back end (the server side) so that when your reader fills out a form, something actually happens. That part requires scripts to be written, tested, and saved on your server. Finally, it's yet another matter to actually entice any of your visitors to fill out the form. This last part, however, is an issue for the marketers and psychologists.

FrontPage and FrontPage Express offer toolbar shortcuts that make it easy to put together forms. Word 2000 likewise makes the client-side of form creation very easy.

Programming the Web

If you want your web pages to do more than just lie there waiting for someone to read every word and click every link, then you've learned all the web design you need to accomplish your goals. If, on the other hand, you want to develop a truly interactive web site that offers a different experience to each user, depending on how the visitor responds and behaves at the site, then you'll need to do some scripting or some program-development to "get things to happen." This scripting can happen on either the server end (where your site is stored) or on the client side (inside your reader's browser).

CGI and Other Server-Side Controls

Both traditional server-side image maps and forms require the cooperation of a server to function properly. The ingredient that tells the server what to do, how to do it, and when to do it is the CGI script. (There are other methods of server-side scripting, such as server-side includes, Active Server Pages (ASP), and Cold Fusion.)

If you've ever worked with macros in a program such as WordPerfect or Word, then you have some idea of what a script does.

CAUTION

If you use a program such as FrontPage to "activate" your web site, you may find yourself locked into Microsoft solutions across the board; not that there's anything wrong with that.

DEFINITION

Server-side Include:
A method for inserting a section of code (or, more usually, a section of a web page) into numerous web pages, using a variable that the server replaces with actual content on the fly.

BOOKMARK

A good general reference for forms (and CGI scripts) is An Instantaneous Introduction To CGI Scripts And HTML Forms (*http://www.cc.ukans.edu/~acs/docs/other/forms-intro.shtml*).

You may also know that the devil is in the details, and understanding what to do in principle is a far cry from writing a script with no bugs in it, putting it in the right place on a server, and getting it to work.

Another common type of script is the sort that negotiates between a simple form and a mail server, enabling people to send replies in a consistent format. Another type of script keeps track of how many visitors have come to a page—"You are visitor number XXXX since our hit-count script last broke down!" A more sophisticated type of script, coupled with a regularly updated index of a site, can enable your readers to search your site by entering keywords into a simple form.

Java, ActiveX, and Other Client-Side Components

The cutting edge of web development involves the development of small modular web-based programs that web browsers actually download from the server site and then run on the user's host computer. This distribution of computing time and resources is much more efficient than enabling each user who hits the site to spin the wheels there.

The two competing approaches to web development are Java and ActiveX. By no means mutually exclusive (ActiveX incorporates Java controls and Java programs can initiate ActiveX events), the two represent fundamentally different philosophies of the desktop and the Web.

Java, developed by Sun Microsystems and embraced by a wide consortium of industry heavyweights, is an open system that can be used to develop object-oriented program modules (called applets) which, in theory, should be able to run equally well on any type of computer platform. ActiveX, by contrast, is Microsoft's baby, and is a standard for creating a component or object, fine-tuned for Windows computers.

Either way, unless you're a programmer, you'll need to hire one to develop programs, routines, components, or plug-ins in any of several

DEFINITION

CGI:
Common gateway interface; a standard set of commands for passing information back and forth between a web server application and other software running on the same system.

Script:
A small-scale program consisting of instructions designed to respond to varying circumstances with different actions and results.

BOOKMARK

For archives of existing scripts, try Matt's Script Archive (*http://worldwidemart.com/scripts/*). For more on CGI scripting, try *http://www.cgi-resources.com*.

languages. Other methods for "hopping up" web pages include developing multimedia content designed for special browser plug-ins, which has the unfortunate side effect of narrowing your audience to only those intrepid enough to install them.

The final way to jazz up web documents—one that's within reach of a normal busy person—is to incorporate scripts into your web document. As with the more advanced programming languages, there are two major competing scripting languages: JavaScript and VBScript.

JavaScript is not the same thing as Java itself, nor is it the same thing as the CGI scripts described in the previous section. Java is a much more fully functional programming language. CGI scripts run on the server side. JavaScript is interpreted by the browser (on the client side) and is generally limited to basic tasks such as checking the contents of a form before submission or creating the always popular roll-over button. Microsoft's VBscript is not nearly as popular as a client-side scripting language, and it tends to be at home only in intranets running mostly Microsoft applications and operating systems. VBScript, however, is very popular as a server-side technology, and most Active Server Page applications use it.

As with CGI scripting, it's not really possible to learn the ins and outs of JavaScript without special training. However, there are a number of useful existing JavaScript routines that you can borrow and adapt for your own pages, the same way you might borrow and adapt someone else's HTML code.

Examples of popular, simple JavaScript routines include a scrolling (possibly annoying to some) marquee message in the browser's status bar, and a script using a command called onMouse Over that puts explanatory text instead of the destination URL in the status bar when the user positions the mouse pointer over a link.

DEFINITION

JavaScript: A set of programming instructions that can be inserted into a web document and interpreted by a browser to produce interactive or variable effects.

Java: A platform-independent object-oriented programming language used to write programs that can be downloaded by web browsers and played on any computer.

BOOKMARK

More JavaScript information can be found online at *http://www.webreference.com/js/*. An organization that calls itself the Bandwidth Conservation Society (*http://www.infohiway.com/faster/*) has a nice archive of cut-and-paste JavaScript examples (*http://www.infohiway.com/javascript/*).

Unless you're a programmer, you have no business messing with Java itself. However, if you have need of a full-fledged application that you can serve up to any web browser who wants to run it, then you should consider hiring a programmer to develop your software in Java.

Dynamic HTML (DHTML)

Another web-design standard you can use to increase the dynamism and interactivity of your pages is Dynamic HTML (DHTML). Dynamic HTML effects can be applied to any page element (such as a word, a picture, a paragraph, or a heading) and set to respond to various "events" (such as the appearance of the element on the page, the mouse pointer passing over the element, the element's being clicked, and so on). DHTML is implemented somewhat differently in the two major web browsers, Internet Explorer and Netscape, but the simplest effects will work about the same way for both. The easiest way to add DHTML effects to a web site is to use a full-featured web site creation and management program such as Microsoft FrontPage 2000, a program in the Office 2000 suite that I'll discuss later in this chapter.

Deciding Where to Publish Your Site

When your site is ready for prime time, you need to find a place for it to live (a server) and then transfer all the files from your staging area (see Chapter 7) to the server. If you plan to publish your site on the World Wide Web at large, you can either set up and maintain your own server or post your pages on someone else's server. If your site has been designed for an intranet, then you can publish it to any local file server that everyone else on the intranet has access to.

EXPERT ADVICE

If you're about to try your first web publishing project, request access to a server at your organization or one run by your Internet service provider. Some providers offer web server access separate from e-mail accounts.

Finding a Server

There are two ways to publish your web site on an Internet server. One is to set up and run your own server on a machine connected to the Net. The other is to pay a provider to host your site for you on an existing server. Depending on the size of your organization and your budget, either solution may work for you.

If you rent space on a provider's server (or web farm), you generally lack security and control of your site. It may be difficult or cumbersome to update your site, and you may not be able to install the software you want there (such as a RealAudio server). On the other hand, the site will probably be faster to access and cheaper to maintain. Cost issues are subtle and have to be considered with the bandwidth you're getting.

Maintaining your own site can be expensive when you take into account all the labor, equipment, lines, servers, and so on that you will need. You also won't be able to have the fastest type of connection (a T3) with your own site. On the positive side, you can integrate your web presence with your other Internet servers, such as e-mail, and you'll have total control over the site.

> **DEFINITION**
>
> **Web farm:**
> A large Internet web server site that hosts many smaller web sites, either because the owner or primary tenant has a huge surplus of resources, or because the owner is in the business of providing web presence.

Running Your Own Server

Running your own server can mean anything from setting up a 386 PC with the free Linux operating system and free Unix web server software (such as Apache or httpd) over a round-the-clock ISDN link to being given access to a directory on a server already set up for your organization. Another do-it-yourself approach might require setting up and maintaining a network with a fast, dedicated gateway to the Internet on a high-end Pentium Pro workstation running Microsoft, Windows NT and Netscape, or other server software.

No matter what solution you choose—and you should solicit as much advice as possible for your specific circumstances—you must be prepared to maintain a 24-hours-a-day, 7-days-a-week Internet presence if you intend to run your own server. Decide what sort of computer you are going to use as your server. Do you have a spare PC? Ideally, you shouldn't share your web server machine with other processor-intensive tasks, such as database management.

EXPERT ADVICE

If you choose one of the more popular servers, then you're more likely to be able to find working examples of useful scripts. With up-and-coming servers, you may have to do more script development yourself.

The type of server software you choose depends primarily on what sort of computer you plan to run it on. I'll tell you about the most popular servers on the most common platforms. More importantly, I'll tell you how to keep up-to-date as these facts change. New developments emerge on the Net all the time, so you'd do well to know how to keep abreast of the news.

Other considerations that will help you decide among servers are cost (some are free, some are cheap, some are expensive), available support, whether the server is commercial (can handle transactions, whether you need this capability now or in the future), and the speed or efficiency (throughput) of the server.

Finding a Host for Your Site

The alternative to maintaining your own server is to hire out the hosting and a good deal of the day-to-day site maintenance (also known as *webmastery*) to a service provider.

It may be possible or preferable to get your web site hosted by your e-mail or Internet access provider, but it's not necessary. You don't even have to limit yourself to providers with local-access phone numbers. As long as you have some sort of Internet access already, you can negotiate a separate hosting arrangement with any provider on the Net.

BOOKMARK

Keep up with web server developments at ServerWatch (*http://www.serverwatch.com/*), which includes an excellent tool for comparing servers by price and rating and makes it easy for you to download free evaluation copies of servers you're considering. Another site that compares servers is WebCompare (*http://webcompare.iworld.com/*). Yahoo!'s server page is *http://dir.yahoo.com/ Computers_and_Internet/Software/Internet/World_Wide_Web/Servers/*.

EXPERT ADVICE

It is also possible to install the freeware Linux operating system (a Unix clone) on PCs, from the 386 up to the Pentium Pro, and then run one of the Unix web servers on a PC.

If you are creating a site for a small division of a large company or organization, and the publishing space available to you is on the server of a bigger part of the company, then your relationship with the administrator of the site will be much like that between a customer and a commercial service provider's administrator.

Service providers can also offer domain name service, providing a domain name for your company (www.*yournamehere*.com) either for a separate fee or as part of your company account package. See "Establishing Your Internet Presence" in the next section for more information on domain names.

The best place online to hunt for service providers is The List (**http://www.thelist.com/**).

Here are some issues to consider and questions to ask when negotiating with a potential host for your site:

- Can I make updates to the site directly myself, or will I have to send changes to a webmaster and wait for them to be posted?
- What type of machine houses the site and what web server software runs on that machine (see the previous section for more on server software)?
- How much traffic does the server handle now? What are the quotas (included in the base charge) for disk storage space and server traffic?
- Will I be permitted to run CGI scripts from the server?
- Is an existing library of common scripts already available at the server?
- Are any supplementary servers or facilities available for building a web presence (such as mailing list software, hypernews or other discussion group tools, and so on)?

EXPERT ADVICE

To get the best network connection, you may not want to limit yourself to local providers. Many Japanese companies, for example, hire providers on the West Coast of the U.S. to provide web mirroring to U.S. customers and, in some cases, to host their primary Internet presence.

EXPERT ADVICE

Perhaps the best advantage of having your own domain name is that it's completely portable. You can change your host provider or move a site to different machines and keep the address exactly the same.

- What provisions, if any, are there for password protection, secure commercial transactions, and other privacy and security needs?
- How dependable is the server? What provisions are in place for backing up the server in case of failure?
- Does the provider offer server support for streaming media formats like RealMedia?
- Is there database access?
- Is there support for advanced server-side scripting languages like ASP or Cold Fusion?
- What level of sustained bandwidth is permitted?
- What level of traffic can I pass per day, week, or month?

Establishing Your Internet Presence

Beyond setting up a web site, to establish a full-fledged Internet presence, you'll probably want to establish your own domain name (that is, if you or your organization has not already done so). Primarily, this has cosmetic advantages. A short URL focused on your company name is more memorable and attractive than a longer one where your company name hangs off the end of your provider's address.

See Appendix A for more about establishing an Internet connection.

As with servers, you can either register and maintain your own domain name or have your provider do it for you. To maintain your own domain, you'll need access to at least two computers on the Internet that are running name-service software (this is why it's often easier for providers or other centralized entities to do this, rather than individuals). You'll also need to fill out the appropriate paperwork for InterNIC (**http://www.internic.net**) and pay $100 for two years of service.

Most providers offer domain-name service as part of a package (particularly for business accounts) or as a separate billable service.

Browsers are getting smarter about guessing URLs, with Netscape leading the way. An address such as http:// www.*yourcompany*.com will be found even if a user simply types yourcompany in the Netscape address box.

This can mean the difference between a nice short URL like http://www.*yourcompany*.com, or something along the lines of http://www.*providername*.com/*yourcompany*/ or, worse yet, http://www.*providername*.com/~*yourcompany*/. Then again, some providers offer a quick-and-dirty method in which your home page URL is not at the root of a server but in a subdirectory, something like http://www.*yourcompany*.com/*your company*. This is not as good, since anyone entering just the www. . .com part will actually end up at your provider's home page instead of yours. The site redirection option (which gives you your own root address) may cost more, but it's worth it.

Publishing Your Web Pages

Whether you maintain your own server or contract for someone else to host you, you'll have to deal with sending (also called publishing or uploading) your web documents and related media files to the server. Traditionally, this was done using either file transfer protocol (FTP), to transfer the files, or Telnet (remote login), to log in directly to the remote site and create the file there. You can still work this way or, if you have a web-editing tool, you can usually post your pages directly from within the program.

To publish web pages to your host server, you'll need to know a username and password for logging in to the site, and the pathname (the folder and subfolders) to which you should transfer your files. Whoever has given you access to the site should be able to give you this information. If you run the server yourself, then this information will depend on how you initially set up the site.

Publishing in Windows with the Web Publishing Wizard

Since Windows 98, Microsoft has bundled a Web Publishing Wizard with the operating system, to help automate the process of publishing web pages. You can run the program directly (on my Start menu it's at Programs | Accessories | Internet Tools | Web Publishing Wizard) and other programs (such as FrontPage Express) can trigger it automatically when you try to save to a web or FTP address. Figure 8.1 shows the first message the Wizard displays.

When you click Next >, the Wizard will prompt you to specify a file and folder location (unless you're publishing a page directly from within a program like FrontPage Express). Then the Wizard will ask you to specify the file-transfer method your host prefers.

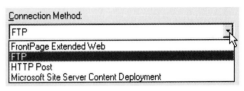

Depending on your choice, the Wizard will walk you through publishing via one of these methods. If it runs into any hitches, it may start prompting you to reenter the destination URL, to specify the path of the web site at the host, for login information, or for other stuff you may not understand. If it's not obvious what to do, contact your system administrator.

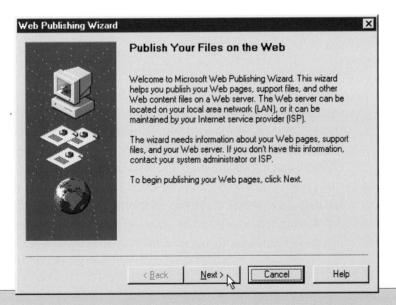

Figure 8.1: The Web Wizard that comes with Windows helps you publish your pages to a web site.

EXPERT ADVICE

FTP is a more efficient protocol for file transfers than the Web's HTTP protocol. Most web servers or service providers who maintain large sites with software or files to download make the files available by FTP, with ftp://... URLs embedded into the web pages.

Publishing a Site via FTP

Generally, any site running a web server will also maintain an FTP server so that the owner or owners of the content on the site can log in (using passwords) and change or add to files. The FTP connection is therefore a sort of back entrance or backstage area to which the public does not have access.

Generally speaking, FTP has always been an expert or "power user" protocol—but when will you need to use it nowadays? Probably the most popular use of FTP these days is for the oversight and management of web sites. Although it can be used to connect to any computer on the Internet (and therefore to any site, as long as you have a password), it's perfect for logging in to the protected area of a web site and adding, changing, downloading, or even deleting files at the site. For Unix sites, Telnet programs are also used for this purpose.

After that, FTP is most often used for transferring or sharing files between collaborators. I used to submit chapters to my editors by courier. More recently, I've been sending them as e-mail attachments. Lately, however, I've been experimenting with posting them at my FTP site and asking my editors to download them directly.

Using FTP with a Web Browser

A few years ago, web browsers generally weren't able to send (upload) files to FTP sites, partly because the Web is set up as a somewhat

---

EXPERT ADVICE

To make an FTP connection to a web site, enter the address in the form ftp://*username@usersite.name*. You'll be presented with a dialog box for entering your password. Once you connect, you can browse to the right folder and start uploading (or downloading) files.

BOOKMARK

You can get WS_FTP (either the free LE version or the commercial Pro version) from *http://www.ipswitch.com/*. You can get CuteFTP as well as other Windows FTP clients from *http://www.tucows.com* or from *http://www.winsite.com/*.

passive medium, with browsers downloading files, not sending files. Now, generally, you can upload files by using the File | Upload File command or by dragging files and dropping them into an FTP directory. The browser will ask you to confirm to file transfer.

Publishing Pages with an FTP Program

Free FTP programs are readily available for both Windows and Macintosh systems. Unix has FTP built in and accessible via the ubiquitous FTP program.

A free program, called Ftp.exe, comes with Windows, but it's no easier to use than the character-based Unix program it's modeled on. A better bet would be WS_FTP or CuteFTP, both shareware products, or WinFTP from Microsoft, which is based on an earlier, licensed version of WS_FTP.

For the Mac, the hands-down favorite FTP program is called Fetch. The free NCSA Telnet program for the Macintosh also includes built-in FTP capabilities.

If you *do* work with Unix machines, see if your system has the more advanced ncftp built in. It has more shortcuts and can save you, at the very least, some typing.

Publishing Pages with Free Programs (Microsoft FrontPage Express or Netscape Composer)

To publish a page with Microsoft FrontPage Express, click the Save button to save a page directly to a web address. It will start up the Web Publishing Wizard, as described a few sections ago. With Netscape Composer, click the Publish button, enter the URL (http:// or ftp:// address), and click OK.

CAUTION

If you tell Netscape Composer to save your password, then anyone using your computer will be able to publish files to your web server, so be careful.

Publishing Pages with Microsoft Office 2000 (or 98)

Word 2000 (along with all the Office 2000 programs) offer two approaches to publishing web pages. One method uses Web Folders, which are intranet or Internet sites you can save to and open files from just like ordinary folders (after you've entered their URLs once). The other is an FTP feature built into the Open and Save dialog boxes. (Word 97 also had the FTP feature.)

To save the current page to a web site in Word, follow the steps shown in Figure 8.2.

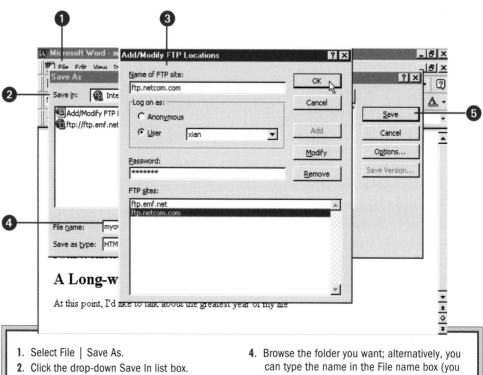

1. Select File | Save As.
2. Click the drop-down Save In list box.
3. Under Internet Locations (FTP), either select your FTP site (if you've already set it up), or select Add/Modify FTP Locations to enter the URL (ftp://*something*) of your site.
4. Browse the folder you want; alternatively, you can type the name in the File name box (you may need your web administrator's help with the exact name of your web directory).
5. Click Save.

Figure 8.2: You can publish pages easily from within Word using either FTP (shown here) or Web Folders.

Publishing Pages with Web Site Management Programs (Including Microsoft FrontPage 2000)

Web site management programs such as Microsoft FrontPage 2000, Macromedia Dreamweaver, Allaire ColdFusion, Macromedia Drumbeat 2000, and Adobe GoLive (among others) offer a more comprehensive system for publishing and updating web pages at a site. They enable you to publish many pages at once, only pages that have changed since the last time you published, or just a single changed page. They also distinguish between saving pages to your local staging area and publishing them to the site's web server.

To publish some or all of the pages in your web site at once with FrontPage 2000, click the Publish button, which brings up the Publish Web dialog box. For servers with FrontPage extensions installed, you can publish directly to a URL beginning with http:// (generally the same URL you'd give out for visitors). Your provider will tell you the URL to use. If you try publishing via HTTP to a server that cannot handle that form of upload, you'll get an error message, and you'll need to find out what FTP address you should be using (FTP always works).

If you want to make sure FrontPage remembers the FTP address to which you publish your web, type it in the Publish Web dialog box. If you'd rather set up the FTP site in a way that other programs can access, click the Browse button and, in the Open Web dialog box that appears, pull down the Look In list and choose Add/Modify FTP Locations, as discussed in the previous section.

Once FrontPage starts publishing your web, it may take some time to complete, especially if there are many large new files to upload. Meanwhile, the program will report to you on its progress and tell you when it's done. Click the underlined hyperlink on the dialog box to visit your published web in your default web browser.

If you try to publish a web that contains components to a server without the extensions to support them, FrontPage will warn you about the features that will not function as advertised.

Promoting Your Web Site

What if you built a storefront and no one came? It can happen on the Web. Sure, you can set up shop on prime real estate, directly across from Time/Warner's web mega-site, but you'll have no visitors unless you promote your site. Without promotion, a public web site is a lonely voice, crying out in the wilderness.

If there are web sites for related issues or interests, you could start promoting your site by sending their webmasters e-mail and offering to exchange links. As for Usenet newsgroups and mailing lists that deal with subjects related to your site, feel free to send brief announcements to them when your site is first published and whenever you make major changes or updates to it. For example, if you have compiled a list of writing resources, you could post a brief announcement describing your page to **news:misc.writing** and/or to **news:comp.internet.net-happenings**.

Next, visit all the directory and search engine sites mentioned in Chapter 3 and submit the URL of your web site to each one. (They all have pages where you can fill out forms to submit web addresses.)

Once you get past the wonder of it all—the fact that you can set up a tidy little web site just "down the road" from CNN, the White House, and Sony—you realize the catch: how will anyone ever find you? The Internet and the Web get more complicated and crowded every day. There's no space to run out of, but you still have to work to make sure that people who might be interested in your site can find it. In other words, publishing is one thing, but findability is the key.

There are really two ways to publicize your site online. The first is to submit the URL of your site to every directory and search engine you can find (excluding perhaps the uncategorized "What's New" pages out there). This is easy, but tedious. The second way is more subtle and is more in line with the traditional meaning of the term *networking*. To make a site visible from the many avenues on the Internet, you have to communicate with other people who publish on the Net or participate in discussion groups. You have to tell them, by

Don't underestimate the importance of promoting your site in the "real world." Be sure to put your URL on business cards and letterhead and mention it in advertising or marketing campaigns to promote your site's address.

NETIQUETTE

Don't spam (send multiple or unwelcome messages to) mailing lists or newsgroups to promote your site. Be careful to keep commercial messages out of noncommercial areas.

e-mail or in public posts, about your site and trade hyperlinks with sites that have common themes or interests. (Another variation on this theme is popular "web rings," related sites all signed onto the same ring server, which permits a user to navigate "horizontally" from site to site, around the ring. Some of these are exclusive while others are open to all comers.)

Submitting Announcements

All directory and search engine sites send robotic indexing programs around to browse the Web, follow links, and add sites to their databases. But why wait until they find you when you can go directly to the source?

The first step is to write an announcement describing your site, what makes it unique, and its intended audience. If your announcement is long (more than a few paragraphs), create a companion, condensed version of it, since many of these sites allow only short statements. (Many of them won't even use your text, for that matter.)

After that, just repeat the following process as many times as you can stand:

1. Browse to a search, directory, or "what's new" site (see the list in Table 8.2).
2. Choose the Submit URL or an equivalent option.
3. Enter your site's web address and as much of your announcement as the form permits.
4. Submit the information.
5. Check back after a week (or whatever lead time the site recommends) to make sure that your site is now listed.

Table 8.1 lists the major sites to which you should consider submitting your URL. New search sites appear all the time, so to make sure you haven't missed any, visit some of the centralized search sites such as Netscape's Internet Search page (**http://home.netscape.com/home/internet-search.html**) or clnet's Search.com (**http://www.search.com**) and scan the sites, adding any new ones to your list.

CAUTION

There are a lot of freelance operators who offer to submit announcements to sites all over the Net. Most of them just drop by the Submit It! site (we'll cover that in a moment), and many don't follow up to make sure that the URL has shown up at all the sites. You're better off doing this task (or supervising it) yourself.

Site Name	URL
AltaVista	http://www.altavista.com/
Excite	http://www.excite.com/
G.O.D.	http://www.god.co.uk/
Goto.com	http://www.goto.com
Google.com	http://www.google.com/
HotBot	http://www.hotbot.com/
InfoSeek Guide	http://infoseek.go.com/
Lycos	http://www.lycos.com/
Northernlight.com	http://www.northernlight.com/
Open Directory Project	http://www.dmoz.com/
Submit It!	http://www.submit-it.com/
WebCrawler	http://www.webcrawler.com
Yahoo!	http://www.yahoo.com/

Table 8.1: Sites for submitting your URL

Your first stop should be Submit It! (**http://www.submit-it.com**), because it contains links to most of the other relevant sites. Submit It! is a sort of mega-form that you can use to submit to multiple search and directory places. It's not quite as easy as it sounds since you still have to submit to each individual site, one after another, but at least many of them are all in one place.

Networking and Trading Links

To really have a presence on the Net, you have to spend time communicating with people one-to-one via e-mail and one-to-many

---

BOOKMARK

Other ways to generate traffic include affiliate programs, by which you agree to drive traffic to a site for a commission (such as a percentage of Amazon.com book sales generated by your visitors), and banner swapping programs. For affiliate links, see *http://www.refer-it.com/* and *http://www.cashpile.com/*. For banner-exchange programs, try *http://www.linkexchange.com/*.

via discussion groups. You need to go beyond just responding to e-mail from visitors to your site; you need to also put the URL of your site in your e-mail signature so that anyone who gets mail from you gets at least a minimal, classified-ad type plug for the site. Here's my signature to give you an idea:

```
Christian Crumlish - xian@pobox.com - http://ezone.org/ - waterside.com
```

Also, you have to be on the lookout for organizations and groups of people on the Net, and other web sites, that deal with topics similar or related to your own. For a business site, this may mean tracking down other vendors, suppliers, and so on whose products and services relate to your own. As long as they're not your competitors, there's no reason why they shouldn't want to trade links with you.

CAUTION

Don't send announcements to every single list, group, or private e-mail address you can find! This is known as spamming and will create more enemies than customers. Make sure that when you post information about your site, especially if your site is a commercial one, you do so only in forums whose members will appreciate the information.

Webmastery: Maintaining a Living, Breathing Web Site

Even after you've finished creating your site, published it to the Net, and worked day and night promoting it, your job is not necessarily done. There's a distinction between designing (and building) a site and webmastery. Every site needs a webmaster in the same sense that every mail server needs a postmaster. Someone has to fix things that go wrong, respond to basic e-mail, keep the server running, and—perhaps most important—post updates and changes to the site as they occur.

You must ask, "Who will do this job? Me? My service provider? An assistant?" If you hire web designers to create or enhance your site, don't assume that they will also take over the webmaster chores unless it's written into the agreement.

If it falls to you to oversee a site, you may want to invest in a site management program such as Adobe GoLive, Microsoft FrontPage, or Macromedia Dreamweaver. These programs, at the very least, make it easier to keep all your internal links up to date if and when you make changes to the overall structure of the site.

Webmastery also involves analyzing the access logs that most servers generate. If you pay a service provider to host your site, ask to

---

BOOKMARK

ServerWatch (bookmarked earlier in this chapter) maintains an up-to-date list of site development and management tools. Yahoo! also has a good section on this subject (*http://dir.yahoo.com/Computers_and_Internet/Software/Internet/World_Wide_Web/Servers/ Log_Analysis_Tools/*).

---

receive your access statistics on a regular basis. (They may just point you to a page at the site that can generate reports for you.)

A web site will wither away if you don't revisit it often to improve its appearance, content, and organization, and to add up-to-date information to it. To avoid chaos, you need to establish a clear, simple system for making updates. Only one person should have the final say regarding what gets posted, and all changes should be made in some safe staging area and tested before being posted to the public site.

Welcome to the Net!

By now you are one of the masters of the Internet! If you've made it this far, you've not only learned how to communicate with people around the globe and download information and files from archives near and far, but also how to create, publish, and maintain your own little corner of cyberspace on the World Wide Web. In fact, with what you've learned so far, you have more than adequate opportunities to advance your learning about the Internet directly from the Net itself.

No matter what degree of participation you choose or how much information you help yourself to, you're now part of a vital and growing global community. There's no reason why the Internet has to eat up all your time and energy. You now know enough to make productive use of the Net, avail yourself of its vast resources, and avoid entangling yourself in technical distractions.

For a shortcut to all of the web pages referred to in this book, be sure to visit the Busy Persons Links (**http://www.opublish.com/ busy2k/bookmarks/**). See you on the Net!

APPENDIX A

Get Connected to the Net

If you're poking around back here in this part of the book, then you're probably confused about something. No problem. I'm here to help.

First of all, you may already be connected to the Internet to some degree. If you are, your first step is to identify the type of connection you have. If you don't yet have an Internet connection, I can help you figure out what kind of connection you want and how to find a service provider offering that kind of hook-up.

Do You Need an ISP?

Even if you have direct access to the Internet at work, you may still want to dial up your network from home or connect to a private Internet service provider (ISP), perhaps to make personal or business use of the Internet that might not be appropriate over your work connection.

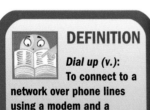

DEFINITION

Dial up (v.):
To connect to a network over phone lines using a modem and a computer.

Dial-up (adj.):
A description of the type of account one accesses by dialing up a network.

Direct access means working on a computer that is connected directly either to the Internet or to a smaller network that is itself directly connected to the Internet. An ISP is a private company that specializes in providing Internet access, especially dial-up access, for individuals.

A direct network connection to the Internet is usually the fastest, but if your access comes by virtue of your employment at a company, or membership in a department or organization, then your participation in the Internet may be limited by your capacity as a representative of your organization. Many companies consider it improper for you to conduct personal business over a company Internet connection (although personal e-mail is usually permitted, within reason, to the same extent that personal phone calls are).

Once you've found some ISPs, grilled them thoroughly, and compared their services and prices, you'll still have to get your computer set up, so I'll cover those details as well.

One final disclaimer: Yes, this stuff is boring. That's why we stuck it in the back of the book. I won't pretty anything up—I'll just tell you the details and move on.

Am I Already Connected to the Internet?

What does "on the Internet" mean? It depends. If you're mainly interested in e-mail, then any type of e-mail system that can send mail to and receive mail from Internet addresses is "on the Internet." If you want to be able to browse the Web, then you'll need either a direct network connection to the Internet or a dial-up connection.

Are You on a Network at Work, School, Prison?

If you use or have access to a computer that's part of a network, and that network is connected in some way to the Internet, then you may be able to run a web browser, for example, and your network will provide the Internet connection. This is often true at universities and at medium-sized and larger corporations.

To find out whether you're computer already has a direct connection to the Internet, you may have to ask whoever maintains your network. If you don't have direct access to the Internet from a local network, jump ahead to "How Can I Get Connected to the Internet?"

Do You Subscribe to an Online Service (AOL, Compuserve, MSN)?

If you have an account at an online service such as America Online or the recently relaunched Microsoft Network, then you already have fairly complete access to the Internet (though you may have to learn some specific rules and methods that are particular to your service). These all offer technical support, although some are occasionally swamped with calls.

If your online service allows you to run a program such as Netscape when connected, then you can also most likely run all the other programs discussed in this book. You may be more comfortable, however, with the interface provided by your service.

What Kind of Connection Do I Have?

If you have a network connection (that is, you're on a network, and the network is connected to the Internet), then you shouldn't have to set up anything yourself (aside from specific programs, as explained throughout the book). Enjoy your network connection. If you want to dial up to connect to your network and run graphical programs from a modem, then you'll be using a PPP (or, possibly, SLIP) connection. This requires configuring some software and possibly putting together a dial-up script. Windows 3.1 requires the most helper software and massaging to get going. Windows 95, 98, NT, and 2000, and MacOS 7 and 8 are pretty easy to set up for PPP, and so is the spanking-new BeOS, which runs on both PowerPC (Mac) and Intel (Windows) chips. You should be able to get technical support to do this.

By the way, PPP stands for point-to-point protocol, and it's the preferable method for handling Internet traffic over a modem. SLIP stands for serial line Internet protocol and is nearly as good a method for the same thing (but not quite as well supported by Windows 95). PPP is faster and more efficient than SLIP.

If you subscribe to an online service, make sure that you're getting full Internet access. You shouldn't have to do any setup beyond installing the service's software. Here's the key question: Ask if you have full PPP access. If they say yes, then you can run any of the software mentioned in this book.

If you already have an ISP, then you either have a PPP account perfectly suited for all the instructions in this book, or you have a dial-up Unix shell account. If the latter is the case, then you'll be using mostly different software than that described in this book (mainly a terminal/communications program on your personal computer and then a number of Unix programs at the other end, all in a character-only interface).

How Can I Get Connected to the Internet?

Okay, now say you don't yet have Internet access. That means you need to find an ISP, which is a company that specializes in hooking up individuals to the Internet. If there is more than one in the local area, so much the better. Competition does wonders for Internet rates. You shouldn't have to spend more than $30 a month for a reasonable amount of Internet access, and you can spend closer to $20 in larger metropolitan areas. Many providers offer a range of accounts, each with its own pricing plan, such as:

- A flat-rate, unlimited access account (for $20 to $30 per month)
- A basic-rate account with per-minute charges and (often 40) free hours (for $10 to $20 per month plus $1 to $2 per hour over the allotted free time)
- A low-rate, light-usage account with (sometimes high) per-minute charges and few (perhaps 10) or no free hours (for $5 to $10 per month plus $2 to $2.50 per minute)

Shopping for a Service Provider

Shop around before choosing a provider. Compare the rates of direct-access Internet service providers (ISPs) such as Netcom, Hooked, Portal, Pipeline, Crl, and so on, to those of online services such as CompuServe, AOL, and MSN. If you want to keep the computer out of the equation, consider the TV set-top box service called WebTV. See if there is a Free-Net in your area (a public access network) or if any local universities are offering access. In some areas, newspapers, libraries, and other civic entities are evolving into service providers as well.

If you have to compromise more than you want on price for a provider, you can get an additional forwarding address with an e-mail forwarding company such as Pobox.com (e-mail **info@pobox.com** or **http://pobox.com/** on the Web) and give out the pobox address. Then you can move your provider when a better deal becomes available and not have to inform everyone you know or do business with that your address has changed. The pobox service costs $15 for three years.

Some people prefer to start exploring the Net through the more controlled environment of an online service. The big online services are sometimes more expensive than ISPs, but they do offer additional content of their own and, in most regions, their prices are now competitive. They also offer more hand-holding and all-in-one interfaces that, while sometimes limited, can be easier to use.

If you can get or borrow web access, visit The List (**http://www.thelist.com/**). You can enter your area code there and search for service providers who offer local-call access in your area. Local access is essential to keeping your costs down. (Another list of providers, for comparison's sake, can be found at **http://www.tagsys.com/Providers/index.html**.) Look in local newspapers and computer periodicals for other listings of providers.

What Questions to Ask

When you're looking for access to the Internet, here are some specific questions to ask a service provider:

- Do you offer affordable high-speed access (via cable, ISDN, or DSL)?
- Will I have a PPP connection?
- Will I be able to browse the Web (and see pictures), send and receive e-mail, subscribe to Usenet newsgroups, and so on?
- Is there flat-rate access (a rate for unlimited time)?
- How busy are your modems? Will I ever have trouble getting through? When are the peak usage hours?
- Do you include a disk of useful software (such as connection software, a web browser, an FTP program, a mail reader, and so on) with the service?
- Do you also offer a manual? Free training classes? Technical support?

- Will the service be easy to set up? Will you or the installation software do all the geek work (such as IP configuration)?

- What is the top dial-in modem speed? The top dial-in modem speed should be at least as fast as your modem—the slower modem in a connection controls the speed. Today, the fastest modems are 57.6 Kbps (kilobits per second), but very few (if any) ISPs have modems that fast. With compression, the fastest practical modems are 33.6 Kbps, but 28.8 Kbps modems are still standard. (Another, faster, more expensive alternative is ISDN.)

- Is there a local dial-up number? Are there nationwide numbers for when I'm traveling? Is there an 800 number, and if so, how much does it cost?

- Are there any hidden or extra charges?

- Are there any quotas or limits on disk storage, e-mail, or other Internet traffic?

- Do you offer space on the World Wide Web as part of the account?

- What's the file-transfer allowance (100 megabytes per month? 500?)?

Also, if you encounter people on the Internet with the domain name of a provider you're considering, ask them (by mail) what they think of the service.

What Kinds of Connections Do I Want?

Your best bet is a direct (PPP) account, or some other sort of account that is equivalent (such as online service accounts, which amount to full PPP access).

Depending on availability (and your budget), the fastest connection available to you might be a T3 (screaming), a T1 (also rather fast), a cable modem (you wait for the rest of the Net to catch up), one of the many new flavors of DSL (a fast, dedicated—meaning it's on all the time—digital connection over ordinary phone lines), ISDN (a special type of digital phone line that's at best twice as fast as the fastest ordinary modems today), or an ordinary analog modem connection.

Setting Up Different Types of Connections

Here are the essentials of setting up an Internet connection. You'll need to get specific details from your service provider, but most likely they'll offer the information and may possibly set up your software for you, saving you the trouble. If you get stuck anywhere, your provider can walk you through the problem and get you set up (some charge a premium for this service).

The first time you get these numbers from your provider or host, don't just jot them down by the phone, write them into the blank spaces on the "Connect to the Net and Set Up Mail" blueprint at the beginning of this book. Then, the next time you have to set up a new connection, you'll already have the information handy.

A Network with an Internet Gateway

Your network system administrator should be able to tell you whether you can simply go ahead and run Internet software, such as Netscape, and send Internet e-mail out from your network e-mail program. Maybe you'll have to set up a TCP/IP network connection or, for Windows 3.1, obtain a Winsock driver to enable Internet software to run. A Winsock driver enables a PC that's not network connected to send and receive TCP/IP packets. (Windows 95 comes with a Winsock driver.)

Setting up TCP/IP will mainly entail typing certain numerical Internet addresses (your system administrator can give them to you) into specific boxes, to indicate specific gateways and servers (see Figure A.1).

Windows 95 and 98 come with Winsock.

On a Macintosh, if you have system 7.5 or later, then you have the MacTCP control panel already installed on your computer. You'll have to purchase MacTCP from Apple for earlier versions of the Macintosh operating system.

CAUTION

Windows 3.1 Winsocks such as Trumpet are 16-bit, whereas Windows 95's Winsock is 32-bit. You can't run 16-bit Internet software over a 32-bit Winsock, nor vice versa.

Dial-Up PPP

To get a PPP (or SLIP) connection going, you need to have the same software and settings in place as are needed for a network connection. (That is, you'll need TCP/IP software running, and on Windows

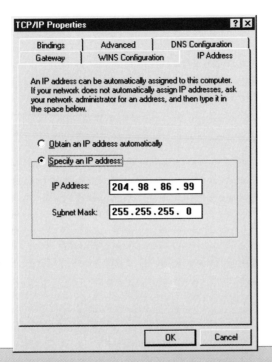

Figure A.1: The specific program and dialog box may look different in Windows 3.1, MacOS, and BeOS, but the type of information you have to supply remains the same.

machines, you'll need Winsock.) You'll also need a dial-up program to make and maintain your phone connection to the Internet. Windows 98 has built-in software for PPP (and you can get the SLIP driver from **http://www.microsoft.com**). Also, Windows 95's Plus! Pack comes with a dial-up networking scripting tool for putting together a simple dial-up script, so you won't have to log in by hand every time.

No matter what conglomeration of programs you're using to maintain your PPP connection, you'll need to tell it the correct modem settings and numerical Internet addresses for nameservers, e-mail, and news.

So, for example, to set up a PPP account on Windows 98, first double-click the Make New Connection icon in the Dial-Up Networking folder. Type your provider's name, select your modem, and click Next. Enter the phone number and click Next again. Then

Windows 98's Internet Connection Wizard can also walk you through a questionnaire and then set up your Internet connection for you.

click Finish. (That's the easy part.) Next, right-click the new connection icon, which appears in the Dial-Up Networking folder, and select Properties.

In the dialog box that appears, click the Server Types tab. Make sure PPP is chosen as the connection type. Click the TCP/IP Settings button. If your provider assigns you a new address every time you connect (you can ask them this), make sure Server Assigned IP Address is checked. Otherwise, your provider should give you primary and secondary name-server addresses, and you should enter them in the boxes provided in this dialog box. Then click OK repeatedly to close the windows.

Cable Modems, ISDN, and DSL

If your local cable company starts to offer Internet access, they'll sell or rent you a cable modem ,and you'll pay a monthly fee of something like $40 (1999 dollars) for both cable TV and round-the-clock cable Internet access. (This is not to be confused with WebTV or AOL TV, which run over ordinary telephone modem lines but use your television instead of a computer as the Internet access point.)

Integrated Services Digital Network (ISDN) accounts require a special kind of modem and a special kind of phone line coming into the house or office, but they are faster than any other type of dial-up modem connection. (They connect at a minimum of 57.6 Kbps and in some circumstances can go at 128 Kbps—more than four times as fast as a 28.8 Kbps modem.)

ISDN modems are faster than analog modems and can make voice *and* data connections at the same time, but they're more expensive (they have higher setup fees, higher monthly fees, and per-minute phone usage charges) and more difficult to set up. ISDN service is still unavailable in many areas and might become obsolete when cable modem technology comes along, any year now.

I've been using ISDN for the last few years and frankly, it's expensive, since my phone company/service provider (Pacbell) charges me about $1 per minute for the connection. I'm considering changing to the new DSL service Pacbell is offering, as it will give 24/7 (round the clock) access for a flat monthly rate. DSL makes use of existing

Look for cable-modem services springing up within the next year, as cable companies start to get serious about offering Net access and their own web programming. For bigger-budget, higher-demand corporate solutions, try comparing frame relay and dedicated lines for costs, dependability, and speed.

phone lines (requiring neither fiber optics nor cable) but provides a digital connection (simultaneous with a voice connection, if need be) that's 20 times faster than a 56K modem. (I will have to purchase special equipment (yet again) though, to take advantage of this digital solution.)

Another alternative to standard modem connections are direct satellite—yes, satellite—Internet hookups, such as the service available from DirectPC.

That should be enough to get you up and running.

Index

References to figures and illustrations are in italics.